Dreams of Fear:
Poetry of Terror and the Supernatural

DREAMS OF FEAR
Poetry of Terror and the Supernatural

Edited by S. T. Joshi and Steven J. Mariconda

Hippocampus Press

New York

Published by Hippocampus Press
P.O. Box 641, New York, NY 10156.
www.hippocampuspress.com

Cover art: Charles E. Burchfield (1893–1967), "The Tree"
(1946), 35½ × 28½ in. watercolor on paper. Reproduced by
permission of the Charles E. Burchfield Foundation.

Cover design by Barbara Briggs Silbert.
Hippocampus Press logo designed by Anastasia Damianakos.

First Edition
1 3 5 7 9 8 6 4 2

ISBN 978-1-61498-027-8

Contents

Introduction

The poetry of weirdness, terror, and the supernatural has been remarkably, and lamentably, understudied. In spite of the fact that, as this volume shows, a substantial number of the leading poets of Western literature have indulged in weird poetry on at least a single occasion, and several noteworthy poets have specialized in the genre, our understanding of the scope and extent of the field is sketchy at best. August Derleth's anthology *Dark of the Moon: Poems of Fantasy and the Macabre* (1947)—compiled with significant assistance from Donald Wandrei, whose knowledge of poetry was substantially superior to Derleth's—was a notable achievement, but it contained some curious omissions and is of course now far out of date. Derleth went on to edit a volume of more recent weird poetry, *Fire and Sleet and Candlelight* (1961), but the quality of the material was very uneven. More recent compilations, such as Michael Hayes's *Supernatural Poetry: A Selection, 16th Century to 20th Century* (1978) and John Hollander's *Poems Bewitched and Haunted* (2005), are suggestive but do not claim comprehensiveness. Actual criticism or scholarship on the field is even rarer: aside from a splendid but highly compressed chapter by Steve Eng in Marshall Tymn's *Horror Literature* (1981) and a slim booklet by S. T. Joshi, *Emperors of Dreams: Some Notes on Weird Poetry* (2008), there are no general studies of the field, although any number of critical articles on individual authors offer insights large and small.

Poetry is, by common consensus, the oldest mode of human expression, and it is no surprise that the oldest literary documents in Western literature, the epics of Homer, contain their share of supernatural episodes. (If we wished, we could go back a millennium before Homer and note the numerous weird elements in the Epic of Gilgamesh.) Although ghosts of the dead appear sporadically in the *Iliad*, our interest in Homer must focus on the *Odyssey*, especially on Odysseus' remarkable tale of his adventures after the Trojan War (books 9–12), in which he meets a succession of remarkable monsters and supernatural creatures ranging from the sorceress Circe to the hideous Cyclops. To be sure, it is unlikely that these bizarre creatures are the invention of a single creative artist; rather, they were no doubt the product of a long tradition of mythopoeic creation, although why and how the Greek imagination fashioned such distinctive monsters—especially those in the Herakles cycle, a tradition separate from that of the Homeric poems, and which features such creatures as the Lernean hydra, the Stymphalian birds, and so forth—has not been satisfactorily explained. Greek tragedy is also full of spectral phenomena, the most striking of which is the hideous death of Creon and his daughter by the magic potion of Medea in Euripides' *Medea*. The Romans were less given to imaginative flights than the Greeks, but they adopted and adapted Greek myth to their own purposes; Virgil, Ovid, and others took their epic heroes on weird explorations of the underworld in the manner of Homer and other Greek poets.

To be a viable literary mode, the supernatural in literature must be segregated from religion and myth. For authors (and, more significantly, for readers) to have a proper understanding of the supernatural, there must be a concrete and widely accepted understanding of the natural. This process, in the West, took several centuries, and in the course of that evolution certain religiously based works—such as Dante's *Inferno* and Milton's *Paradise Lost*—contributed imagery and conceptions that later supernatural writers would draw upon in largely secular writings. For all that Dante and Milton believed themselves to be expressing Christian orthodoxy in their work, their vivid and terrifying descriptions of Hell seem largely the product of their own imaginations. Nor were the Elizabethan playwrights silent where the supernatural is concerned. Although Shakespeare's inclusion of ghosts and witches in *Hamlet* and *Macbeth* has attracted the greatest attention and significantly influenced later writing, it was Marlowe's *Dr. Faustus* that constituted perhaps the first major literary work whose entire premise rested upon a supernatural foundation.

The later seventeenth and early eighteenth centuries were in fact not notable for their contribution to the supernatural, either in prose or in verse. The dominance of science and rationalist philosophy—this was the heyday of Newton, Hume, Pope, and Samuel Johnson—appears to have cast a certain shadow of disrepute upon the expression of weirdness or terror in literature, a shadow that in some ways remains to this day. The so-called Graveyard Poets of the early to mid-eighteenth century did not indulge in horror or the supernatural so much as on gloomy reflections on the inevitability of death, and their poetry does not appear to have been a notable influence on later work.

Things began to change when Thomas Percy compiled *Reliques of Ancient English Poetry* (1765), a three-volume assemblage of old ballads that was seized upon by the public and contributed significantly to the Gothic movement that Horace Walpole's short novel *The Castle of Otranto* (1764) initiated. Both writers and readers recognized that the ballad form was an ideal vehicle for the expression of supernatural terror, since it combined the narrative drive of prose with the compactness, poignancy, and symbolizing faculty of lyric poetry. It is no surprise that, in the later eighteenth and early nineteenth centuries, many noteworthy authors— ranging from Robert Burns ("Tam o'Shanter") to James Hogg ("The Witch of the Gray Thorn") to Sir Walter Scott ("William and Helen" and "The Wild Huntsman," translations of the two celebrated German ballads by Bürger)—used the ballad form for supernatural verse. The Gothic novelist M. G. Lewis compiled an entire volume of such poems, *Tales of Wonder* (1800), perhaps the first anthology of weird poetry ever published. The supernatural ballad achieved its apex of literary artistry in Coleridge's *Rime of the Ancient Mariner* (1798), the greatest weird poem ever written. Other Romantic poets such as Byron, Keats, and Shelley used more orthodox lyric poetry to express weirdness.

But just as he effected a revolution in supernatural fiction by the virtually single-handed invention of the short story, so did

Edgar Allan Poe effect a revolution in weird poetry by his monomaniacal focus on terror and the supernatural in verse. Virtually the entirety of Poe's poetry would deserve inclusion here for its systematic treatment of nearly every phase of weirdness, from grim reflections on death ("The Conqueror Worm") to evocations of fantastic landscapes ("Dream-Land," "Ulalume") to the symbolic use of the supernatural for psychological analysis ("The Haunted Palace," where the palace of the title clearly stands for a disordered mind). But Poe was by no means alone among nineteenth-century artists in infusing horror into verse. Even aside from Thomas Lovell Beddoes's vivid evocation of Elizabethan tragedy in *Death's Jest-Book* (1850), we find the most notable—and respectable—Victorian poets, from Longfellow to Tennyson to Browning to Holmes to Lowell, summoning witches, haunted houses, and sea monsters to convey messages that could not be conveyed in any other fashion. Among the French, a fair proportion of Victor Hugo's abundant array of poetry features elements of weirdness. Baudelaire's *Les Fleurs du mal* (1857) has perhaps gained a misleading reputation as a fount of weirdness, when in fact its focus is on the iconoclastic scorn of conventional morality by the evocation of images of death and eroticism, but some of Baudelaire's poems are actually supernatural in their orientation.

The later nineteenth century continued the trend. Swinburne, Hardy, Meredith, and other poets—some of whom were primarily novelists—vivified their verse with brief doses of weirdness, while such writers of supernatural fiction as Ambrose Bierce and Julian Hawthorne extended their investigations of terror from prose to verse. Two lesser-known American writers, Thomas Bailey Aldrich and Madison Cawein, incorporated the supernatural into their poetry to such an extent that they could be considered specialists in the form; an entire volume of Cawein's weird verse could—and should—be compiled. It is no surprise that such writers as A. E. Housman, whose *Shropshire Lad* is so cheerlessly focused on the baleful figure of death, and W. B. Yeats, whose imagination seemed to dwell eternally in a never-never-land of his own creating, would indulge in weird verse; and among Franco-phone writers, the Belgian Emile Verhaeren contributed his mite. Verhaeren is an unjustly forgotten poet whose verse is laced with weirdness.

With the dawning of the twentieth century—and, more pertinently, the emergence of supernatural fiction as an increasingly viable literary form—weird poetry came into its own. Whether it be the work of such Californians as George Sterling and Clark Ashton Smith, or such New Englanders as Edwin Arlington Robinson, Robert Frost, and H. P. Lovecraft, or such Englishmen as Walter de la Mare, John Masefield, and Robert Graves, supernatural verse flourished as never before. It is of course significant that a number of these writers also wrote supernatural fiction, but the surprise is that so many poets whose work seems so grounded in mundane reality, such as Robinson and Frost, would indulge in weirdness even for a single poem or two. The form had now become an international phenomenon, as testified by the Canadian Robert W. Service, the Australian Christopher Brennan, the German Georg Heym, and the Irishman Lord Dunsany. For all that, it was Clark Ashton Smith who, in a poetic career that spanned five decades, established himself as perhaps the greatest weird poet in all literature, if gauged by both the extent and the pungency of his work.

It would be fair to say that, by the early to mid-twentieth century, supernatural verse had become a subgenre of its own. The pulp magazine *Weird Tales* did much to foster the form, publishing work by Lovecraft, Smith, and younger writers such as Frank Belknap Long, Robert E. Howard, and Donald Wandrei. A later generation of weird fiction writers also indulged in verse, among them Joseph Payne Brennan, Stanley McNail, and Richard L. Tierney.

In the present day, any number of poets—Bruce Boston, Ann K. Schwader, G. Sutton Breiding, the late Keith Allen Daniels—specialize in weird verse, and they and others continue to nurture this literary alcove even if they stand to gain little in celebrity or remuneration from it. Poetry itself has become the province of the few, and even fewer are those who gain genuine pleasure and insight by reading the poetry of the supernatural. But if this volume serves no other purpose, it is hoped that it displays the extent to which poets of the highest distinction have found in the supernatural a means to express moods, images, and conceptions that conventional mimetic realism cannot encompass. As such, it is likely that weird poetry will remain a permanent form of expression for the delectation of those sensitive enough to appreciate both its delicacy and its emotive power.

—S. T. JOSHI AND STEVEN J. MARICONDA

A Note on This Edition

In this volume, the editors have sought to include representative samples of weird, horrific, and supernatural poetry from classical antiquity to the present day. The focus has been on verse that actually depicts supernatural phenomena; instances of non-supernatural terror have been generally excluded, as have poems whose emphasis is merely on the inevitability of death. Some long poems that one might expect to be included in such a volume—e.g., Keats's *Lamia*, Clark Ashton Smith's *The Hashish-Eater*, Donald Wandrei's complete *Sonnets of the Midnight Hours*, H. P. Lovecraft's complete *Fungi from Yuggoth* sequence—have been omitted or abridged to make space for lesser-known items. The poems have been arranged by the life dates of the author; in some cases this has resulted in poems being presented out of chronological sequence, but in general a chronological arrangement has resulted. The editors have supplied headnotes that provide concise biographical and critical overviews of the author, with an emphasis on their weird poetry and publication details on the poems included. The poems themselves have not been annotated. We have sought to use the most accurate texts of the poems in question. Translators of foreign-language poems are identified at the end of the poem; in some cases the editors have produced new translations.

The editors are grateful to the several living poets, and to the publishers and estates of poems still under copyright, for permission to reprint the works in question.

—S. T. J. / S. J. M.

I. The Ancient World

Homer (c. 750 B.C.E.)

It is not clear that there ever was a poet named Homer, but the ancient Greeks believed that he was the author of two epic poems, the *Iliad* (about the Trojan War) and the *Odyssey* (about the wanderings of Odysseus after the Trojan War). Both poems may have originated as early as 1200 B.C.E. and were apparently assembled by oral tradition by 750 or 700 B.C.E. The *Odyssey* contains numerous supernatural episodes, ranging from the sorceress Circe to the monsters Scylla and Charybdis to Odysseus' descent to the underworld, which takes up the entirety of Book 11. An extract from this last segment is presented here.

From the Odyssey

"Then I beheld the illustrious son of Jove,
Minos, a golden sceptre in his hand,
Sitting to judge the dead, who round the king
Pleaded their causes. There they stood or sat
In Pluto's halls,—a pile with ample gates.
    "And next I saw the huge Orion drive,
Across the meadows green with asphodel,
The savage beast whom he had slain; he bore
The brazen mace, which no man's power could break.
    "And Tityus there I saw,—the mighty earth
His mother,—overspreading, as he lay,
Nine acres, with two vultures at his side,
That, plucking at his liver, plunged their beaks
Into the flesh; nor did his hands avail
To drive them off, for he had offered force
To Jove's proud wife Latona, as she went
To Pytho, through the pleasant Panopeus.
    "And next I looked on Tantalus, a prey
To grievous torments, standing in a lake
That reached his chin. Though painfully athirst,

He could not drink; as often as he bowed
His aged head to take into his lips
The water, it was drawn away, and sank
Into the earth, and the dark soil appeared
Around his feet; a god had dried it up.
And lofty trees drooped o'er him, hung with fruit,—
Pears and pomegranates, apples fair to sight,
And luscious figs, and olives green of hue.
And when that ancient man put forth his hands
To pluck them from their stems, the wind arose
And whirled them far among the shadowy clouds.
    "There I beheld the shade of Sisyphus
Amid his sufferings. With both hands he rolled
A huge stone up a hill. To force it up,
He leaned against the mass with hands and feet;
But, ere it crossed the summit of the hill
A power was felt that sent it rolling back,
And downward plunged the unmanageable rock
Before him to the plain. Again he toiled
To heave it upward, while the sweat in streams
Ran down his limbs, and dust begrimed his brow.
    "Then I beheld the mighty Hercules,—
The hero's image,—for he sits himself
Among the deathless gods, well pleased to share
Their feasts, and Hebe of the dainty feet—
A daughter of the mighty Jupiter
And golden-sandalled Juno—is his wife.
Around his image flitted to and fro
The ghosts with noise, like fear-bewildered birds.
His look was dark as night. He held in hand
A naked bow, a shaft upon the string,
And fiercely gazed, like one about to send
The arrow forth. Upon his breast he wore
The formidable baldric, on whose band
Of gold were sculptured marvels,—forms of bears,
Wild boars, grim lions, battles, skirmishings,
And death by wounds, and slaughter. He who wrought
That band had never done the like before,
Nor could thereafter. As I met his eye,
The hero knew me, and, beholding me

With pity, said to me in winged words:—
    "'Son of Laertes, nobly born and wise,
And yet unhappy; surely thou dost bear
A cruel fate, like that which I endured
While yet I saw the brightness of the sun.
The offspring of Saturnian Jupiter
Am I, and yet was I compelled to serve
One of a meaner race than I, who set
Difficult tasks. He sent me hither once
To bring away the guardian hound; he deemed
No harder task might be. I brought him hence;
I led him up from Hades, with such aid
As Hermes and the blue-eyed Pallas gave.'
    "Thus having spoken, he withdrew again
Into the abode of Pluto. I remained
And kept my place, in hope there yet might come
Heroes who perished in the early time,
And haply I might look on some of those,—
The ancients, whom I greatly longed to see,—
On Theseus and Pirithoüs, glorious men,
The children of the gods. But now there flocked
Already round me, with a mighty noise,
The innumerable nations of the dead;
And I grew pale with fear, lest from the halls
Of Pluto the stern Proserpine should send
The frightful visage of the monster-maid,
The Gorgon. Hastening to my ship, I bade
The crew embark, and cast the hawsers loose.
Quickly they went on board, and took their seats
Upon the benches. Through Océanus
The current bore my galley, aided first
By oars, and then by favorable gales."
                  [tr. William Cullen Bryant (1871)]

Euripides (485?–406 B.C.E.)

Euripides was the third of the great Athenian tragic playwrights of the 5th century B.C.E., slightly younger than his contemporaries, Aeschylus and Sophocles. Nineteen of his plays (out of an estimated 92) survive, more than that of any other playwright of the period. Several of his plays involve the supernatural, but the most concentrated segment is the Messenger's speech that concludes *Medea* (431 B.C.E.), about the sorceress who was brought from Colchis (in Asia Minor) by Jason after he obtained the Golden Fleece. He married her, but subsequently scorned her for a younger woman, Creusa. The Messenger now describes the murder of Creusa and her father, Creon, by Medea.

From Medea

Medea: Friends, this long hour I wait on Fortune's eyes,
And strain my senses in a hot surmise
What passeth on that hill.—Ha! even now
There comes . . . 'tis one of Jason's men, I trow.
His wild-perturbèd breath doth warrant me
The tidings of some strange calamity.

[*Enter* Messenger.

Messenger: O dire and ghastly deed! Get thee away,
Medea! Fly! Nor let behind thee stay
One chariot's wing, one keel that sweeps the seas. . . .

Medea: And what hath chanced, to cause such frights as these?

Messenger: The maiden princess lieth—and her sire,
The king—both murdered by thy poison-fire.

Medea: Most happy tiding! Which thy name prefers
Henceforth among my friends and well-wishers.

Messenger: What say'st thou? Woman, is thy mind within
Clear, and not raving? Thou art found in sin
Most bloody wrought against the king's high head,
And laughest at the tale, and hast no dread?

Medea: I have words also that could answer well
Thy word. But take thine ease, good friend, and tell,
How died they? Hath it been a very foul
Death, prithee? That were comfort to my soul.

Messenger: When thy two children, hand in hand entwined,
Came with their father, and passed on to find
The new-made bridal rooms, Oh, we were glad,
We thralls, who ever loved thee well, and had
Grief in thy grief. And straight there passed a word
From ear to ear, that thou and thy false lord
Had poured peace offering upon wrath foregone.
A right glad welcome gave we them, and one
Kissed the small hand, and one the shining hair:
Myself, for very joy, I followed where
The women's rooms are. There our mistress . . . she
Whom now we name so . . . thinking not to see
Thy little pair, with glad and eager brow
Sate waiting Jason. Then she saw, and slow
Shrouded her eyes, and backward turned again,
Sick that thy children should come near her. Then
Thy husband quick went forward, to entreat
The young maid's fitful wrath. "Thou wilt not meet
Love's coming with unkindness? Nay, refrain
Thy suddenness, and turn thy face again,
Holding as friends all that to me are dear,
Thine husband. And accept these robes they bear
As gifts: and beg thy father to unmake
His doom of exile on them—for my sake."
When once she saw the raiment, she could still
Her joy no more, but gave him all his will.
And almost ere the father and the two
Children were gone from out the room, she drew
The flowerèd garments forth, and sate her down
To her arraying: bound the golden crown
Through her long curls, and in a mirror fair
Arranged their separate clusters, smiling there
At the dead self that faced her. Then aside
She pushed her seat, and paced those chambers wide
Alone, her white foot poising delicately—

So passing joyful in those gifts was she!—
And many a time would pause, straight-limbed, and wheel
Her head to watch the long fold to her heel
Sweeping. And then came something strange. Her cheek
Seemed pale, and back with crooked steps and weak
Groping of arms she walked, and scarcely found
Her old seat, that she fell not to the ground.
     Among the handmaids was a woman old
And grey, who deemed, I think, that Pan had hold
Upon her, or some spirit, and raised a keen
Awakening shout; till through her lips was seen
A white foam crawling, and her eyeballs back
Twisted, and all her face dead pale for lack
Of life: and while that old dame called, the cry
Turned strangely to its opposite, to die
Sobbing. Oh, swiftly then one woman flew
To seek her father's rooms, one for the new
Bridegroom, to tell the tale. And all the place
Was loud with hurrying feet.
               So long a space
As a swift walker on a measured way
Would pace a furlong's course in, there she lay
Speechless, with veilèd lids. Then wide her eyes
She oped, and wildly, as she strove to rise,
Shrieked: for two diverse waves upon her rolled
Of stabbing death. The carcanet of gold
That gripped her brow was molten in a dire
And wondrous river of devouring fire.
And those fine robes, the gift thy children gave—
God's mercy!—everywhere did lap and lave
The delicate flesh; till up she sprang, and fled,
A fiery pillar, shaking locks and head
This way and that, seeking to cast the crown
Somewhere away. But like a thing nailed down
The burning gold held fast the anadem,
And through her locks, the more she scattered them,
Came fire the fiercer, till to earth she fell
A thing—save to her sire—scarce nameable,
And strove no more. That cheek of royal mien,
Where was it—or the place where eyes had been?

Only from crown and temples came faint blood
Shot through with fire. The very flesh, it stood
Out from the bones, as from a wounded pine
The gum starts, where those gnawing poisons fine
Bit in the dark—a ghastly sight! And touch
The dead we durst not. We had seen too much.
        But that poor father, knowing not, had sped,
Swift to his daughter's room, and there the dead
Lay at his feet. He knelt, and groaning low,
Folded her in his arms, and kissed her: "Oh,
Unhappy child, what thing unnatural hath
So hideously undone thee? Or what wrath
Of gods, to make this old grey sepulchre
Childless of thee? Would God but lay me there
To die with thee, my daughter!" So he cried.
But after, when he stayed from tears, and tried
To uplift his old bent frame, lo, in the folds
Of those fine robes it held, as ivy holds
Strangling among your laurel boughs. Oh, then
A ghastly struggle came! Again, again,
Up on his knee he writhed; but that dead breast
Clung still to his: till, wild, like one possessed,
He dragged himself half free; and, lo, the live
Flesh parted; and he laid him down to strive
No more with death, but perish; for the deep
Had risen above his soul. And there they sleep,
At last, the old proud father and the bride,
Even as his tears had craved it, side by side.
        For thee—Oh, no word more! Thyself will know
How best to baffle vengeance. . . . Long ago
I looked upon man's days, and found a grey
Shadow. And this thing more I surely say,
That those of all men who are counted wise,
Strong wits, devisers of great policies,
Do pay the bitterest toll. Since life began,
Hath there in God's eye stood one happy man?
Fair days roll on, and bear more gifts or less
Of fortune, but to no man happiness.

[tr. Gilbert Murray (1906)]

Catullus (84?–54 B.C.E.)

C. Valerius Catullus was one of the premier poets of the late first century B.C.E. in Rome. He was a contemporary of Julius Caesar and the philosophical poet Lucretius and a predecessor of the Augustan poets Horace and Virgil. Although chiefly a love poet (he wrote many poems about a woman he called Lesbia—probably Clodia, the wife of P. Claudius Pulcher), his poem 63, written in an unusual meter found almost nowhere in ancient literature, deals horrifically with the self-castration of the demigod Attis, son and lover of the Phrygian goddess Cybele.

Attis

Over ocean Attis sailing in a swift ship charioted
When he reached the Phrygian forests, and with rash foot violently
Trod the dark and shadowy regions of the goddess, wood-
    garlanded,
And with ravening madness ravished, and his reason abandoning him,
Seized a pointed flint and sundered from his flesh his virility.
Then in all his limbs realising his manhood irrevocable,
Seeing earth with blood besprinkled, with fresh blood, the blood of
    him,
In his snow-white hands he snatches the light tambourine suddenly,
Tambourine that thou, Cybele, madest, mother, for thy mysteries,
And, between his tender fingers the hide's hollow agitating,
Stricken through with trembling shudders, thus sings to his com-
    panions:
"Corybantes, all together, up, on to the woods of Cybele;
All together, on, ye wandering herds of Dindymus' shepherdess,
Ye that seeking foreign shores, and, in an exile voluntary,
Following me and guided by me, on my ways my companions,
Having overcome the rapid main and the floods' savagery,
And in passing hate of Venus having overcome the man in you,
Now your mistress' heart gladden ye with the speed of courses pre-
    cipitate.
Slow delay be cast behind you, follow all together, follow me,
To the Phrygian home of Cybele, Phrygian woods, the goddess's,
Where the cymbals utter their voices to the tambourines echoing,

Where the curved reed makes grave music for the Phrygian flute-
    player,
Where the Maenads toss together wild heads ivy-filleted,
Where with piercing ululations the sacred signs are agitated,
Where in wonted wake the wandering cohort follows the deity,
Thither meet it as we hasten, thither with dances swift-footed."
Scarcely had the would-be woman Attis ceased to his followers
When at once the Corybantes shrieked, and their tongues palpitated,
And their tambourines re-bellowed, and their cymbals crackled hol-
    lowly,
And the chorus swiftly leaping rushed towards Ida's summits ver-
    durous.
Whereat Attis, raging, wavering, goes unsteadily, breath forsaking
    him,
Tambourining through the dark woods the tumultuous company,
As, the yoke's weight shouldered off it, surges the heifer untamable.
Him their leader all the Bacchantes follow with feet precipitate;
But no sooner Cybele's threshold touched, together languorously
Fall in sleep, tired out with journeying, and without Ceres' suste-
    nance.
Sluggish slumber shuts their eyelids in a languor hesitating,
From their souls the raging madness passes away in quietude.
But, when the golden-visaged sun with bright eyes illuminated
Cloudless ether and the solid earth and ocean tumultuous,
And with sounding hoofs of morning trampled night's shadows
    away,
Then did Sleep with flying footsteps remove from Attis awakening
And divine Pasithea took him back to her bosom tremulous.
Then awakening out of quiet suddenly without delirium
All at once his deed returning comes again to his memory,
And himself he sees, and where, and without what now abidingly,
And with mind at ebb and flow he turns him seaward and, surveying
    it,
All the mighty vast of ocean, through eyes weeping incessantly,
He his fatherland addresses with sad crying dejectedly:
"Fatherland, O my mother! fatherland the begetter of me,
Have I, wretch above all wretched, cast thee off as a runagate
Slave his master, and on Ida sought these groves, this icy dwelling-
    place
Of the snow and savage region of the wild beasts' sovereignty?

Where, O where and in what region shall my thoughts imagine thee,
  fatherland?
Still the light within my eyelids longs for thee, turning thitherward,
When my mind a little season scatters these pangs ravaging me.
Am I then condemned for ever to these distant woods, abandoning
Fatherland and friends and chattels and the forefathers of me,
These abandoning, forum, race-course, wrestling-place, and gym-
  nasium?
Miserable, ah miserable soul lamenting herself perpetually!
For what form of bodily feature is there that I had it not?
I a woman! I adolescent, I a stripling, I all but a man,
I the seemliest at the wrestling, at the gymnasium I the flower of
  them?
Once my doors were thronged my thresholds warm with footprints
  uncountable,
Once my dwelling was with flowery wreaths and tokens engar-
  landed,
When I used to leave my chamber, and the rising sun arose with me.
I a priestess of the gods now, and a waiting-woman of Cybele?
I a Maenad, I this remnant left of a man emasculate?
I inhabit the cold green places, Ida's summit snow-garmented?
I beneath the heights of Phrygian mountains scatter my life away,
Where the woodland-haunting hind is and the wild-boar wood-
  wandering?
Now, now the deed I sorrow for; now, now I repent of it."
Scarcely from the rosy lips the sound had gone and, flitting rapidly
To both the ears of the gods the new rumour communicated,
When the lions from the traces of her chariot-yoke unharnessing
Cybele thus spake, and stung with words the left flock-terrifier:
"Go," she cries, "and with the fury of thy going, my fierce minister,
Let a madness harry, a madness drive him to my wood-fastnesses
Who desires to be delivered from my intolerable slavery.
Go thou, beat thy flanks with thy tail, and endure thy own blows
  lashing thee,
Roar, roar till all the region round resounds with thy bellowing,
Toss thy brawny neck and toss abroad thy fierce mane rutilant."
Thus spake the pitiless goddess, with her hands the yoke un-
  trammelling.
Whereat, loosed, the beast to swiftness in his fury lashing himself,

Rushes, roars, and breaks the thickets all in pieces with his galloping.
Then he, coming to the sea-wet margin where the foam whitens it,
Seeing there the tender Attis, where the flood curdless, luminous,
Rushes on him: he in terror flies, the savage woods envelop him;
Who his whole life long inhabits them, the goddess's waiting-
    woman.
Goddess, mighty goddess, Cybele, lady goddess of Dindymus,
Keep, mistress, all thy fury far, far from my dwelling-place,
Others urge thou headlong, others with thy madness intoxicate.
[tr. Arthur Symons (1913)]

Horace (65–8 B.C.E.)

Q. Horatius Flaccus was the leading lyric poet of the Augustan Age (the reign of the Emperor Augustus (31 B.C.E.–14 C.E.), just as his friend Virgil was the leading epic poet. His earliest works were the *Epodes* (short poems in various metres) and *Satires,* probably written in the 30s. They were followed by his greatest work, the *Odes,* ultimately published in four books. He also wrote *Epistles* and the *Carmen Saeculare.* Epode 5 is an evocative poem about the witch Canidia.

Epode 5

"Oh, by all the Gods that, high sitting throned above the sky,
    Bear dominion o'er the earth, the human race,
What means this fierce attack?—why with scowling fury black
    On me, me only, turned is every face?

In your little children's name,—if the Birth-queen ever came
    To aid you in your travail when you cried,—
By this my purple gay, that avails me not, I pray!—
    By Jove, who looketh down indignant-eyed,
Why like a stepdame glare upon me, or a bear
    That has felt the hunter's javelin in his side?"

While, with lips for fear that quivered, in their midst he stood, and
    shivered,
    Stripped of toga, stripped of medal, helpless child,

A tender frame—you might have thought that such a sight
    Would have melted hearts of Thracians stern and wild,—

Canidia—vipers crawling mid the elf-locks tangled falling
    From a head that never once had known the comb—
Bids them bring the barren fig that from sepulchres they dig,
    Bring the cypresses that grow beside the tomb,
And the spawn a loathly toad had voided, smeared with blood,
    And the feather of a screech-owl, bird of gloom,

And the herbs of deadly bane from Iolcos and from Spain
    Brought, from lands where only poisons rankly grow,
And the bone snatched from its jaw ere the famished hound could
    gnaw—
    All these upon the witch-fires bade she throw.

But Sagana, with gown girded high, runs up and down,
    Sprinkling waters of Avernus on the floor,
With her shaggy head a-bristle like the shell of some sea-thistle,
    Or the back, when he is charging, of a boar.

By no conscience-pang deterred, Veia, by no pity stirred,
    Fell to digging—and she grunted with the toil—
Digging—harder-hearted she than her iron spade could be—
    A burial-pit in that accursèd soil,

Where, from his living grave, his dying gaze might crave
    Food changed and changed throughout the weary day,
While, as one that swims chin-deep where the waters round him
    sweep,
    The child-face only rose above the clay;

That the hunger famine-anguished, and the thirst that burned and
    languished
    Might be mingled in her philtre of desire,
Soon as, yearning on the food aye forbidden, aye renewed,
    In their sockets his eyes shrivelled, as in fire.

Ay, and Folia too was there, the virago, from her lair
    In the city by the Adriatic sea,
As every gossip tells in Neapolis that dwells;
    And all the neighbouring alley-folk agree,

How her incantation-cry drew the planets from on high,
    And plucked the moon from heaven impiously.

But the savage witch, with brow scowling rage, is gnawing now,
    With those blackened teeth of hers, her talon-nails;
And she said—what said she not?—"Oh ye that o'er my lot
    Rule supreme, whose protection never fails,

O Night, O Hecat, come! thou who rulest o'er the gloom
    When the sacred rites of darkness have their hour,
Come, be present now at mine! Oh descend in wrath divine
    On my foes, and blast their dwellings by your power.

While the forest's savage brood yet are lurking in the wood,
    While slumber o'er them waves her wings of down,
Let the dogs with barking greet, as he totters up our street,
    That old debauchee, derision of the town,

While his perfumes load the air—even I, with all my care,
    Cannot make them stronger, sweeter—How is this?
What is wrong? The very charms that were fell Medea's arms
    In the old time, are they working now amiss?—

The charms that, ere she fled, bowed in dust the haughty head
    Of her rival, who could vaunt a king her sire,
When the bridal-present, steeped in the drugs of murder, leaped
    Into flame, and she died a death of fire?

I forgot no flower nor fruit, neither any evil root
    Lurking guiltily in tangled thickets lone:—
Why, the bed on which he sleeps my infernal unguent steeps
    In oblivion of all beauty save my own!

Ha, I have it! He's been set free from my enchantment's net
    By the spells of some one cunninger than I;
And he strolls abroad at ease!—But I'll bring you to your knees
    By the stranger, direr hell-broth I will try,

Varus! Hasten back you shall, and your soul be brought in thrall,
    By no hackneyed incantations, to my bower.
I will mix a deadlier draught: yea, a deadlier shall be quaffed
    By the spirit that in scorn defies my power.

Ay, and sooner shall the sky 'neath the floor of ocean lie,
    And the earth be stretched a canopy above,
Than you for me shall fail—as bitumen through the veil
    Of its smoke is quenchless flame—to burn in love!"

Then the hapless boy, no more begging mercy as before
    Of the devilish hags with humble plea and prayer,—
Pausing but to find a curse than the ban of Atreus worse,
    Hurled his malison upon the shuddering air:

"There's no damnèd drug so strong that the laws of Right and
    Wrong
    From their course, like plans of men, thereby are driven.
My curse shall dog you ever: flame of sacrifice shall never
    Expiate the maledictions heard in heaven.

Nay, when thus condemned to death I have gasped away my breath,
    I will haunt you still, a demon of the night;
And my ghost with talon-nail your faces shall assail.
    Ay, the Gods of Hell shall make you feel their might!

For, with horror-stricken breast by my nightmare weight oppressed,
    You shall start from troubled sleep, and sleep no more.
And the mob with volleyed sleet of their stones from street to street,
    Filthy hags, shall drive you down to Hades' door.

And, for burial, where you fall shall the wolves hold carnival,
    And the vultures of the Esquiline shall rend:
And my parents, living on—woe is me!—when I am gone,
    Shall with bitter exultation see your end!"

                                [tr. Arthur S. Way (1898)]

II. From the Middle Ages to the Eighteenth Century

Dante Alighieri (1265–1321)

Dante Alighieri is the leading epic poet of medieval Europe. His *Divina commedia* (*Divine Comedy*), in three books ("Inferno," "Purgatorio," "Paradiso"), depicts the metaphorical voyage of a man from Hell (Inferno) to purgatory to Paradise, in the company of the poet Virgil. The *Divine Comedy* was probably completed around 1314. The "Inferno" includes numerous vivid descriptions of Hell, its nine circles, and its inhabitants. Two cantos from "Inferno" are presented here.

From Inferno

Canto 3

"Through me the way is to the city dolent;
 Through me the way is to eternal dole;
 Through me the way among the people lost.
Justice incited my sublime Creator;
 Created me divine Omnipotence,
 The highest Wisdom and the Primal Love.
Before me there were no created things,
 Only eterne, and I eternal last.
 All hope abandon, ye who enter in!"
These words in sombre color I beheld
 Written upon the summit of a gate;
 Whence I: "Their sense is, Master, hard to me!"
And he to me, as one experienced:
 "Here all suspicion needs must be abandoned,
 All cowardice must needs be here extinct.
We to the place have come, where I have told thee
 Thou shalt behold the people dolorous
 Who have foregone the good of intellect."
And after he had laid his hand on mine

With joyful mien, whence I was comforted,
    He led me in among the secret things.
There sighs, complaints, and ululations loud
    Resounded through the air without a star,
    Whence I, at the beginning, wept thereat.
Languages diverse, horrible dialects,
    Accents of anger, words of agony,
    And voices high and hoarse, with sound of hands,
Made up a tumult that goes whirling on
    Forever in that air forever black,
    Even as the sand doth, when the whirlwind breathes.
And I, who had my head with horror bound,
    Said: "Master, what is this which now I hear?
    What folk is this, which seems by pain so vanquished?"
And he to me: "This miserable mode
    Maintain the melancholy souls of those
    Who lived withouten infamy or praise.
Commingled are they with that caitiff choir
    Of Angels, who have not rebellious been,
    Nor faithful were to God, but were for self.
The heavens expelled them, not to be less fair;
    Nor them the nethermore abyss receives,
    For glory none the damned would have from them."
And I: "O Master, what so grievous is
    To these, that maketh them lament so sore?"
    He answered: "I will tell thee very briefly.
These people have not any hope of death;
    And this blind life of theirs is so debased,
    They envious are of every other fate.
No fame of them the world permits to be;
    Misericord and Justice both disdain them.
    Let us not speak of them, but look, and pass."
And I, who looked again, beheld a banner,
    Which, whirling round, ran on so rapidly,
    That of all pause it seemed to me indignant;
And after it there came so long a train
    Of people, that I ne'er would have believed
    That ever Death so many had undone.
When some among them I had recognized,
    I looked, and I beheld the shade of him

Who made through cowardice the great refusal.
Forthwith I comprehended, and was certain,
    That this the sect was of the caitiff wretches
    Hateful to God and to his enemies.
These miscreants, who never were alive,
    Were naked, and were stung exceedingly
    By gadflies and by hornets that were there.
These did their faces irrigate with blood,
    Which, with their tears commingled, at their feet
    By the disgusting worms was gathered up.
And when to gazing farther I betook me,
    People I saw on a great river's bank;
    Whence said I: "Master, now vouchsafe to me,
That I may know who these are, and what law
    Makes them appear so ready to pass over,
    As I discern athwart the feeble light."
And he to me: "These things shall all be known
    To thee, as soon as we our footsteps stay
    Upon the dismal shore of Acheron."
Then with mine eyes ashamed and downward cast,
    Fearing my words might irksome be to him,
    From speech refrained I till we reached the river.
And lo! towards us coming in a boat
    An old man, hoary with the hair of eld,
    Crying: "Woe unto you, ye souls depraved!
Hope nevermore to look upon the heavens;
    I come to lead you to the other shore,
    To the eternal shades in heat and frost.
And thou, that yonder standest, living soul,
    Withdraw thee from these people, who are dead!"
    But when he saw that I did not withdraw,
He said: "By other ways, by other ports
    Thou to the shore shalt come, not here, for passage;
    A lighter vessel needs must carry thee."
And unto him the Guide: "Vex thee not, Charon;
    It is so willed there where is power to do
    That which is willed; and ask no further question."
Thereat were quieted the fleecy cheeks
    Of him the ferryman of the livid fen,
    Who round about his eyes had wheels of flame.

But all those souls who weary were and naked
      Their color changed and gnashed their teeth together,
      As soon as they had heard those cruel words.
God they blasphemed and their progenitors,
      The human race, the place, the time, the seed
      Of their engendering and of their birth!
Thereafter all together they withdrew,
      Bitterly weeping, to the accursed shore,
      Which waiteth every man who fears not God.
Charon the demon, with the eyes of glede,
      Beckoning to them, collects them all together,
      Beats with his oar whoever lags behind.
As in the autumn-time the leaves fall off,
      First one and then another, till the branch
      Unto the earth surrenders all its spoils;
In similar wise the evil seed of Adam
      Throw themselves from that margin one by one,
      At signals, as a bird unto its lure.
So they depart across the dusky wave,
      And ere upon the other side they land,
      Again on this side a new troop assembles.
"My son," the courteous Master said to me,
      "All those who perish in the wrath of God
      Here meet together out of every land;
And ready are they to pass o'er the river,
      Because celestial Justice spurs them on,
      So that their fear is turned into desire.
This way there never passeth a good soul;
      And hence if Charon doth complain of thee,
      Well mayst thou know now what his speech imports."
This being finished, all the dusk champaign
      Trembled so violently, that of that terror
      The recollection bathes me still with sweat.
The land of tears gave forth a blast of wind,
      And fulminated a vermilion light,
      Which overmastered in me every sense,
And as a man whom sleep doth seize I fell.

Canto 18

There is a place in Hell called Malebolge,
 Wholly of stone and of an iron color,
  As is the circle that around it turns.
Right in the middle of the field malign
 There yawns a well exceeding wide and deep,
  Of which its place the structure will recount.
Round, then, is that enclosure which remains
 Between the well and foot of the high, hard bank,
  And has distinct in valleys ten its bottom.
As where for the protection of the walls
 Many and many moats surround the castles,
  The part in which they are a figure forms,
Just such an image those presented there;
 And as about such strongholds from their gates
  Unto the outer bank are little bridges,
So from the precipice's base did crags
 Project, which intersected dikes and moats,
  Unto the well that truncates and collects them.
Within this place, down shaken from the back
 Of Geryon, we found us; and the Poet
  Held to the left, and I moved on behind.
Upon my right hand I beheld new anguish,
 New torments, and new wielders of the lash,
  Wherewith the foremost Bolgia was replete.
Down at the bottom were the sinners naked;
 This side the middle came they facing us,
  Beyond it, with us, but with greater steps;
Even as the Romans, for the mighty host,
 The year of Jubilee, upon the bridge,
  Have chosen a mode to pass the people over;
For all upon one side towards the Castle
 Their faces have, and go unto Saint Peter's;
  On the other side they go towards the Mountain.
This side and that, along the livid stone
 Beheld I hornëd demons with great scourges,
  Who cruelly were beating them behind.
Ah me! how they did make them lift their legs
 At the first blows! and sooth not any one

The second waited for, nor for the third.
While I was going on, mine eyes by one
    Encountered were; and straight I said: "Already
    With sight of this one I am not unfed."
Therefore I stayed my feet to make him out,
    And with me the sweet Guide came to a stand,
    And to my going somewhat back assented;
And he, the scourged one, thought to hide himself,
    Lowering his face, but little it availed him;
    For said I: "Thou that castest down thine eyes,
If false are not the features which thou bearest,
    Thou art Venedico Caccianimico;
    But what doth bring thee to such pungent sauces?"
And he to me: "Unwillingly I tell it;
    But forces me thine utterance distinct,
    Which makes me recollect the ancient world.
I was the one who the fair Ghisola
    Induced to grant the wishes of the Marquis,
    Howe'er the shameless story may be told.
Not the sole Bolognese am I who weeps here;
    Nay, rather is this place so full of them,
    That not so many tongues to-day are taught
'Twixt Reno and Savena to say *sipa;*
    And if thereof thou wishest pledge or proof,
    Bring to thy mind our avaricious heart."
While speaking in this manner, with his scourge
    A demon smote him, and said: "Get thee gone,
    Pander, there are no women here for coin."
I joined myself again unto mine Escort;
    Thereafterward with footsteps few we came
    To where a crag projected from the bank.
This very easily did we ascend,
    And turning to the right along its ridge,
    From those eternal circles we departed.
When we were there, where it is bellowed out
    Beneath, to give a passage to the scourged,
    The Guide said: "Wait, and see that on thee strike
The vision of those others evil-born,
    Of whom thou hast not yet beheld the faces,
    Because together with us they have gone."

From the old bridge we looked upon the train
     Which tow'rds us came upon the other border,
     And which the scourges in like manner smite.
And the good Master, without my inquiring,
     Said to me: "See that tall one who is coming,
     And for his pain seems not to shed a tear;
Still what a royal aspect he retains!
     That Jason is, who by his heart and cunning
     The Colchians of the Ram made destitute.
He by the isle of Lemnos passed along
     After the daring women pitiless
     Had unto death devoted all their males.
There with his tokens and with ornate words
     Did he deceive Hypsipyle, the maiden
     Who first, herself, had all the rest deceived.
There did he leave her pregnant and forlorn;
     Such sin unto such punishment condemns him,
     And also for Medea is vengeance done.
With him go those who in such wise deceive;
     And this sufficient be of the first valley
     To know, and those that in its jaws it holds."
We were already where the narrow path
     Crosses athwart the second dike, and forms
     Of that a buttress for another arch.
Thence we heard people, who are making moan
     In the next Bolgia, snorting with their muzzles,
     And with their palms beating upon themselves.
The margins were encrusted with a mould
     By exhalation from below, that sticks there,
     And with the eyes and nostrils wages war.
The bottom is so deep, no place suffices
     To give us sight of it, without ascending
     The arch's back, where most the crag impends.
Thither we came, and thence down in the moat
     I saw a people smothered in a filth
     That out of human privies seemed to flow;
And whilst below there with mine eye I search,
     I saw one with his head so foul with ordure,
     It was not clear if he were clerk or layman.

He screamed to me: "Wherefore art thou so eager
     To look at me more than the other foul ones?"
     And I to him: "Because, if I remember,
I have already seen thee with dry hair,
     And thou'rt Alessio Interminei of Lucca;
     Therefore I eye thee more than all the others."
And he thereon, belaboring his pumpkin:
     "The flatteries have submerged me here below,
     Wherewith my tongue was never surfeited."
Then said to me the Guide: "See that thou thrust
     Thy visage somewhat farther in advance,
     That with thine eyes thou well the face attain
Of that uncleanly and dishevelled drab,
     Who there doth scratch herself with filthy nails,
     And crouches now, and now on foot is standing.
Thais the harlot is it, who replied
     Unto her paramour, when he said, 'Have I
     Great gratitude from thee?'—'Nay, marvellous';
And herewith let our sight be satisfied."
                    [tr. Henry Wadsworth Longfellow (1867)]

Christopher Marlowe (1564–1593)

Christopher Marlowe is the foremost Elizabethan tragedian next to
William Shakespeare. He was not merely the first major English
dramatist to use blank verse, but also a master of the form; and his
dramatic works are particularly memorable for their ambitious, char-
ismatic, and conflicted protagonists. His verse dramas include *Dido,
Queen of Carthage* (c. 1586); *Tamburlaine* (in two parts, 1587–88);
The Jew of Malta (c. 1589); *Edward the Second* (c. 1592); and *The
Massacre at Paris* (c. 1593). Most famous of all is *The Tragical His-
tory of Doctor Faustus,* based on a sixteenth-century chapbook by an
anonymous German author—the first dramatized version of the leg-
end of a scholar's dealings with the devil. It exists in two manuscript
variants (c. 1589, 1593). At various times an informant to the Brit-
ish government, a counterfeiter, and a petty criminal, Marlowe was
stabbed to death at the age of twenty-nine in a meeting-house brawl
under ambiguous circumstances.

From Dr. Faustus

Enter FAUSTUS *to conjure.*

FAUSTUS: Now that the gloomy shadow of the earth,
Longing to view Orion's drizzling look,
Leaps from the antarctic world unto the sky,
And dims the welkin with her pitchy breath,
Faustus, begin thine incantations,
And try if devils will obey thy hest,
Seeing thou hast prayed and sacrificed to them.
Within this circle is Jehovah's name,
Forward and backward anagrammatized,
The breviated names of holy saints,
Figures of every adjunct to the Heavens,
And characters of signs and erring stars,
By which the spirits are enforced to rise:
Then fear not, Faustus, but be resolute,
And try the uttermost magic can perform.

Sint mihi Dei Acherontis propitii! Valeat numen triplex Jehova!
Ignei, aërii, acquatani spiritus, salvete? Orientis princeps Belzezub, in-
ferni ardentis monarcha, et Demogorgon, propitiamus vos, ut apparet et
surgat Mephistophilis, quod tumeraris; per Jehovam, Gehennam, et conse-
cratam aquam quam nunc spargo, signumque crucis quod nunc facio, et
per vota nostra, ipse nunc surgat nobis dicatus Mephistophilis!

Enter MEPHISTOPHILIS.

I charge thee to return and change thy shape;
Thou art too ugly to attend on me:
Go, and return an old Franciscan friair;
That holy shape becomes a devil best.

Exit MEPHISTOPHILIS.

I see there's virtue in my heavenly words:
Who would not be proficient in this art?
How pliant is this Mephistophilis,
Full of obedience and humility!
Such is the force of magic and my spells:
Now, Faustus, thou art conjuror laureat,
That canst command great Mephistophilis:

Quin regis Mephistophilis fratris imagine.

                                  Enter MEPHISTOPHILIS, *like a Franciscan friar.*
MEPHISTOPHILIS: Now, Faustus, what would'st thou have
me do?

FAUSTUS: I charge thee wait upon me whilst I live,
To do whatever Faustus shall command,
Be it to make the moon drop from her sphere,
Or the ocean to overwhelm the world.

MEPHISTOPHILIS: I am a servant to great Lucifer,
And may not follow thee without his leave:
No more than he commands must we perform.

FAUSTUS: Did not he charge thee to appear to me?

MEPHISTOPHILIS: No. I came hither of mine own accord.

FAUSTUS: Did not my conjuring speeches raise thee? Speak.

MEPHISTOPHILIS: That was the cause, but yet *per accidens;*
For, when we hear one rack the name of God,
Abjure the Scriptures and his Saviour Christ,
We fly, in hope to get his glorious soul;
Nor will we come, unless he use such means
Whereby he is in danger to be damn'd.
Therefore the shortest cut for conjuring
Is stoutly to abjure the Trinity,
And pray devoutly to the prince of Hell.

FAUSTUS: So Faustus hath
Already done; and holds this principle,
There is no Chief but only Belzebub,
To whom Faustus doth dedicate himself.
This word "damnation" terrifies not him,
For he confounds hell in Elysium;
His ghost be with the old philosophers!
But, leaving these vain trifles of men's souls,
Tell me what is that Lucifer, thy Lord?

MEPHISTOPHILIS: Arch-regent and commander of all spirits.

FAUSTUS: Was not that Lucifer an angel once?

MEPHISTOPHILIS: Yes, Faustus, and most dearly loved of God.

FAUSTUS: How comes it, then, that he is Prince of devils?

MEPHISTOPHILIS: O, by aspiring pride and insolence;
For which God threw him from the face of Heaven.

FAUSTUS: And what are you that live with Lucifer?

MEPHISTOPHILIS: Unhappy spirits that fell with Lucifer,
Conspired against our God with Lucifer,
And are for ever damned with Lucifer.

FAUSTUS: Where are you damned?

MEPHISTOPHILIS: In Hell.

FAUSTUS: How comes it, then, that thou art out of Hell?

MEPHISTOPHILIS: Why this is Hell, nor am I out of it:
Think'st thou that I, who saw the face of God,
And tasted the eternal joys of Heaven,
Am not tormented with ten thousand hells,
In being deprived of everlasting bliss?
Oh, Faustus, leave these frivolous demands,
Which strike a terror to my fainting soul.

FAUSTUS: What, is great Mephistophilis so passionate
For being deprivèd of the joys of heaven?
Learn thou of Faustus manly fortitude,
And scorn those joys thou never shalt possess.
Go bear these tidings to great Lucifer:
Seeing Faustus hath incurred eternal death
By desperate thoughts against Jove's deity,
Say he surrenders up to him his soul,
So he will spare him four and twenty years,
Letting him live in all voluptuousness;
Having thee ever to attend on me,
To give me whatsoever I shall ask,
To tell me whatsoever I demand,
To slay mine enemies, and aid my friends,

And always be obedient to my will.
Go and return to mighty Lucifer,
And meet me in my study at midnight,
And then resolve me of thy master's mind.

    MEPHISTOPHILIS: I will, Faustus.   *Exit.*

    FAUSTUS: Had I as many souls as there be stars,
I'd give them all for Mephistophilis.
By him I'll be great Emperor of the world,
And make a bridge thorough the moving air,
To pass the ocean with a band of men;
I'll join the hills that bind the Afric shore,
And make that country continent to Spain,
And both contributory to my crown:
The Emperor shall not live but by my leave,
Nor any potentate of Germany.
Now that I have obtained what I desire,
I'll live in speculation of this art
Till Mephistophilis return again.

William Shakespeare (1564–1616)

William Shakespeare joined an acting company at age twenty-one; his first plays began to be presented around five years later. In 1599 he helped found the Globe Theatre, the most famous of Elizabethan playhouses, where his work was subsequently featured. Later plays were staged at Blackfriars Theatre, a more intimate setting that encouraged Shakespeare's development of more sophisticated dramatic technique. In 1593–94, with theatres closed because of the plague, Shakespeare turned his hand to narrative poetry. He also composed upwards of 150 finely turned sonnets throughout his career, apparently for private readership. The playwright flourished financially and socially; by 1610 he was a landed gentleman, retiring to Stratford where he died six years later. Shakespeare's thirty-eight plays (some in collaboration) are typically classified as comedies, histories, and tragedies. The supernatural is a recurring element in all three types—presentiments abound, and ghosts, fairies, sprites, and witches make varied appearances—and it serves to centrally motivate the action in *Hamlet* (c. 1603) and *Macbeth* (c. 1605–06).

From Hamlet

Enter Ghost.

MARCELLUS: Peace, break thee off. Look where it comes again.

BERNARDO: In the same figure like the king that's dead.

MARCELLUS: Thou art a scholar; speak to it, Horatio.

BERNARDO: Looks 'a not like the king? Mark it, Horatio.

HORATIO: Most like. It harrows me with fear and wonder.

BERNARDO: It would be spoke to.

MARCELLUS: Speak to it, Horatio.

HORATIO: What art thou that usurp'st this time of night
Together with that fair and warlike form
In which the majesty of buried Denmark
Did sometimes march? By heaven I charge thee, speak.

MARCELLUS: It is offended.

BERNARDO: See, it stalks away.

HORATIO: Stay. Speak, speak. I charge thee, speak. *Exit Ghost.*

MARCELLUS: 'Tis gone and will not answer.

BERNARDO: How now, Horatio? You tremble and look pale.
Is not this something more than fantasy?
What think you on't?

HORATIO: Before my God, I might not this believe
Without the sensible and true avouch
Of mine own eyes.

MARCELLUS: Is it not like the king?

HORATIO: As thou art to thyself.
Such was the very armor he had on

When he th'ambitious Norway combated.
So frowned he once when, in an angry parle,
He smote the sledded Polacks on the ice.
'Tis strange.

MARCELLUS: Thus twice before, and jump at this dead hour,
With martial stalk hath he gone by our watch.

HORATIO: In what particular thought to work I know not;
But, in the gross and scope of my opinion,
This bodes some strange eruption to our state.

MARCELLUS: Good now, sit down, and tell me he that knows,
Why this same strict and most observant watch
So nightly toils the subject of the land,
And why such daily cast of brazen cannon
And foreign mart for implements of war,
Why such impress of shipwrights, whose sore task
Does not divide the Sunday from the week.
What might be toward that this sweaty haste
Doth make the night joint-laborer with the day?
Who is't that can inform me?

HORATIO: That can I.
At least the whisper goes so. Our last king,
Whose image even but now appeared to us,
Was as you know by Fortinbras of Norway,
Thereto pricked on by a most emulate pride,
Dared to the combat; in which our valiant Hamlet
(For so this side of our known world esteemed him)
Did slay this Fortinbras; who, by a sealed compact
Well ratified by law and heraldry,
Did forfeit, with his life, all those his lands
Which he stood seized of to the conqueror;
Against the which a moiety competent
Was gagèd by our king, which had returned
To the inheritance of Fortinbras
Had he been vanquisher, as, by the same comart
And carriage of the article designed,
His fell to Hamlet. Now, sir, young Fortinbras,
Of unimprovèd mettle hot and full,

Hath in the skirts of Norway here and there
Sharked up a list of lawless resolutes
For food and diet to some enterprise
That hath a stomach in't; which is no other,
As it doth well appear unto our state,
But to recover of us by strong hand
And terms compulsatory those foresaid lands
So by his father lost; and this, I take it,
Is the main motive of our preparations,
The source of this our watch, and the chief head
Of this posthaste and romage in the land.

     BERNARDO: I think it be no other but e'en so.
Well may it sort that this portentous figure
Comes armèd through our watch so like the king
That was and is the question of these wars.

     HORATIO: A mote it is to trouble the mind's eye.
In the most high and palmy state of Rome,
A little ere the mightiest Julius fell,
The graves stood tenantless and the sheeted dead
Did squeak and gibber in the Roman streets;
As stars with trains of fire and dews of blood,
Disasters in the sun; and the moist star
Upon whose influence Neptune's empire stands
Was sick almost to doomsday with eclipse.
And even the like precurse of feared events,
As harbingers preceding still the fates
And prologue to the omen coming on,
Have heaven and earth together demonstrated
Unto our climatures and countrymen.

Enter Ghost.

But soft, behold, lo where it comes again!
I'll cross it, though it blast me.—Stay, illusion.

He spreads his arms.

If thou hast any sound or use of voice,
Speak to me.
If there be any good thing to be done
That may to thee do ease and grace to me,
Speak to me.
If thou art privy to thy country's fate,

Which happily foreknowing may avoid,
O, speak! Or if thou hast uphoarded in thy life
Extorted treasure in the womb of earth,
For which, they say, you spirits oft walk in death,

The cock crows.

Speak of it. Stay and speak. Stop it, Marcellus.

MARCELLUS: Shall I strike at it with my partisan?

HORATIO: Do, if it will not stand.

BERNARDO: 'Tis here.

HORATIO: 'Tis here.

MARCELLUS: 'Tis gone.   *Exit Ghost.*
We do it wrong, being so majestical,
To offer it the show of violence,
For it is as the air invulnerable,
And our vain blows malicious mockery.

BERNARDO: It was about to speak when the cock crew.

HORATIO: And then it started, like a guilty thing
Upon a fearful summons. I have heard
The cock, that is the trumpet to the morn,
Doth with his lofty and shrill-sounding throat
Awake the god of day, and at his warning,
Whether in sea or fire, in earth or air,
Th'extravagant and erring spirit hies
To his confine; and of the truth herein
This present object made probation.

MARCELLUS: It faded on the crowing of the cock.
Some say that ever 'gainst that season comes
Wherein our Saviour's birth is celebrated,
This bird of dawning singeth all night long,
And then, they say, no spirit dare stir abroad,
The nights are wholesome, then no planets strike,
No fairy takes, nor witch hath power to charm.
So hallowed and so gracious is that time.

HORATIO: So have I heard and do in part believe it.

But look, the morn in russet mantle clad
Walks o'er the dew of yon high eastward hill.
Break we our watch up, and by my advice
Let us impart what we have seen to-night
Unto young Hamlet, for upon my life
This spirit, dumb to us, will speak to him.
Do you consent we shall acquaint him with it,
As needful in our loves, fitting our duty?

MARCELLUS: Let's do't, I pray, and I this morning know
Where we shall find him most conveniently.

Exeunt.

[. . .]

Enter Ghost.

HORATIO: Look, my lord, it comes.

HAMLET: Angels and ministers of grace defend us!
Be thou a spirit of health or goblin damned,
Bring with thee airs from heaven or blasts from hell,
Be thy intents wicked or charitable,
Thou com'st in such a questionable shape
That I will speak to thee. I'll call thee Hamlet,
King, father, royal Dane. O, answer me!
Let me not burst in ignorance, but tell
Why thy canonized bones, hearsèd in death,
Have burst their cerements, why the sepulchre
Wherein we saw thee quietly interred
Hath oped his ponderous and marble jaws
To cast thee up again. What may this mean
That thou, dead corse, again in complete steel,
Revisits thus the glimpses of the moon,
Making night hideous, and we fools of nature
So horridly to shake our disposition
With thoughts beyond the reaches of our souls?
Say, why is this? wherefore? what should we do?

[Ghost] beckons.

HORATIO: It beckons you to go away with it,
As if it some impartment did desire
To you alone.

MARCELLUS: Look with what courteous action

It waves you to a more removèd ground.
But do not go with it.

HORATIO: No, by no means.

HAMLET: It will not speak. Then will I follow it.

HORATIO: Do not, my lord.

HAMLET: Why, what should be the fear?
I do not set my life at a pin's fee,
And for my soul, what can it do to that,
Being a thing immortal as itself?
It waves me forth again. I'll follow it.

HORATIO: What if it tempt you toward the flood, my lord,
Or to the dreadful summit of the cliff
That beetles o'er his base into the sea,
And there assume some other horrible form,
Which might deprive your sovereignty of reason
And draw you into madness? Think of it.
The very place puts toys of desperation,
Without more motive, into every brain
That looks so many fathoms to the sea
And hears it roar beneath.

HAMLET: It waves me still.
Go on. I'll follow thee.

MARCELLUS: You shall not go, my lord.

HAMLET: Hold off your hands.

HORATIO: Be ruled. You shall not go.

HAMLET: My fate cries out
And makes each petty artere in this body
As hardy as the Nemean lion's nerve.
Still am I called. Unhand me, gentlemen.
By heaven, I'll make a ghost of him that lets me!
I say, away! Go on. I'll follow thee.

Exit Ghost, and Hamlet.

From Macbeth

Thunder. Enter the three Witches.

1. WITCH: Thrice the brinded cat hath mewed.

2. WITCH: Thrice, and once the hedge-pig whined.

3. WITCH: Harpier cries.—'Tis time, 'tis time!

1. WITCH: Round about the cauldron go;
In the poisoned entrails throw.
Toad, that under cold stone
Days and nights has thirty-one
Swelt'red venom, sleeping got,
Boil thou first i' th' charmèd pot.
Double, double, toil and trouble,
Fire burn and cauldron bubble.

2. WITCH: Fillet of a fenny snake,
In the cauldron boil and bake;
Eye of newt, and toe of frog,
Wool of bat, and tongue of dog,
Adder's fork, and blindworm's sting,
Lizard's leg, and howlet's wing—
For a charm of pow'rful trouble
Like a hell-broth boil and bubble.

ALL: Double, double, toil and trouble,
Fire burn and cauldron bubble.

3. WITCH: Scale of dragon, tooth of wolf,
Witch's mummy, maw and gulf
Of the ravined salt-sea shark,
Root of hemlock digged i' th' dark,
Liver of blaspheming Jew,
Gall of goat, and slips of yew
Slivered in the moon's eclipse,
Nose of Turk, and Tartar's lips,
Finger of birth-strangled babe
Ditch-delivered by a drab
Make the gruel thick and slab.

Add thereto a tiger's chaudron
For th' ingredience of our cauldron.

    ALL: Double, double, toil and trouble,
Fire burn and cauldron bubble.

    2. WITCH: Cool it with a baboon's blood,
Then the charm is firm and good.
                  [Enter Hecate and the other three Witches.

    HECATE: O, well done! I commend your pains,
And every one shall share i' th' gains.
And now about the cauldron sing
Like elves and fairies in a ring,
Enchanting all that you put in.
          Music and a song, "Black spirits," &c.
                Exeunt Hecate and singers.]

    2. WITCH: By the pricking of my thumbs,
Something wicked this way comes.
Open locks,
Whoever knocks!

                    Enter Macbeth.

    MACBETH: How now, you secret, black, and midnight hags,
What is't you do?

    ALL: A deed without a name.

    MACBETH: I conjure you by that which you profess,
Howe'er you come to know it, answer me.
Though you untie the winds and let them fight
Against the churches, though the yesty waves
Confound and swallow navigation up,
Though bladed corn be lodged and trees blown down,
Though castles topple on their warders' heads,
Though palaces and pyramids do slope
Their heads to their foundations, though the treasure
Of Nature's germains tumble all together
Even till destruction sicken, answer me
To what I ask you.

    1. Witch: Speak.

2. Witch: Demand.

3. WITCH: We'll answer.

1. WITCH: Say if th' hadst rather hear it from our mouths
Or from our masters.

MACBETH: Call 'em. Let me see 'em.

1. WITCH: Pour in sow's blood, that hath eaten
Her nine farrow; grease that's sweaten
From the murderer's gibbet throw
Into the flame.

ALL: Come, high or low,
Thyself and office deftly show!

                    Thunder. First Apparition, an Armed Head.

MACBETH: Tell me, thou unknown power—

1. WITCH: He knows thy thought:
Hear his speech, but say thou naught.

1. APPARITION: Macbeth, Macbeth, Macbeth, beware Macduff!
Beware the Thane of Fife! Dismiss me.—Enough.

                             He descends.

MACBETH: Whate'er thou art, for thy good caution thanks:
Thou hast harped my fear aright. But one word more—

1. WITCH: He will not be commanded. Here's another,
More potent than the first.

               Thunder. Second Apparition, a Bloody Child.

2. APPARITION: Macbeth, Macbeth, Macbeth—

MACBETH: Had I three ears, I'ld hear thee.

2. APPARITION: Be bloody, bold, and resolute! Laugh to scorn
The pow'r of man, for none of woman born
Shall harm Macbeth.

                             Descends.

MACBETH: Then live, Macduff,—what need I fear of thee?
But yet I'll make assurance double sure

And take a bond of fate. Thou shalt not live;
That I may tell pale-hearted fear it lies
And sleep in spite of thunder.
Thunder. Third Apparition, a Child Crowned, with a tree in his hand.
                              What is this
That rises like the issue of a king
And wears upon his baby-brow the round
And top of sovereignty?

      ALL: Listen, but speak not to't.

      3. APPARITION: Be lion-mettled, proud, and take no care
Who chafes, who frets, or where conspirers are!
Macbeth shall never vanquished be until
Great Birnam Wood to high Dunsinane Hill
Shall come against him.

                                           Descends.

      MACBETH: That will never be.
Who can impress the forest, bid the tree
Unfix his earth-bound root? Sweet bodements, good!
Rebellious dead rise never till the Wood
Of Birnam rise, and our high-placed Macbeth
Shall live the lease of nature, pay his breath
To time and mortal custom. Yet my heart
Throbs to know one thing. Tell me, if your art
Can tell so much: Shall Banquo's issue ever
Reign in this kingdom?

      ALL: Seek to know no more.

      MACBETH: I will be satisfied. Deny me this,
And an eternal curse fall on you! Let me know.
Why sinks that cauldron? and what noise is this?

                                           Hautboys.

      1. Witch: Show!

      2. Witch: Show!

      3. Witch: Show!

      ALL: Show his eyes, and grieve his heart!

Come like shadows, so depart!
  A show of eight Kings and Banquo, last [King] with a glass in his hand.

     MACBETH: Thou art too like the spirit of Banquo. Down!
Thy crown does sear mine eyeballs. And thy hair,
Thou other gold-bound brow, is like the first.
A third is like the former. Filthy hags,
Why do you show me this? A fourth? Start, eyes!
What, will the line stretch out to th' crack of doom?
Another yet? A seventh? I'll see no more.
And yet the eighth appears, who bears a glass
Which shows me many more; and some I see
That twofold balls and treble sceptres carry.
Horrible sight! Now I see 'tis true;
For the blood-boltered Banquo smiles upon me
And points at them for his. What? Is this so?

     [1. WITCH: Ay, sir, all this is so. But why
Stands Macbeth thus amazedly?
Come, sisters, cheer we up his sprites
And show the best of our delights.
I'll charm the air to give a sound
While you perform your antic round,
That this great king may kindly say
Our duties did his welcome pay.
                Music. The Witches dance, and vanish.]

     MACBETH: Where are they? Gone? Let this pernicious hour
Stand aye accursèd in the calendar!

John Donne (1572–1631)

British poet John Donne was the leading member of what came to be called the Metaphysical Poets, a group of poets of the early seventeenth century who were derisively thought to have incorporated obscure learning and far-fetched analogies in their poems. Donne's earliest poems, his *Satires* and *Elegies,* date to the 1590s. He also wrote many "songs and sonnets." His prose works include essays, sermons, and devotions. "The Apparition," one of his "songs and sonnets," was first published in a posthumous edition of 1633.

The Apparition

When by thy scorne, O murdresse, I am dead,
And that thou thinkst thee free
From all solicitation from mee,
Then shall my ghost come to thy bed,
And thee, fain'd vestall, in worse armes shall see;
Then thy sicke taper will begin to winke,
And he, whose thou art then, being tyr'd before,
Will, if thou stirre, or pinch to wake him, thinke
    Thou call'st for more,
And in false sleepe will from thee shrinke,
Amd then poore Aspen wretch, neglected thou
Bath'd in a cold quicksilver sweat wilt lye
    A veryer ghost then I;
What I will say, I will not tell thee now,
Lest that preserve thee; and since my love is spent,
I'had rather thou shouldst painfully repent,
Then by my threatnings rest still innocent.

John Milton (1608–1674)

British poet and pamphleteer John Milton attended Christ's College, Cambridge, during which time he wrote poetry in both English and Latin, including the celebrated "On the Morning of Christ's Nativity" (1629). The masque *Comus* was written in 1634 and published in 1637, the same year that he wrote the famous lyric poem "Lycidas." For the next twenty years Milton wrote little poetry, instead devoting himself to prose pamphlets on important religious and political questions of the day, including the celebrated defense of freedom of the press, *Areopagitica* (1644). He supported the overthrow of King Charles I by Oliver Cromwell, becoming Latin secretary of the Council of State. In 1651 he went blind. He began working on *Paradise Lost* around 1658, although he had conceived it as early as 1639. It was completed around 1663 and published in 1667. *Para-*

dise Regain'd appeared in 1671. *Paradise Lost,* although an attempt to "justify the ways of God to men," contains stirring passages on Satan and other devils in Hell. One such passage, from Book II, is printed here.

From Paradise Lost

> The *Stygian* Council thus dissolv'd; and forth
> In order came the grand infernal Peers:
> Midst came thir mighty Paramount, and seem'd
> Alone th' Antagonist of Heav'n, nor less
> Than Hell's dread Emperor with pomp Supreme,
> And God-like imitated State; him round
> A Globe of fiery Seraphim inclos'd
> With bright imblazonry, and horrent Arms.
> Then of thir Session ended they bid cry
> With Trumpet's regal sound the great result:
> Toward the four winds four speedy Cherubim
> Put to thir mouths the sounding Alchymy
> By Herald's voice explain'd: the hollow Abyss
> Heard far and wide, and all the host of Hell
> With deaf'ning shout, return'd them loud acclaim.
> Thence more at ease thir minds and somewhat rais'd
> By false presumptuous hope, the ranged powers
> Disband, and wand'ring, each his several way
> Pursues, as inclination or sad choice
> Leads him perplext, where he may likeliest find
> Truce to his restless thoughts, and entertain
> The irksome hours, till this great Chief return.
> Part on the Plain, or in the Air sublime
> Upon the wing, or in swift Race contend,
> As at th' *Olympian* Games or *Pythian* fields;
> Part curb thir fiery Steeds, or shun the Goal
> With rapid wheels, or fronted Brígads form.
> As when to warn proud Cities war appears
> Wag'd in the troubl'd Sky, and Armies rush
> To Battle in the Clouds, before each Van
> Prick forth the Aery Knights, and couch thir spears
> Till thickest Legions close; with feats of Arms
> From either end of Heav'n the welkin burns.

Others with vast *Typhœan* rage more fell
Rend up both Rocks and Hills, and ride the Air
In whirlwind; Hell scarce holds the wild uproar.
As when *Alcides* from *Oechalia* Crown'd
With conquest, felt th' envenom'd robe, and tore
Through pain up by the roots *Thessalian* Pines,
And *Lichas* from the top of *Oeta* threw
Into th' *Euboic* Sea. Others more mild,
Retreated in a silent valley, sing
With notes Angelical to many a Harp
Thir own Heroic deeds and hapless fall
By doom of Battle; and complain that Fate
Free Virtue should enthrall to Force or Chance.
Thir Song was partial, but the harmony
(What could it less when Spirits immortal sing?)
Suspended Hell, and took with ravishment
The thronging audience. In discourse more sweet
(For Eloquence the Soul, Song charms the Sense,)
Others apart sat on a Hill retir'd,
In thoughts more elevate, and reason'd high
Of Providence, Foreknowledge, Will, and Fate,
Fixt Fate, Free will, Foreknowledge absolute,
And found no end, in wand'ring mazes lost.
Of good and evil much they argu'd then,
Of happiness and final misery,
Passion and Apathy, and glory and shame,
Vain wisdom all, and false Philosophie:
Yet with a pleasing sorcery could charm
Pain for a while or anguish, and excite
Fallacious hope, or arm th' obdured breast
With stubborn patience as with triple steel.
Another part in Squadrons and gross Bands,
On bold adventure to discover wide
That dismal World, if any Clime perhaps
Might yield them easier habitation, bend
Four ways thir flying March, along the Banks
Of four infernal Rivers that disgorge
Into the burning Lake thir baleful streams;
Abhorred *Styx* the flood of deadly hate,
Sad *Acheron* of sorrow, black and deep;

Cocytus, nam'd of lamentation loud
Heard on the rueful stream; fierce *Phlegeton*
Whose waves of torrent fire inflame with rage.
Far off from these a slow and silent stream,
Lethe the River of Oblivion rolls
Her wat'ry Labyrinth, whereof who drinks,
Forthwith his former state and being forgets,
Forgets both joy and grief, pleasure and pain.
Beyond this flood a frozen Continent
Lies dark and wild, beat with perpetual storms
Of Whirlwind and dire Hail, which on firm land
Thaws not, but gathers heap, and ruin seems
Of ancient pile; all else deep snow and ice,
A gulf profound as that *Serbonian* Bog
Betwixt *Damiata* and Mount *Casius* old,
Where Armies whole have sunk: the parching Air
Burns frore, and cold performs th' effect of Fire.
Thither by harpy-footed Furies hal'd,
At certain revolutions all the damn'd
Are brought: and feel by turns the bitter change
Of fierce extremes, extremes by change more fierce,
From Beds of raging Fire to starve in Ice
Thir soft Ethereal warmth, and there to pine
Immovable, infixt, and frozen round,
Periods of time, thence hurried back to fire.
They ferry over this *Lethean* Sound
Both to and fro, thir sorrow to augment,
And wish and struggle, as they pass, to reach
The tempting stream, with one small drop to lose
In sweet forgetfulness all pain and woe,
All in one moment, and so near the brink;
But Fate withstands, and to oppose th' attempt
Medusa with *Gorgonian* terror guards
The Ford, and of itself the water flies
All taste of living wight, as once it fled
The lip of *Tantalus.* Thus roving on
In confus'd march forlorn, th' advent'rous Bands
With shudd'ring horror pale, and eyes aghast
View'd first thir lamentable lot, and found
No rest: through many a dark and dreary Vale

They pass'd, and many a Region dolorous,
O'er many a Frozen, many a Fiery Alp,
Rocks, Caves, Lakes, Fens, Bogs, Dens, and shades of death,
A Universe of death, which God by curse
Created evil, for evil only good,
Where all life dies, death lives, and Nature breeds,
Perverse, all monstrous, all prodigious things,
Abominable, inutterable, and worse
Than Fables yet have feign'd, or fear conceiv'd,
Gorgons and *Hydras,* and *Chimeras* dire.
      Meanwhile the Adversary of God and Man,
Satan with thoughts inflam'd of highest design,
Puts on swift wings, and towards the Gates of Hell
Explores his solitary flight; sometimes
He scours the right hand coast, sometimes the left,
Now shaves with level wing the Deep, then soars
Up to the fiery concave tow'ring high.
As when far off at Sea a Fleet descri'd
Hangs in the Clouds, by *Equinoctial* Winds
Close sailing from *Bengala,* or the Isles
Of *Ternate* and *Tidore,* whence Merchants bring
Thir spicy Drugs: they on the Trading Flood
Through the wide *Ethiopian* to the Cape
Ply stemming nightly toward the Pole. So seem'd
Far off the flying Fiend: at last appear
Hell bounds high reaching to the horrid Roof,
And thrice threefold the Gates; three folds were Brass,
Three Iron, three of Adamantine Rock,
Impenetrable, impal'd with circling fire,
Yet unconsum'd. Before the Gates there sat
On either side a formidable shape;
The one seem'd Woman to the waist, and fair,
But ended foul in many a scaly fold
Voluminous and vast, a Serpent arm'd
With mortal sting: about her middle round
A cry of Hell Hounds never ceasing bark'd
With wide *Cerberean* mouths full loud, and rung
A hideous Peal: yet, when they list, would creep,
If aught disturb'd thir noise, into her womb,
And kennel there, yet there still bark'd and howl'd

Within unseen. Far less abhorr'd than these
Vex'd *Scylla* bathing in the Sea that parts
Calabria from the hoarse *Trinacrian* shore:
Nor uglier follow the Night-Hag, when call'd
In secret, riding through the Air she comes
Lur'd with the smell of infant blood, to dance
With *Lapland* Witches, while the laboring Moon
Eclipses at thir charms. The other shape,
If shape it might be call'd that shape had none
Distinguishable in member, joint, or limb,
Or substance might be call'd that shadow seem'd,
For each seem'd either; black it stood as Night,
Fierce as ten Furies, terrible as Hell,
And shook a dreadful Dart; what seem'd his head
The likeness of a Kingly Crown had on.
Satan was now at hand, and from his seat
The Monster moving onward came as fast,
With horrid strides; Hell trembled as he strode.
Th' undaunted Fiend what this might be admir'd,
Admir'd, not fear'd; God and his Son except,
Created thing naught valu'd he nor shunn'd;
And with disdainful look thus first began.
　　　Whence and what are thou, execrable shape,
That dar'st, though grim and terrible, advance
Thy miscreated Front athwart my way
To yonder Gates? through them I mean to pass,
That be assured, without leave askt of thee:
Retire, or taste thy folly, and learn by proof,
Hell-born, not to contend with Spirits of Heav'n.
　　　To whom the Goblin full of wrath repli'd:
Art thou that Traitor Angel, art thou hee,
Who first broke peace in Heav'n and Faith, till then
Unbrok'n, and in proud rebellious Arms
Drew after him the third part of Heav'n's Sons
Conjur'd against the Highest, for which both Thou
And they outcast from God, are here condemn'd
To waste Eternal days in woe and pain?
And reck'n'st thou thyself with Spirits of Heav'n,
Hell-doom'd, and breath'st defiance here and scorn,
Where I reign King, and to enrage thee more,

Thy King and Lord? Back to thy punishment,
False fugitive, and to thy speed add wings,
Lest with a whip of Scorpions I pursue
Thy ling'ring, or with one stroke of this Dart
Strange horror seize thee, and pangs unfelt before.
     So spake the grisly terror, and in shape,
So speaking and so threat'ning, grew tenfold
More dreadful and deform: on th' other side
Incens't with indignation *Satan* stood
Unterrifi'd, and like a Comet burn'd,
That fires the length of *Ophiucus* huge
In th' Artic Sky, and from his horrid hair
Shakes Pestilence and War. Each at the Head
Levell'd his deadly aim; thir fatal hands
No second stroke intend, and such a frown
Each cast at th' other, as when two black Clouds
With Heav'n's Artillery fraught, come rattling on
Over the *Caspian,* then stand front to front
Hov'ring a space, till Winds the signal blow
To join thir dark Encounter in mid air:
So frown'd the mighty Combatants, that Hell
Grew darker at thir frown, so matcht they stood;
For never but once more was either like
To meet so great a foe: and now great deeds
Had been achiev'd, whereof all Hell had rung . . .

John Gay (1685–1732)

British poet and dramatist John Gay initially gained celebrity as the author of satirical and parodic poems; many of these were collected in *Trivia* (1716) and *Poems* (1720). He subsequently wrote *The Beggar's Opera* (1728), an immensely successful comic ballad opera. Gay occasionally collaborated with Alexander Pope and other leading poets of the age; he also wrote the libretto to Handel's operetta *Acis and Galatea* (1732). "A True Story of an Apparition" was first published in *Poems* (1720).

A True Story of an Apparition

Scepticks (whose strength of argument makes out
That wisdom's deep enquirys end in doubt)
Hold this assertion positive and clear,
That sprites are pure delusions rais'd by fear.
Not that fam'd ghost, which in presaging sound
Call'd *Brutus* to *Philippi's* fatal ground;
Nor can *Tiberius Gracchus'* goary shade
These ever-doubting disputants persuade.
Strait they with smiles reply; those tales of old
By visionary Priests were made and told:
Oh might some ghost at dead of night appear,
And make you own conviction by your fear!
I know your sneers my easy faith accuse,
Which with such idle legends scares the Muse:
But think not that I tell those vulgar sprites,
Which frighted boys relate on winter nights;
How cleanly milk-maids meet the fairy train,
How headless horses drag the clinking chain,
Night-roaming ghosts, by saucer eye-balls known,
The common spectres of each country town.
No, I such fables can like you despise,
And laugh to hear these nurse-invented lies.
Yet has not oft the fraudful guardian's fright
Compell'd him to restore an orphan's right?
And can we doubt that horrid ghosts ascend,
Which on the conscious murd'rer's steps attend?
Hear then, and let attested truth prevail,
From faithful lips I learnt the dreadful tale.

      Where *Arden's* forest spreads its limits wide,
Whose branching paths the doubtful road divide,
A trav'ler took his solitary way;
When low beneath the hills was sunk the day.
And now the skies with gath'ring darkness lour,
The branches rustle with the threaten'd shower;
With sudden blasts the forest murmurs loud,
Indented lightnings cleave the sable cloud,
Thunder on thunder breaks, the tempest roars,
And heav'n discharges all its watry stores.

The wand'ring trav'ler shelter seeks in vain,
And shrinks and shivers with the beating rain;
On his steed's neck the slacken'd bridle lay,
Who chose with cautious step th' uncertain way;
And now he checks the rein, and halts to hear
If any noise foretold a village near.
At length from far a stream of light he sees
Extend its level ray between the trees;
Thither he speeds, and as he nearer came
Joyfull he knew the lamp's domestick flame
That trembled through the window; cross the way
Darts forth the barking cur, and stands at bay.
        It was an ancient lonely house, that stood
Upon the borders of the spacious wood;
Here towers and antique battlements arise,
And there in heaps the moulder'd ruine lyes;
Some Lord this mansion held in days of yore,
To chase the wolf, and pierce the foaming boar:
How chang'd, alas, from what it once had been!
'Tis now degraded to a publick Inn.
        Strait he dismounts, repeats his loud commands;
Swift at the gate the ready landlord stands;
With frequent cringe he bows, and begs excuse,
His house was full, and ev'ry bed in use.
What not a garret, and no straw to spare?
Why then the kitchin fire, and elbow-chair
Shall serve for once to nod away the night.
The kitchin ever is the servant's right,
Replys the host; there, all the fire around,
The Count's tir'd footmen snore upon the ground.
        The maid, who listen'd to this whole debate,
With pity learnt the weary stranger's fate.
Be brave, she crys, you still may be our guest,
Our haunted room was ever held the best;
If then your valour can the fright sustain
Of rattling curtains, and the clinking chain,
If your couragious tongue have power to talk,
When round your bed the horrid ghost shall walk;
If you dare ask it, why it leaves its tomb,
I'll see your sheets well-air'd, and show the room.

Soon as the frighted maid her tale had told,
The stranger enter'd, for his heart was bold.
　　　The damsel led him through a spacious hall,
Where Ivy hung the half-demolish'd wall;
She frequent look'd behind, and chang'd her hue,
While fancy tipt the candle's flame with blue.
And now they gain'd the winding stairs ascent,
And to the lonesome room of terrors went.
When all was ready, swift retir'd the maid,
The watch-lights burn, tuckt warm in bed was laid
The hardy stranger, and attends the sprite
Till his accustom'd walk at dead of night.
　　　At first he hears the wind with hollow roar
Shake the loose lock, and swing the creaking door;
Nearer and nearer draws the dreadful sound
Of rattling chains, that dragg'd upon the ground:
When lo, the spectre came with horrid stride,
Approach'd the bed, and drew the curtains wide!
In human form the ghastful Phantom stood,
Expos'd his mangled bosom dy'd with blood,
Then silent pointing to his wounded breast,
Thrice wav'd his hand. Beneath the frighted guest
The bed-cords trembled, and with shudd'ring fear,
Sweat chill'd his limbs, high rose his bristled hair;
Then mutt'ring hasty pray'rs, he mann'd his heart,
And cry'd aloud; Say, whence and who thou art.
The stalking ghost with hollow voice replys,
Three years are counted, since with mortal eyes
I saw the sun, and vital air respir'd.
Like thee benighted, and with travel tir'd,
Within these walls I slept. O thirst of gain!
See, still the planks the bloody mark retain;
Stretch'd on this very bed, from sleep I start,
And see the steel impending o'er my heart;
The barb'rous hostess held the lifted knife,
The floor ran purple with my gushing life.
My treasure now they seize, the golden spoil
They bury deep beneath the grass-grown soil,
Far in the common field. Be bold, arise,
My steps shall lead thee to the secret prize;

There dig and find; let that thy care reward:
Call loud on justice, bid her not retard
To punish murder; lay my ghost at rest,
So shall with peace secure thy nights be blest;
And when beneath these boards my bones are found,
Decent interr them in some sacred ground.
    Here ceas'd the ghost. The stranger springs from bed,
And boldly follows where the Phantom led;
The half-worn stony stairs they now descend,
Where passages obscure their arches bend
Silent they walk; and now through groves they pass,
Now through wet meads their steps imprint the grass;
At length amidst a spacious field they came:
There stops the spectre, and ascends in flame.
Amaz'd he stood, no bush, no briar was found,
To teach his morning search to find the ground;
What cou'd he do? the night was hideous dark,
Fear shook his joints, and nature dropt the mark:
With that he starting wak'd, and rais'd his head,
But found the golden mark was left in bed.
    What is the statesman's vast ambitious scheme,
But a short vision, and a golden dream?
Power, wealth, and title elevate his hope;
He wakes. But for a garter finds a rope.

David Mallet (1705?–1765)

Scottish poet David Mallet was the author of the long poem *The Excursion* (1728) and several tragedies, including *Elvira* (1763). He also wrote a *Life of Francis Bacon* (1740). He gained celebrity with the publication of the ballad "William and Margaret," written in 1723 and first published in Aaron Hill's periodical, the *Plain Dealer* (July 1724). It was included in Thomas Percy's *Reliques of Ancient English Poetry* (1765) under the title "Margaret's Ghost."

William and Margaret

'Twas at the silent, solemn hour,
  When night and morning meet;
In glided MARGARET'S grimly ghost,
  And stood at WILLIAM'S feet.

Her face was like an *April* morn,
  Clad in a wintry cloud:
And clay-cold was her lily-hand,
  That held her sable shroud.

So shall the fairest face appear,
  When youth and years are flown:
Such is the robe that kings must wear,
  When death has reft their crown.

Her bloom was like the springing flower,
  That sips the silver dew;
The rose was budded in her cheek,
  Just opening to the view.

But *Love* had, like the canker-worm,
  Consum'd her early prime:
The rose grew pale, and left her cheek;
  She died before her time.

"Awake!" *she* cried, "thy *True Love* calls,
  Come from her midnight grave;
Now let thy *Pity* hear the maid,
  Thy *Love* refus'd to save.

This is the dumb and dreary hour,
  When injur'd ghosts complain;
When yawning graves give up their dead,
  To haunt the faithless swain.

Bethink thee, WILLIAM, of thy fault,
  Thy pledge and broken oath:
And give me back my maiden-vow,
  And give me back my troth.

Why did you promise love to me,
　　And not that promise keep?
Why did you swear my eyes were bright,
　　Yet leave those eyes to weep?

How could you say my face was fair,
　　And yet that face forsake?
How could you win my virgin heart,
　　Yet leave that heart to break?

Why did you say my lip was sweet,
　　And made the scarlet pale?
And why did I, young witless maid!
　　Believe the flattering tale?

That face, alas! no more is fair;
　　Those lips no longer red:
Dark are my eyes, now clos'd in death,
　　And every charm is fled.

The hungry *worm* my *sister* is;
　　This *winding-sheet* I wear:
And cold and weary lasts our *night,*
　　Till that *last morn* appear.

But, hark! the *cock* has warn'd me hence;
　　A long and late adieu!
Come see, false *man,* how low *she* lies,
　　Who died for love of you."

The lark. sung loud; the morning smil'd,
　　With beams of rosy red:
Pale WILLIAM quak'd in every limb,
　　And raving left his bed.

He hied him to the fatal place
　　Where MARGARET'S body lay:
And stretch'd him on the grass-green turf
　　That wrap'd her breathless clay.

And thrice he call'd on MARGARET'S name,
　　And thrice he wept full sore:
Then laid his cheek to her cold grave,
　　And word spoke never more!

William Collins (1721–1759)

British poet William Collins was a "pre-Romantic" poet whose works adhered to Neoclassical forms but were Romantic in theme and feeling. Though his literary output was small, the imaginative quality of his work has earned him a reputation as one of the finest lyric poets of the eighteenth century. His four *Persian Eclogues* (1742) were followed by *Odes on Several Descriptive and Allegoric Subjects* (1746, dated 1747). The "Ode on the Superstitions of the Highlands" (1749) is an important poem at the vanguard of the Romantic movement. Other works include *Verses Address'd to Sir Thomas Hanmer* (1743), *Ode on the Death of Thomson* (1749), *Dirge in Cymbeline* (1749), and the unfinished *Superstitions of the Scottish Highlands* (1749). In this thirties his bouts with depression and alcoholism, apparently exacerbated by his lack of literary recognition, deepened into mental illness. He spent a year in an asylum around 1754 and died forgotten five years later, his reputation flourishing only after his death. "Ode to Fear" first appeared in *Odes on Several Descriptive and Allegoric Subjects*.

Ode to Fear

Thou, to whom the World unknown
With all its shadowy Shapes is shown;
Who see'st appall'd th' unreal Scene,
While Fancy lifts the Veil between:
      Ah, *Fear!* Ah frantic *Fear!*
      I see, I see Thee near.
I know thy hurried Step, thy haggard Eye!
Like Thee I start, like Thee disorder'd fly,
For lo what *Monsters* in thy Train appear!
Danger, whose Limbs of Giant Mold
What mortal Eye can fix'd behold?
Who stalks his Round, an hideous Form,
Howling amidst the Midnight Storm,
Or throws him on the ridgy Steep
Of some loose hanging Rock to sleep:
And with him thousand Phantoms join'd,
Who prompt to Deeds accurs'd the Mind:

And those, the Fiends, who near allied,
O'er Nature's Wounds, and Wrecks preside;
Whilst *Vengeance,* in the lurid Air,
Lifts her red Arm, expos'd and bare:
On whom that rav'ning Brood of Fate,
Who lap the Blood of Sorrow, wait;
Who, *Fear,* this ghastly Train can see,
And look not madly wild, like Thee?

EPODE
In earliest *Grece* to Thee with partial Choice,
      The Grief-full Muse addrest her infant Tongue;
The Maids and Matrons, on her awful Voice,
      Silent and pale in wild Amazement hung.

Yet He the Bard who first invok'd thy Name,
      Disdain'd in *Marathon* its Pow'r to feel:
For not alone he nurs'd the Poet's flame,
      But reach'd from Virtue's Hand the Patriot's Steel.

But who is He whom later Garlands grace,
      Who left a-while o'er *Hybla's* Dews to rove,
With trembling Eyes thy dreary Steps to trace,
      Where Thou and *Furies* shar'd the baleful Grove?

Wrapt in thy cloudy Veil th' *Incestuous Queen*
      Sigh'd the sad Call her Son and Husband hear'd,
When once alone it broke the silent Scene,
      And He the Wretch of *Thebes* no more appear'd.

O *Fear,* I know Thee by my throbbing Heart,
      Thy with'ring Pow'r inspir'd each mournful Line,
Tho' gentle *Pity* claim her mingled Part,
      Yet all the Thunders of the Scene are thine!

ANTISTROPHE
Thou who such weary Lengths hast past,
Where wilt thou rest, mad Nymph, at last?
Say, wilt thou shroud in haunted Cell,
Where gloomy *Rape* and *Murder* dwell?
Or in some hollow'd Seat,
'Gainst which the big Waves beat,

Hear drowning Sea-men's Cries in Tempests brought!
Dark Pow'r, with shudd'ring meek submitted Thought
Be mine, to read the Visions old,
Which thy awak'ning Bards have told:
And lest thou meet my blasted View,
Hold each strange Tale devoutly true;
Ne'er be I found, by Thee o'eraw'd,
In that thrice-hallow'd Eve abroad,
When Ghosts, as Cottage-Maids believe,
Their pebbled Beds permitted leave,
And *Gobblins* haunt from Fire, or Fen,
Or Mine, or Flood, the Walks of Men!
     O Thou whose Spirit most possest
The sacred Seat of *Shakespear's* Breast!
By all that from thy Prophet broke,
In thy Divine Emotions spoke:
Hither again thy Fury deal,
Teach me but once like Him to feel:
His *Cypress Wreath* my Meed decree,
And I, O *Fear,* will dwell with *Thee!*

III. The Gothics and Romantics

Johann Wolfgang von Goethe (1749–1832)

German poet, playwright, and critic Johann Wolfgang von Goethe published his first collection of poems, *Annette*, in 1770. In 1774 he published the novel *The Sorrows of Young Werter*, a prototypical work of German Romanticism. The first part of *Faust*, his imperishable poetic drama about the temptation of Faust by Mephistopheles, appeared in 1808; the second part appeared in 1832, shortly after his death. His multifaceted literary work, as well as his work as a scientist and philosopher, has made him the most significant author in German literary history and one of the titanic figures in world literature. "The Erl-King" ("Der Erlkönig") was first published in 1782; "The Bride of Corinth" ("Die Braut von Korinth"; based on an anecdote found in the ancient Greek writer Phlegon, 1st century C.E.) was first published in 1797; "The Dance of Death" ("Totentanz") was first published in 1813.

The Erl-King

Who rides there so late through the night dark and drear?
The father it is, with his infant so dear;
He holdeth the boy tightly clasp'd in his arm,
He holdeth him sadly, he keepeth him warm.

"My son, wherefore seek'st thou thy face thus to hide?"
"Look, father, the Erl-King is close by our side!
Dost see not the Erl-King with crown and with train?"
"My son, 'tis the mist rising over the plain."

"Oh come, thou dear infant! oh come thou with me!
Full many a game I will play there with thee;
On my strand, lovely flowers their blossoms unfold,
My mother shall grace thee with garments of gold."

"My father, my father, and dost thou not hear
The words that the Erl-King now breathes in mine ear?"

"Be calm, dearest child, 'tis thy fancy deceives;
'Tis the sad wind that sighs through the withering leaves."

"Wilt go, then, dear infant, wilt go with me there?
My daughters shall tend thee with sisterly care;
My daughters by night their glad festival keep,
They'll dance thee, and rock thee, and sing thee to sleep."

"My father, my father, and dost thou not see,
How the Erl-King his daughters has brought here for me?"
"My darling, my darling, I see it aright,
'Tis the aged grey willows deceiving thy sight.

"I love thee, I'm charm'd by thy beauty, dear boy!
And if thou'rt unwilling, then force I'll employ."
"My father, my father, he seizes me fast,
Full sorely the Erl-King has hurt me at last."

The father now gallops, with terror half wild,
He grasps in his arms the poor shuddering child;
He reaches his courtyard with toil and with dread—
The child in his arms he finds motionless, dead.

The Bride of Corinth

Once a stranger youth to Corinth came,
      Who in Athens lived, but hoped that he
From a certain townsman there might claim,
      As his father's friend, kind courtesy.
          Son and daughter, they
          Had been wont to say
Should thereafter bride and bridegroom be.

But can he that boon so highly prized,
      Save 'tis dearly bought, now hope to get?
They are Christians and have been baptized,
      He and all of his are heathens yet.
          For a newborn creed,
          Like some loathsome weed,
Love and truth to root out oft will threat.

Father, daughter, all had gone to rest,
    And the mother only watches late;
She receives with courtesy the guest,
    And conducts him to the room of state.
        Wine and food are brought,
        Ere by him besought;
    Bidding him good night, she leaves him straight.

But he feels no relish now, in truth,
    For the dainties so profusely spread;
Meat and drink forgets the wearied youth,
    And, still dress'd, he lays on the bed.
        Scarce are closed his eyes,
        When a form in-hies
    Through the open door with silent tread.

By his glimmering lamp discerns he now
    How, in veil and garment white array'd,
With a black and gold band round her brow,
    Glides into the room a bashful maid.
        But she, at his sight,
        Lifts her hand so white,
    And appears as though full sore afraid.

"Am I," cries she, "such a stranger here,
    That the guest's approach they could not name?
Ah, they keep me in my cloister drear,
    Well nigh feel I vanquish'd by my shame.
        On thy soft couch now
        Slumber calmly thou!
    I'll return as swiftly as I came."

"Stay, thou fairest maiden!" cries the boy,
    Starting from his couch with eager haste:
"Here are Ceres', Bacchus' gifts of joy;
    Amor bringest thou, with beauty grac'd!
        Thou art pale with fear!
        Loved one, let us here
    Prove the raptures the Immortals taste."

"Draw not nigh, O Youth! afar remain!
    Rapture now can never smile on me;

For the fatal step, alas! is ta'en,
    Through my mother's sick-bed phantasy.
       Cured, she made this oath:
       'Youth and nature both
    Shall henceforth to Heav'n devoted be.'"

"From the house, so silent now, are driven
    All the gods who reign'd supreme of yore;
One Invisible now rules in heaven,
    On the cross a Saviour they adore.
       Victims slay they here,
       Neither lamb nor steer,
    But the altars reek with human gore."

And he lists, and ev'ry word he weighs,
    While his eager soul drinks in each sound:
"Can it be that now before my gaze
    Stands my loved one on this silent ground?
       Pledge to me thy troth!
       Through our father's oath,
    With Heav'n's blessing will our love be crown'd."

"Kindly youth, I never can be thine!
    'Tis my sister they intend for thee.
When I in the silent cloister pine,
    Ah, within her arms remember me!
       Thee alone I love,
       While love's pangs I prove;
    Soon the earth will veil my misery."

"No! for by this glowing flame I swear,
    Hymen hath himself propitious shown:
Let us to my father's house repair,
    And thou'lt find that joy is not yet flown.
       Sweetest, here then stay,
       And without delay
    Hold we now our wedding feast alone!"

Then exchange they tokens of their truth;
    She gives him a golden chain to wear,
And a silver chalice would the youth

Give her in return of beauty rare.
        "That is not for me;
        Yet I beg of thee,
One lock only give me of thy hair."

Now the ghostly hour of midnight knell'd,
        And she seem'd right joyous at the sign;
To her pallid lips the cup she held
        But she drank of nought but blood-red wine.
                For to taste the bread
                There before them spread,
        Nought he spoke could make the maid incline.

To the youth the goblet then she brought,—
        He too quaff'd with eager joy the bowl.
Love to crown the silent feast he sought,
        Ah! full love-sick was the stripling's soul.
                From his prayer she shrinks,
                Till at length he sinks
        On the bed and weeps without control.

And she comes and lays her near the boy:
        "How I grieve to see thee sorrowing so!
If thou think'st to clasp my form with joy,
        Thou must learn this secret sad to know.
                Yes! the maid, whom thou
                Call'st thy loved one now,
        Is as cold as ice, though white as snow."

Then he clasps her madly in his arm,
        While love's youthful might pervades his frame:
"Thou might'st hope, when with me, to grow warm,
        E'en if from the grave thy spirit came!
                Breath for breath, and kiss!
                Overflow of bliss!
        Dost not thou, like me, feel passion's flame?"

Love still closer rivets now their lips,
        Tears they mingle with their rapture blest;
From his mouth the flame she wildly sips,
        Each is with the other's thought possess'd.
                His hot ardor's flood

Warms her chilly blood,
But no heart is beating in her breast.

In her care to see that nought went wrong,
    Now the mother happen'd to draw near;
At the door long hearkens she, full long,
    Wond'ring at the sounds that greet her ear.
        Tones of joy and sadness,
        And love's blissful madness,
    As of bride and bridegroom they appear.

From the door she will not now remove,
    Till she gains full certainty of this;
And with anger hears she vows of love,
    Soft caressing words of mutual bliss.
        "Hush! the cock's loud strain!
        But thou'lt come again,
    When the night returns!"—then kiss on kiss.

Then her wrath the mother cannot hold,
    But unfastens straight the lock with ease:—
"In this house are girls become so bold,
    As to seek e'en strangers' lusts to please?"
        By her lamp's clear glow
        Looks she in,—and oh!
    Sight of horror!—'tis her child she sees.

Fain the youth would, in his first alarm,
    With the veil that o'er her had been spread,
With the carpet, shield his love from harm;
    But she casts them from her, void of dread,
        And with spirit's strength,
        In its spectre length,
    Lifts her figure slowly from the bed.

"Mother! mother!"—Thus her wan lips say:
    "May not I one night of rapture share?
From the warm couch am I chased away?
    Do I waken only to despair?
        It contents not thee
        To have driven me
    An untimely shroud of death to wear?"

"But from out my coffin's prison-bounds
        By a wond'rous fate I'm forced to rove,
While the blessings and the chaunting sounds
        That your priests delight in, useless prove.
                Water, salt, are vain
                Fervent youth to chain,
        Ah, e'en earth can never cool down love!"

"When that infant vow of love was spoken,
        Venus' radiant temple smiled on both.
Mother! thou that promise since has broken,
        Fetter'd by a strange, deceitful oath.
                Gods, though, hearken ne'er,
                Should a mother swear
        To deny her daughter's plighted troth."

"From my grave to wander I am forc'd,
        Still to seek The God's long-sever'd link,
Still to love the bridegroom I have lost,
        And the life-blood of his heart to drink;
                When his race is run,
                I must hasten on,
        And the young must 'neath my vengeance sink.

"Beauteous youth! no longer mayst thou live;
        Here must shrivel up thy form so fair;
Did not I to thee a token give,
        Taking in return this lock of hair?
                View it to thy sorrow!
                Grey thou'lt be to-morrow,
        Only to grow brown again when *there*."

"Mother, to this final prayer give ear!
        Let a funeral pile be straightway dress'd;
Open then my cell so sad and drear,
        That the flames may give the lovers rest!
                When ascends the fire
                From the glowing pyre,
        To the gods of old we'll hasten, blest."

The Dance of Death

The warder looks down at the mid hour of night,
    On the tombs that lie scattered below;
The moon fills the place with her silvery light,
    And the churchyard like day seems to glow.
When see! first one grave, then another opes wide,
And women and men stepping forth are descried,
    In cerements snow-white and trailing.

In haste for the sport soon their ankles they twitch,
    And whirl round in dances so gay;
The young and the old, and the poor, and the rich,
    But the cerements stand in their way;
And as modesty cannot avail them aught here,
They shake themselves all, and the shrouds soon appear
    Scatter'd over the tombs in confusion.

Now waggles the leg, and now wriggles the thigh,
    As the troop with strange gestures advance,
And a rattle and clatter anon rises high,
    As of one beating time to the dance.
The sight to the warder seems wondrously queer,
When the villainous Tempter speaks thus in his ear:
    "Seize one of the shrouds that lie yonder!"

Quick as thought it was done! and for safety he fled
    Behind the church-door with all speed;
The moon still continues her clear light to shed
    On the dance that they fearfully lead.
But the dancers at length disappear one by one,
And their shrouds, ere they vanish, they carefully don,
    And under the turf all is quiet.

But one of them stumbles and shuffles there still,
    And gropes at the graves in despair;
Yet 'tis by no comrade he's treated so ill;—
    The shroud he soon scents in the air.
So he rattles the door—for the warder 'tis well
That 'tis bless'd, and so able the foe to repel,
    All cover'd with crosses in metal.

The shroud he must have, and no rest will allow,
    There remains for reflection no time;
On the ornaments Gothic the wight seizes now,
    And from point on to point hastes to climb.
Alas for the warder! his doom is decreed!
Like a long-legged spider, with ne'er-changing speed,
    Advances the dreaded pursuer.

The warder he quakes, and the warder turns pale,
    The shroud to restore fain had sought;
When the end,—now can nothing to save him avail,—
    In a tooth formed of iron is caught.
With vanishing lustre the moon's race is run,
When the bell thunders loudly a powerful One,
    And the skeleton falls, crushed to atoms.

[tr. Edgar Alfred Bowring (1874)]

Mary Robinson (1757–1800)

Mary Robinson was a leading British actress of the period, starring in many Shakespeare plays. She also became for a time the mistress of King George IV. Later in her career she wrote a substantial amount of poetry along with six novels, two plays, and other works. "The Haunted Beach" was first collected in Robinson's *Lyrical Tales* (1800).

The Haunted Beach

Upon a lonely desart Beach
    Where the white foam was scatter'd,
A little shed uprear'd its head
    Though lofty Barks were shatter'd.
The Sea-weeds gath'ring near the door,
    A sombre path display'd;
And, all around, the deaf'ning roar,
    Re-echo'd on the chalky shore,
By the green billows made.

Above, a jutting cliff was seen
        Where Sea Birds hover'd, craving;
And all around, the craggs were bound
        With weeds—for ever waving.
And here and there, a cavern wide
        Its shad'wy jaws display'd;
And near the sands, at ebb of tide,
        A shiver'd mast was seen to ride
Where the green billows stray'd.

And often, while the moaning wind
        Stole o'er the Summer Ocean,
The moonlight scene was all serene,
        The waters scarce in motion:
Then, while the smoothly slanting sand
        The tall cliff wrapp'd in shade,
The Fisherman beheld a band
        Of Spectres, gliding hand in hand—
Where the green billows play'd.

And pale their faces were, as snow,
        And sullenly they wander'd:
And to the skies with hollow eyes
        They look'd as though they ponder'd.
And sometimes, from their hammock shroud,
        They dismal howlings made,
And while the blast blew strong and loud
The clear moon mark'd the ghastly croud,
        Where the green billows play'd!

And then, above the haunted hut
        The Curlews screaming hover'd;
And the low door with furious roar
        The frothy breakers cover'd.
For, in the Fisherman's lone shed
        A MURDER'D MAN was laid,
With ten wide gashes in his head
And deep was made his sandy bed
        Where the green billows play'd.

A Shipwreck'd Mariner was he,
        Doom'd from his home to sever;
Who swore to be thro' wind and sea
        Firm and undaunted ever!
And when the wave resistless roll'd,
        About his arm he made
A packet rich of Spanish gold,
And, like a British sailor, bold,
        Plung'd, where the billows play'd!

The Spectre band, his messmates brave
        Sunk in the yawning ocean,
While to the mast he lash'd him fast
        And brav'd the storm's commotion.
The winter moon, upon the sand
        A silv'ry carpet made,
And mark'd the Sailor reach the land,
And mark'd his murd'rer wash his hand
        Where the green billows play'd.

And since that hour the Fisherman
        Has toil'd and toil'd in vain!
For all the night, the moony light
        Gleams on the specter'd main!
And when the skies are veil'd in gloom,
        The Murd'rer's liquid way
Bounds o'er the deeply yawning tomb,
And flashing fires the sands illume,
        Where the green billows play!

Full thirty years his task has been,
        Day after day more weary;
For Heav'n design'd, his guilty mind
        Should dwell on prospects dreary.
Bound by a strong and mystic chain,
        He has not pow'r to stray;
But, destin'd mis'ry to sustain,
He wastes, in Solitude and Pain—
        A loathsome life away.

William Blake (1757–1827)

British poet, painter, and mystic William Blake published his first volume of poetry, *Poetical Sketches,* in 1783. Much of his career was, however, occupied by painting and illustration; he illustrated works by Mary Wollstonecraft, Edward Young, and Milton (*Paradise Lost,* 1808), as well as such of his own works as *Songs of Innocence and Experience* (1789), *The Marriage of Heaven and Hell* (1793), *Visions of the Daughters of Albion* (1793), and *The Book of Los* (1795). These and other volumes of poetry embody a private mythology that Blake evolved, based in part on visions he claimed to have experienced. Overall, his work as both poet and painter constitutes a sharp break from Enlightenment rationalism and classical rhetoric. "Fair Elenor" was first published in *Poetical Sketches.*

Fair Elenor

The bell struck one and shook the silent tower;
The graves give up their dead: fair Elenor
Walked by the castle gate, and looked in.
A hollow groan ran through the dreary vaults.

She shrieked aloud, and sunk upon the steps
On the cold stone her pale cheek. Sickly smells
Of death issue as from a sepulchre,
And all is silent but the sighing vaults.

Chill death withdraws his hand, and she revives;
Amazed, she finds herself upon her feet,
And, like a ghost, through narrow passages
Walking, feeling the cold walls with her hands.

Fancy returns, and now she thinks of bones,
And grinning skulls, and corruptible death,
Wrapped in his shroud; and now fancies she hears
Deep sighs and sees pale sickly ghosts gliding.

At length, no fancy, but reality
Distracts her. A rushing sound, and the feet
Of one that fled, approaches—Ellen stood,
Like a dumb statue, froze to stone with fear.

The wretch approaches, crying, "The deed is done;
Take this, and send it by whom thou wilt send;
It is my life—send it to Elenor—
He's dead, and howling after me for blood!

"Take this," he cried; and thrust into her arms
A wet napkin, wrapped about; then rushed
Past, howling: she received into her arms
Pale death and followed on the wings of fear.

They passed swift through the outer gate; the wretch,
Howling, leaped o'er the wall into the moat,
Stifling in mud. Fair Ellen passed the bridge,
And heard a gloomy voice cry, "Is it done?"

As the deer wounded, Ellen flew over
The pathless plain; as the arrows that fly
By night, destruction flies and strikes in darkness.
She fled from fear, till at her house arrived.

Her maids await her; on her bed she falls,
That bed of joy, where erst her lord hath pressed:
"Ah, woman's fear!" she cried; "Ah, cursed duke!
Ah, my dear lord! ah, wretched Elenor!

"My lord was like a flower upon the brows
Of lusty May! Ah, life as frail as flower!
O ghastly death, withdraw thy cruel hand,
Seek'st thou that flower to deck thy horrid temples?

"My lord was like a star in the highest heaven,
Drawn down to earth by spells and wickedness;
My lord was like the opening eyes of day,
When western winds creep softly o'er the flowers.

"But he is darkened; like the summer's noon,
Clouded; fallen like the stately tree cut down;
The breath of heaven dwelt among his leaves.
O Elenor, weak woman, filled with woe!"

Thus having spoke, she raised up her head,
And saw the bloody napkin by her side,

Which in her arms she brought; and now, tenfold
More terrified, saw it unfold itself.

Her eyes were fixed; the bloody cloth unfolds,
Disclosing to her sight the murdered head
Of her dear lord, all ghastly pale, clotted
With gory blood; it groaned, and thus it spake:

"O Elenor, behold thy husband's head,
Who, sleeping on the stones of yonder tower,
Was reft of life by the accursed duke!
A hired villain turned my sleep to death.

"O Elenor, beware the cursed duke,
O give not him thy hand, now I am dead;
He seeks thy love—who, coward, in the night
Hired a villain to bereave my life."

She sat with dead cold limbs, stiffened to stone;
She took the gory head up in her arms;
She kissed the pale lips; she had no tears to shed;
She hugged it to her breast, and groaned her last.

Robert Burns (1759–1796)

Scottish poet Robert Burns received relatively little schooling aside
from tutoring from his father. Most of his poetry is written in a
richly evocative Scots dialect; his first volume, *Poems, Chiefly in the
Scottish Dialect,* appeared in 1786 and established his reputation. He
continued to write poems, but died of an infection at the age of
thirty-seven. Burns is now seen as a pioneer of British Romanticism
and republicanism. "Tam o' Shanter" was written in 1790 and first
published in the *Edinburgh Magazine* (March 1791).

Tam o' Shanter

When chapman billies leave the street,
And drouthy neebors neebors meet;
As market-days are wearing late,

An' folk begin to tak the gate;
While we sit bousing at the nappy,
An' getting fou and unco happy,
We think na on the lang Scots miles,
The mosses, waters, slaps, and styles,
That lie between us and our hame,
Whare sits our sulky, sullen dame,
Gathering her brows like gathering storm,
Nursing her wrath to keep it warm.

      This truth fand honest Tam o' Shanter,
As he frae Ayr ae night did canter:
(Auld Ayr, wham ne'er a town surpasses,
For honest men and bonie lasses).

      O Tam, had'st thou but been sae wise,
As taen thy ain wife Kate's advice!
She tauld thee weel thou was a skellum,
A blethering, blustering, drunken blellum;
That frae November till October,
Ae market-day thou was nae sober;
That ilka melder wi' the miller,
Thou sat as lang as thou had siller;
That ev'ry naig was ca'd a shoe on,
The smith and thee gat roaring fou on;
That at the Lord's house, even on Sunday,
Thou drank wi' Kirkton Jean till Monday.
She prophesied, that, late or soon,
Thou would be found deep drown'd in Doon,
Or catch'd wi' warlocks in the mirk
By Alloway's auld, haunted kirk.

      Ah! gentle dames, it gars me greet,
To think how monie counsels sweet,
How monie lengthen'd, sage advices
The husband frae the wife despises!

      But to our tale: Ae market-night,
Tam had got planted unco right,
Fast by an ingle, bleezing finely,
Wi' reaming swats, that drank divinely;

And at his elbow, Souter Johnie,
His ancient, trusty, drouthy cronie:
Tam lo'ed him like a very brither;
They had been fou for weeks thegither.
The night drave on wi' sangs and clatter;
And ay the ale was growing better:
The landlady and Tam grew gracious
Wi' secret favours, sweet and precious:
The Souter tauld his queerest stories;
The landlord's laugh was ready chorus:
The storm without might rair and rustle,
Tam did na mind the storm a whistle.

    Care, mad to see a man sae happy,
E'en drown'd hinisel amang the nappy.
As bees flee hame wi' lades o' treasure,
The minutes wing'd their way wi' pleasure:
Kings may be blest but Tam was glorious,
O'er a' the ills o' life victorious!

    But pleasures are like poppies spread:
You seize the flow'r, its bloom is shed;
Or like the snow falls in the river,
A moment white—then melts for ever;
Or like the borealis race,
That flit ere you can point their place;
Or like the rainbow's lovely form
Evanishing amid the storm.
Nae man can tether time or tide;
The hour approaches Tam mann ride:
That hour, o' night's black arch the key-stane,
That dreary hour Tam mounts his beast in;
And sic a night he taks the road in,
As ne'er poor sinner was abroad in.

    The wind blew as 't wad blawn its last;
The rattling showers rose on the blast;
The speedy gleams the darkness swallow'd;
Loud, deep, and lang the thunder bellow'd:
That night, a child might understand,
The Deil had business on his hand.

Weel mounted on his gray mare Meg,
A better never lifted leg,
Tam skelpit on thro' dub and mire,
Despising wind, and rain, and fire;
Whiles holding fast his guid blue bonnet,
Whiles crooning o'er some auld Scots sonnet,
Whiles glow'ring round wi' prudent cares,
Lest bogles catch him unawares:
Kirk-Alloway was drawing nigh,
Whare ghaists and houlets nightly cry.

By this time he was cross the ford,
Whare in the snaw the chapman smoor'd;
And past the birks and meikle stane,
Whare drunken Charlie brak 's neck-bane;
And thro' the whins, and by the cairn,
Whare hunters fand the murder'd bairn;
And near the thorn, aboon the well,
Whare Mungo's mither hang'd hersel.
Before him Doon pours all his floods;
The doubling storm roars thro' the woods;
The lightnings flash from pole to pole;
Near and more near the thunders roll:
When, glimmering thro' the groaning trees,
Kirk-Alloway seem'd in a bleeze,
Thro' ilka bore the beams were glancing,
And loud resounded mirth and dancing.

Inspiring bold John Barleycorn,
What dangers thou canst make us scorn!
Wi' tippenny, we fear nae evil;
Wi' usquabae, we'll face the Devil!
The swats sae ream'd in Tammie's noddle,
Fair play, he car'd na deils a boddle.
But Maggie stood, right sair astonish'd,
Till, by the heel and hand admonish'd,
She ventur'd forward on the light;
And, vow! Tam saw an unco sight!

Warlocks and witches in a dance:
Nae cotillion, brent new frae France,

But hornpipes, jigs, strathspeys, and reels,
Put life and mettle in their heels.
A winnock-bunker in the east,
There sat Auld Nick, in shape o' beast;
A tousie tyke, black, grim, and large,
To gie them music was his charge:
He screw'd the pipes and gart them skirl,
Till roof and rafters a' did dirl.
Coffins stood round, like open presses,
That shaw'd the dead in their last dresses;
And, by some devilish cantraip sleight,
Each in its cauld hand held a light:
By which heroic Tam was able
To note upon the haly table,
A murderer's banes, in gibbet-airns;
Twa span-lang, wee, unchristen'd bairns;
A thief new-cutted frae a rape—
Wi' his last gasp his gab did gape;
Five tomahawks wi' bluid red-rusted;
Five scymitars wi' murder crusted;
A garter which a babe had strangled;
A knife a father's throat had mangled—
Whom his ain son o' life bereft—
The grey-hairs yet stack to the heft;
Wi' mair of horrible and awefu',
Which even to name wad be unlawfu'.

      As Tammie glowr'd, amaz'd, and curious,
The mirth and fun grew fast and furious;
The piper loud and louder blew,
The dancers quick and quicker flew,
They reel'd, they set, they cross'd, they cleekit,
Till ilka carlin swat and reekit,
And coost her duddies to the wark,
And linket at it in her sark!

      Now Tam, O Tam! had thae been queans,
A' plump and strapping in their teens!
Their sarks, instead o' creeshie flannen,
Been snaw-white seventeen hunder linen!—
Thir breeks o' mine, my only pair,

That ance were plush, o' guid blue hair,
I wad hae gi'en them off my hurdies
For ae blink o' the bonie burdies!

     But wither'd beldams, auld and droll,
Rigwoodie bags wad spean a foal,
Louping and flinging on a crummock,
I wonder did na turn thy stomach!

     But Tam kend what was what fu' brawlie:
There was ae winsome wench and wawlie,
That night enlisted in the core,
Lang after kend on Carrick shore
(For monie a beast to dead she shot,
An' perish'd monie a bonie boat,
And shook baith meikle corn and bear,
And kept the country-side in fear).
Her cutty sark, o' Paisley harn,
That while a lassie she had worn,
In longitude tho' sorely scanty,
It was her best, and she was vauntie. . . .
Ah! little kend thy reverend grannie,
That sark she coft for her wee Nannie,
Wi' twa pund Scots ('t was a' her riches),
Wad ever grac'd a dance of witches!

     But here my Muse her wing maun cour,
Sic flights are far beyond her power:
To sing how Nannie lap and flang
(A souple jad she was and strang),
And how Tam stood like ane bewitch'd,
And thought his very een enrich'd;
Even Satan glowr'd, and fidg'd fu' fain,
And hotch'd and blew wi' might and main;
Till first ae caper, syne anither,
Tam tint his reason a' thegither,
And roars out: "Weel done, Cutty-sark!"
And in an instant all was dark;
And scarcely had he Maggie rallied,
When out the hellish legion sallied.

As bees bizz out wi' angry fyke,
When plundering herds assail their byke;
As open pussie's mortal foes,
When, pop! she starts before their nose;
As eager runs the market-crowd,
When "Catch the thief!" resounds aloud:
So Maggie runs, the witches follow,
Wi' monie an eldritch skriech and hollo.

Ah, Tam! ah, Tam! thou 'll get thy fairin!
In hell they'll roast thee like a herrin!
In vain thy Kate awaits thy comin!
Kate soon will be a woefu' woman!
Now, do thy speedy utmost, Meg,
And win the key-stane of the brig;
There, at them thou thy tail may toss,
A running stream they dare na cross!
But ere the key-stane she could make,
The fient a tail she had to shake;
For Nannie, far before the rest,
Hard upon noble Maggie prest,
And flew at Tam wi' furious ettle;
But little wist she Maggie's mettle!
Ae spring brought off her master hale,
But left behind her ain grey tail:
The carlin claught her by the rump,
And left poor Maggie scarce a stump.

Now, wha this tale o' truth shall read,
Ilk man, and mother's son, take heed:
Whene'er to drink you are inclin'd,
Or cutty sarks ran in your mind,
Think! ye may buy the joys o'er dear:
Remember Tam o' Shanter's mare.

Friedrich von Schiller (1759–1805)

German writer Johann Christoph Friedrich von Schiller is most re-
membered for such dramas as *Die Räuber* (1781; The Robbers), the

Wallenstein cycle (a prefatory poem, a dramatic prologue, and two five-act plays; 1800–01), *Maria Stuart* (1801), and *Wilhelm Tell* (1804). *Don Carlos,* Schiller's first major poetic drama and written in resonant blank verse, was published in book form in 1787. Five years later his health collapsed due to overwork as a university professor; but during his recovery he delved deeply into the metaphysics and aesthetics of German Idealism. He went on to create a string of "philosophical lyrics" such as "Das Ideal und das Leben" ("Life and the Ideal"), "Der Spaziergang" ("The Walk"), "Die Macht des Gesanges" ("The Power of Song"), which exult art as the means for man to attain a *schöne Seele* (beautiful soul). Other works followed, but Schiller lost his battle with tuberculosis in 1805 as he was at work on the drama *Demetrius.* "A Funeral Fantasie" ("Eine Leichenfantasie") was first published in Schiller's early volume *Anthologie auf des Jahr 1782* (1782). It was set to music by Franz Schubert.

A Funeral Fantasie

    Pale, at its ghastly noon,
Pauses above the death-still wood—the moon;
The night-sprite, sighing, through the dim air stirs;
    The clouds descend in rain;
    Mourning, the wan stars wane,
Flickering like dying lamps in sepulchres!
Haggard as spectres—vision-like and dumb,
    Dark with the pomp of death, and moving slow,
Towards that sad lair the pale procession come
    Where the grave closes on the night below.

    With dim, deep-sunken eye,
Crutched on his staff, who trembles tottering by?
As wrung from out the shattered heart, one groan
    Breaks the deep hush alone!
Crushed by the iron fate, he seems to gather
    All life's last strength to stagger to the bier,
And hearken—Do these cold lips murmur "Father"?
    The sharp rain, drizzling through that place of fear,
Pierces the bones gnawed fleshless by despair,
And the heart's horror stirs the silver hair.

Fresh bleed the fiery wounds
Through all that agonising heart undone—
Still on the voiceless lips "my Father" sounds,
And still the childless Father murmurs "Son!"
Ice-cold—ice-cold, in that white shroud he lies—
Thy sweet and golden dreams all vanished there—
The sweet and golden name of "Father" dies
Into thy curse,—ice-cold—ice-cold—he lies!
Dead, what thy life's delight and Eden were!

Mild, as when, fresh from the arms of Aurora,
While the air like Elysium is smiling above,
Steeped in rose-breathing odours, the darling of Flora
Wantons over the blooms on his winglets of love.
So gay, o'er the meads, went his footsteps in bliss,
The silver wave mirrored the smile of his face;
Delight like a flame, kindled up at his kiss,
And the heart of the maid was the prey of his chase.

Boldly he sprang to the strife of the world,
As a deer to the mountain-top carelessly springs;
As an eagle whose plumes to the sun are unfurled,
Swept his hope round the heaven on its limitless wings.

Proud as a war-horse that chafes at the rein,
That, kingly, exults in the storm of the brave;
That throws to the wind the wild stream of its mane,
Strode he forth by the prince and the slave!

Life like a spring day, serene and divine,
In the star of the morning went by as a trance;
His murmurs he drowned in the gold of the wine,
And his sorrows were borne on the wave of the dance.

Worlds lay concealed in the hopes of his youth;—
When once he shall ripen to manhood and fame!
Fond father exult!—In the germs of his youth
What harvests are destined for manhood and fame!

Not to be was that manhood!—The death-bell is knelling,
The hinge of the death-vault creaks harsh on the ears—
How dismal, O Death, is the place of thy dwelling!

Not to be was that manhood!—Flow on, bitter tears!
Go, belovèd, thy path to the sun,
    Rise, world upon world, with the perfect to rest;
Go—quaff the delight which thy spirit has won,
    And escape from our grief in the Halls of the Blest.

Again (in that thought what a healing is found!)
    To meet in the Eden to which thou art fled!—
Hark, the coffin sinks down with a dull, sullen sound,
    And the ropes rattle over the sleep of the dead.
And we cling to each other!—O Grave, he is thine!
    The eye tells the woe that is mute to the ears—
And we dare to resent what we grudge to resign,
    Till the heart's sinful murmur is choked in its tears.
    Pale at its ghastly noon,

Pauses above the death-still wood—the moon!
The night-sprite, sighing, through the dim air stirs:
    The clouds descend in rain;
    Mourning, the wan stars wane,
Flickering like dying lamps in sepulchres.
The dull clods swell into the sullen mound;
    Earth, one look yet upon the prey we gave!
The grave locks up the treasure it has found;
Higher and higher swells the sullen mound—
    Never gives back the grave!

                  [tr. E. P. Arnold-Forster (1902)]

Nathan Drake (1766–1836)

Nathan Drake was a British medical doctor and writer. His most cele-
brated work was the critical study *Shakespeare and His Times* (1817).
He also wrote *Literary Hours* (1798–1800; 2 vols.), the first volume
of which contains the essays "On Objects of Terror" and "On Gothic
Superstition." Also in that volume is the following poem.

Ode to Superstition

Quid iste fert tumultus? Aut quid omnium
Vultus in unum me truces?
HORATIUS.

Saw ye that dreadful shape? heard ye the scream
    That shook my trembling soul?
E'en now, e'en now, where yon red lightnings gleam
    Wan forms of terror scowl—
I know thee, Superstition, fiend whose breath
    Poisons the passing hours,
Pales the young cheek, and o'er the bed of death
    The gloom of horror pours;
Of ghastly Fear, and darkest Midnight born,
    Far in a blasted dale,
Mid Lapland's woods, and noisome wastes forlorn,
Where lurid hags the moon's pale orbit hail:
There, in some vast, some wild and cavern'd cell,
    Where flits the dim blue flame,
They drink warm blood, and act the deed of hell,
    The "deed without a name."
    With hollow shriek and boding cry,
    Round the wither'd witches hie,
    On their uncouth features dire,
    Gleams the pale and livid fire;
    The charm begins, and now arise
    Shadows foul, and piercing cries,
    Storm and tempest loud assail,
    Beating wind and rattling hail;
    Thus, within th' infernal wood,
    Dance they round the bubbling blood,
    Till sudden from the wond'ring eye,
    Upborne on harpy wing they fly,
Where, on the rude inhospitable wild,
    Fir'd by the lightning's arrowy stroke,
Oft at the balmy close of evening mild,
They're seen to hurry round the blasted oak:
Then rise strange spectres to the pilgrim's view,
    With horrid lifeless stare,

And gliding float upon the noxious dew,
        And howling rend the air.
Oft near yon leaf-clad solitary fane,
        Whilst morn yet clasps the night,
Some ghost is heard to sound his clanking chain,
Beheld mid moon-beam pale and dead to sight;
Nor less unfrequent the lone trav'ller hears
        The sullen-sounding bell,
And the dim-lighted tow'r awakes to fears
Of haunted mansion, brake, or darkling dell.
        Haste thee, Superstition fly!
        Perish this thy sorcery!
   Why in these gorgon terrors clad,
   But to affright, afflict the bad,
   'Tis thee, O Goddess! thee I hail,
   Of Hesper born, and Cynthia pale,
   That wont the same rude name to bear,
   Yet gentle all and void of fear;
   O come, in Fancy's garb array'd,
   In all her lovely forms display'd,
   And o'er the poet's melting soul,
   Bid the warm tide of rapture roll,
   To dying music, warbling gales,
   Mid moon-light scenes, and woody vales,
   Where Elves, and Fays, and Sprites disport,
   And nightly keep their festive court;
   There, mid the pearly flood of light,
   In tincts cerulean richly dight,
   Light-sporting o'er the trembling green,
   Glance they quick thro' the magic scene,
   And from the sparkling moss receive,
   Shed by the fragrant hand of Eve,
   The silver dew, of matchless pow'r,
   To guard from harm, at midnight hour,
   The lonely wight, who lost, from far,
   Views not one friendly guiding star,
   Or one kind lowly cottage door,
   To point his track across the moor;
   Whilst the storm howling, prompts his mind
   Dark Demons ride the northern wind,

And, 'plaining, mourn their cruel doom,
On tempest hurl'd, and wint'ry gloom:
Oft too, along the vales at eve,
Shall Sprites the songs of gladness weave,
With many a sweet and varied flight,
Soft warbling hymn the setting light,
Heard far th' echoing hills among,
Whilst chaunting wild their heav'nly song,
Till lost in ether dies away,
The last, long, faint and murm'ring lay;
These on the lonely Bard attend,
With him the mountain's side ascend,
Or in the valley's lowly plain,
To Rapture breathe the melting strain;
These lift his soul beyond her clime,
To daring flights of thought sublime,
Where, warm'd by Fancy's brightest fire,
He boldly sweeps the sounding lyre:
Come then, with wild flow'rs, come array'd,
O Superstition, magic maid!
And welcome then, suggesting pow'r!
At evening close, or midnight hour.

––––––––––––––––

James Hogg (1770–1835)

Scottish poet and fiction writer James Hogg produced a substantial amount of supernatural literature, including the pioneering novel *The Private Memoirs and Confessions of a Justified Sinner* (1824). His weird short stories were included in *The Shepherd's Calendar* (1829) and other volumes. "The Witch of the Gray Thorn" was first published in *Blackwood's Edinburgh Magazine* (June 1825) and collected in *A Queer Book* (1832).

The Witch of the Gray Thorn

"Thou old wrinkled beldam, thou crone of the night,
Come read me my vision and read it aright;
For 'tis said thou hast insight the future to scan

Far onward beyond the existence of man,
And hid'st thee for ever from eye of the day,
But rid'st on the night wind, away and away
Over cloud, over valley, on hemlock or reed,
To burrow in churchyards and harrass the dead.
Old beldam declare thee, and give me to wis
If I stand at the side of such being as this?"

 "Proud priest of Inchaffery I know thee too well,
Though thus in disguise thou hast come to my cell:
What is it to thee if through darkness I fly,
Like bird to carreer round the skirts of the sky,
Or sail o'er the seas in my shallop of shell
To do what the tongue of flesh dares not to tell?
Suffice it, I know what thy vision hath been,
Ere a word I have heard or a sign I have seen;
Besides its high import distinctly I see;
And, priest of Inchaffery, I'll tell it to thee,
Not for love or reward, but it troubles me sore
To have one in my presence I scorn and abhor.

 Thou did'st dream of a coronet blazing with gold,
That was hailed by the young and admired by the old;
And thou had'st a longing the thing to obtain,
But all thy bold efforts to reach it were vain;
When lo! thine own mitre arose from thy crown,
And mounted aloft whil'st the other sank down;
It mounted and rose in a circle of flame,
'Mid clamours of wonder and shouts of acclaim;
The crown into darkness descended apace,
And thine was exalted on high in its place.
Thou saw'st till the red blood ran down in a stream,
Then awakened'st in terror, and all was a dream!
Priest that was thy dream—And thou must—'Tis decreed—
Put down the Archbishop, and rise in his stead."

 "Thou lie'st thou old hag. With the cunning of hell
Thou lurest me to practice what thou dost foretell;
But there both thy master and thee I'll defy:
Yet that was my vision, I may not deny.
Mysterious being, unblest and unshriven!
Pray had'st thou that secret from hell or from heaven?"

 "I had it proud priest from a fountain sublime,

That wells beyond nature, and streams beyond time;
And though from the same source thy warning might come,
Yet mine was the essence and thine but the scum.
I heard and I saw what if thou had'st but seen,
A terror thy mortal existence had been,
For thou had'st grown rigid as statue of lead,
A beacon of terror for sinners to dread!
Thou think'st thou hast learning, and knowledge inborn,
Proud priest of Inchaffery I laugh them to scorn!
Thou know'st less of nature where spirits roam free,
Than a mole does of heav'n, or a worm does of thee.
  Begone with thy gold, thy ambition, and pride.
I have told thee thy vision, and solved it beside.
But dare not to doubt the event I foretel,
The thing is decreed both in heaven and hell
That thou—an arch traitor—must do a good deed,
Put down the Archbishop, and rise in his stead."
  Away went the abbot with crosier and cowl,
And visions of grandeur disturbing his soul,
And as he rode on to himself thus he said.
"The counsels of heaven must all be obeyed;
Nor throne, church, nor state can security have,
Till that haughty prelate be laid in his grave.
Let that nerve my arm and my warrantise be."
Well said thou good abbot of Inchafferye!
  The Archbishop had plotted too deep in the state;
The nobles were moved 'gainst the man of their hate;
The monarch was roused, and pronounced in his wrath
A sentence unseemly, the Archbishop's death!
But that very night that his doom was decreed,
A private assassin accomplished the deed.
The court was amazed—for loud whisperings came
Of a deed too unhallowed and horrid to name,
Abroad rushed the rumour, and would not be stem'd;
The murderer is captured, convicted, condemn'd;
Condemn'd to be hung like a dog on a tree.
Who is the assassin?—Pray who may it be?
Ha! The worthy good abbot of Inchafferye!
  In darkness and chains the poor abbot is laid,
And soon his death-warrant is to him conveyed;

His hour is announced, but he laughs it to scorn,
And sends an express for the Witch of Gray-Thorn.
She came at his call, and though hideous her form
And shrivelled, and crouched, like a crone in a storm,
Yet in her dim eye that was hollowed by time
The joy of a demon was gleaming sublime,
And with a weak laugh 'twixt a scream and a hiss,
She cried "Pray great abbot is all come to this?"

     "Where now thy bright omens thou hag of the night?
Come read me this riddle, and read it aright,
So far thou said'st truth—the Archbishop is dead;
Thy bodement confirm—Shall I rise in his stead?"

     "Yes, up to the gallows," the beldam replied;
"This day the archbishop had suffered and died;
But headlong on death I have caused thee to run.
Ha-ha! I have conquered, and thou art undone!"

     "Oh had I the hands which these fetters degrade,
To sear out thy tongue for the lies it hath made,
I would rend out thy heart with black falsehood so cramm'd
And consign thy old soul, to eternity, damn'd.
May heaven's dread vengeance depart from thee never,
But descend and enthrall thee for ever and ever!"

     "Aye curse thou away, to the theme I agree,
Thy curse is worth ten thousand blessings to me.
Ha-ha thou proud priest, I have won! I have won!
Thy course of ambition and cruelty's run.
Thou tortured'st me once, till my nerves were all torn,
For crimes I was free of as babe newly born;
'Twas that which compelled me, in hour of despair,
To sell soul and body to the prince of the air,
That great dreadful spirit of power and of pride,
His servant I am, and thy curse I deride.
For vengeance I did it, for vengeance alone;
Without that, futurity lurements had none.
I have now had full measure in sight of the sun,
Ha-ha! thou proud priest! I have won! I have won!

     'Tis not thy poor life that my vengeance can tame,
It flies to the future, to regions of flame,
To witness exulting th'extreme of thy doom,
And harass thy being 'mid terror and gloom.

Aye, grind thou thy fetters, and fume as thou wilt,
O how I rejoice in thy rage and thy guilt!
And more. I have promise may well strike thee dumb,
To be nurse to thy spirit for ages to come;
Think how thou wilt joy that the task shall be mine
To wreck and to tan thee with tortures condign,
O'er cataracts of sulphur, and torrents of flame,
And horrors that have not exposure nor name.
Until this vile world of lust and of crime
Have sounded through fire the last trumpet of Time,
Adieu bloody priest, in thy hour of despair,
When thy soul is forthcoming there's *one* shall be there."
    The abbot was borne to the scaffold away,
He stretched out his hands and attempted to pray,
But at that dire moment there sounded a knell
Close to his stun'd ear 'twixt a laugh and a yell,
And a voice said aloud that seem'd creaking with hate.
"Ha-ha! thou proud priest, it's too late! it's too late!"
He shivered, he shrunk, drop'd the sign, and was hung;
He gasp'd, and he died, and that moment there rung
This sound through the welkin so darksome and dun.
"I have thee! I have thee! I've won! I have won!"

Sir Walter Scott (1771–1832)

Scottish novelist Sir Walter Scott attained celebrity with a series of historical novels collectively entitled the Waverley novels, beginning with *Waverley* (1814). Several of these novels, as well as such long poems as *Marmion* (1808) and *The Lady of the Lake* (1810), contain supernatural episodes. Early in his career Scott published *The Chase and William and Helen* (1797), the former (later retitled "The Wild Huntsman") a translation of Gottfried August Bürger's "Die wilde Jäger" (1777) and the latter a translation of Bürger's "Lenore" (1773). Both poems were immensely popular and helped to awaken interest in the supernatural in verse and prose.

William and Helen

From heavy dreams fair Helen rose,
    And eyed the dawning red:
"Alas, my love, thou tarriest long!
    O art thou false or dead?"

With gallant Fred'rick's princely power
    He sought the bold Crusade;
But not a word from Judah's wars
    Told Helen how he sped.

With Paynim and with Saracen
    At length a truce was made,
And every knight return'd to dry
    The tears his love had shed.

Our gallant host was homeward bound
    With many a song of joy;
Green waved the laurel in each plume,
    The badge of victory.

And old and young, and sire and son,
    To meet them crowd the way,
With shouts, and mirth, and melody,
    The debt of love to pay.

Full many a maid her true-love met,
    And sobb'd in his embrace,
And flutt'ring joy in tears and smiles
    Array'd full many a face.

Nor joy nor smile for Helen sad;
    She sought the host in vain;
For none could tell her William's fate,
    If faithless, or if slain.

The martial band is past and gone;
    She rends her raven hair,
And in distraction's bitter mood
    She weeps with wild despair.

"O rise, my child," her mother said,
　　"Nor sorrow thus in vain;
A perjured lover's fleeting heart
　　No tears recall again."

"O mother, what is gone, is gone,
　　What's lost for ever lorn:
Death, death alone can comfort me;
　　O had I ne'er been born!

"O break, my heart—O break at once!
　　Drink my life-blood, Despair!
No joy remains on earth for me,
　　For me in heaven no share."

"O enter not in judgment, Lord!"
　　The pious mother prays;
"Impute not guilt to thy frail child!
　　She knows not what she says.

"O say thy pater noster, child!
　　O turn to God and grace!
His will, that turn'd thy bliss to bale,
　　Can change thy bale to bliss."

"O mother, mother, what is bliss?
　　O mother, what is bale?
My William's love was heaven on earth,
　　Without it earth is hell.

"Why should I pray to ruthless Heaven,
　　Since my loved William's slain?
I only pray'd for William's sake,
　　And all my prayers were vain."

"O take the sacrament, my child,
　　And check these tears that flow;
By resignation's humble prayer,
　　O hallow'd be thy woe!"

"No sacrament can quench this fire,
　　Or slake this scorching pain;

No sacrament can bid the dead
        Arise and live again.

"O break, my heart—O break at once!
        Be thou my god, Despair!
Heaven's heaviest blow has fallen on me,
        And vain each fruitless prayer."

"O enter not in judgment, Lord,
        With thy frail child of clay!
She knows not what her tongue has spoke;
        Impute it not, I pray!

"Forbear, my child, this desperate woe,
        And turn to God and grace;
Well can devotion's heavenly glow
        Convert thy bale to bliss."

"O mother, mother, what is bliss?
        O mother, what is bale?
Without my William what were heaven,
        Or with him what were hell?"

Wild she arraigns the eternal doom,
        Upbraids each sacred power,
Till, spent, she sought her silent room,
        All in the lonely tower.

She beat her breast, she wrung her hands,
        Till sun and day were o'er,
And through the glimmering lattice shone
        The twinkling of the star.

Then, crash! the heavy drawbridge fell
        That o'er the moat was hung;
And, clatter! clatter! on its boards
        The hoof of courser rung.

The clank of echoing steel was heard
        As off the rider bounded;
And slowly on the winding stair
        A heavy footstep sounded.

And hark! and hark! a knock—tap! tap!
    A rustling stifled noise;
Door-latch and tinkling staples ring;
    At length a whispering voice:

"Awake, awake, arise, my love!
    How, Helen, dost thou fare?
Wak'st thou, or sleep'st? laugh'st thou, or weep'st?
    Hast thought on me, my fair?"

"My love! my love!—so late by night!
    I waked, I wept for thee:
Much have I borne since dawn of morn;
    Where, William, couldst thou be?"

"We saddle late—from Hungary
    I rode since darkness fell;
And to its bourne we both return
    Before the matin-bell."

"O rest this night within my arms,
    And warm thee in their fold!
Chill howls through hawthorn bush the wind:
    My love is deadly cold."

"Let the wind howl through hawthorn bush!
    This night we must away;
The steed is wight, the spur is bright;
    I cannot stay till day.

"Busk, busk, and boune! thou mount'st behind
    Upon my black barb steed:
O'er stock and stile, a hundred miles,
    We haste to bridal bed."

"To-night—to-night a hundred miles?
    O dearest William, stay!
The bell strikes twelve—dark, dismal hour!
    O wait, my love, till day!"

"Look here, look here—the moon shines clear—
    Full fast I ween we ride;

Mount and away! for ere the day
    We reach our bridal bed.

"The black barb snorts, the bridle rings;
    Haste, busk, and boune, and seat thee!
The feast is made, the chamber spread,
    The bridal guests await thee."

Strong love prevail'd. She busks, she bounes,
    She mounts the barb behind,
And round her darling William's waist
    Her lily arms she twined.

And, hurry! hurry! off they rode,
    As fast as fast might be;
Spurn'd from the courser's thundering heels
    The flashing pebbles flee.

And on the right, and on the left,
    Ere they could snatch a view,
Fast, fast each mountain, mead, and plain,
    And cot, and castle flew.

"Sit fast—dost fear? The moon shines clear;
    Fleet goes my barb—keep hold!
Fear'st thou?" "O no!" she faintly said;
    "But why so stern and cold?

"What yonder rings? what yonder sings?
    Why shrieks the owlet grey?"
"'Tis death-bells' clang, 'tis funeral song,
    The body to the clay.

"With song and clang, at morrow's dawn,
    Ye may inter the dead:
To-night I ride, with my young bride,
    To deck our bridal bed.

"Come with thy choir, thou coffin'd guest,
    To swell our nuptial song!
Come, priest, to bless our marriage feast!
    Come all, come all along!"

Ceased clang and song; down sunk the bier;
    The shrouded corpse arose:
And, hurry! hurry! all the train
    The thundering steed pursues.

And, forward! forward! on they go;
    High snorts the straining steed;
Thick pants the rider's labouring breath,
    As headlong on they speed.

"O William, why this savage haste?
    And where thy bridal bed?"
"'Tis distant far, low, damp, and chill,
    And narrow, trustless maid."

"No room for me?" "Enough for both;
    Speed, speed, my barb, thy course!"
O'er thundering bridge, through boiling surge
    He drove the furious horse.

Tramp! tramp! along the land they rode,
    Splash! splash! along the sea;
The scourge is wight, the spur is bright,
    The flashing pebbles flee.

Fled past on right and left how fast
    Each forest, grove, and bower!
On right and left fled past how fast
    Each city, town, and tower!

"Dost fear? dost fear? The moon shines clear,
    Dost fear to ride with me?
Hurrah! Hurrah! the dead can ride!"
    "O William, let them be!"

"See there, see there! What yonder swings,
    And creaks 'mid whistling ram?"
"Gibbet and steel, th' accursed wheel;
    A murderer in his chain.

"Hollo! thou felon, follow here
    To bridal bed we ride;

And thou shalt prance a fetter dance
    Before me and my bride."

And, hurry! hurry! clash! clash! clash!
    The wasted form descends;
And fleet as wind through hazel bush
    The wild career attends.

Tramp! tramp! along the land they rode,
    Splash! splash! along the sea;
The scourge is red, the spur drops blood,
    The flashing pebbles flee.

How fled what moonshine faintly show'd!
    How fled what darkness hid!
How fled the earth beneath their feet,
    The heaven above their head!

"Dost fear? dost fear? The moon shines clear.
    And well the dead can ride;
Does faithful Helen fear for them?"
    "O leave in peace the dead!"

"Barb! barb! methinks I hear the cock;
    The sand will soon be run:
Barb! barb! I smell the morning air;
    The race is wellnigh done."

Tramp! tramp! along the land they rode,
    Splash! splash! along the sea;
The scourge is red, the spur drops blood,
    The flashing pebbles flee.

"Hurrah! hurrah! well ride the dead;
    The bride, the bride is come;
And soon we reach the bridal bed,
    For, Helen, here's my home."

Reluctant on its rusty hinge
    Revolved an iron door,
And by the pale moon's setting beam
    Were seen a church and tower.

With many a shriek and cry, whiz round
    The birds of midnight, scared;
And rustling like autumnal leaves
    Unhallow'd ghosts were heard.

O'er many a tomb and tombstone pale
    He spurr'd the fiery horse,
Till sudden at an open grave
    He check'd the wondrous course.

The falling gauntlet quits the rein,
    Down drops the casque of steel,
The cuirass leaves his shrinking side,
    The spur his gory heel.

The eyes desert the naked skull,
    The mould'ring flesh the bone,
Till Helen's lily arms entwine
    A ghastly skeleton.

The furious barb snorts fire and foam,
    And, with a fearful bound,
Dissolves at once in empty air,
    And leaves her on the ground.

Half seen by fits, by fits half heard,
    Pale spectres flit along,
Wheel round the maid in dismal dance,
    And howl the funeral song;

"E'en when the heart's with anguish cleft,
    Revere the doom of Heaven!
Her soul is from her body reft;
    Her spirit be forgiven!"

The Wild Huntsman

The Wildgrave winds his bugle-horn,
    To horse, to horse! halloo, halloo!
His fiery courser snuffs the morn,
    And thronging serfs their lord pursue.

The eager pack, from couples freed,
　　Dash through the bush, the brier, the brake;
While, answering hound, and horn, and steed,
　　The mountain echoes startling wake.

The beams of God's own hallow'd day
　　Had painted yonder spire with gold,
And, calling sinful man to pray,
　　Loud, long, and deep the bell had toll'd.

But still the Wildgrave onward rides;
　　Halloo, halloo! and, hark again!
When, spurring from opposing sides,
　　Two Stranger Horsemen join the train.

Who was each Stranger, left and right,
　　Well may I guess, but dare not tell;
The right-hand steed was silver white,
　　The left, the swarthy hue of hell.

The right-hand Horseman, young and fair,
　　His smile was like the morn of May;
The left, from eye of tawny glare,
　　Shot midnight lightning's lurid ray.

He waved his huntsman's cap on high,
　　Cried, "Welcome, welcome, noble lord!
What sport can earth, or sea, or sky,
　　To match the princely chase, afford?"

"Cease thy loud bugle's clanging knell,"
　　Cried the fair youth, with silver voice;
"And for devotion's choral swell,
　　Exchange the rude unhallow'd noise.

"To-day, the ill-omen'd chase forbear,
　　Yon bell yet summons to the fane;
To-day the Warning Spirit hear,
　　To-morrow thou mayst mourn in vain."

"Away, and sweep the glades along!"
　　The Sable Hunter hoarse replies;

"To muttering monks leave matin-song,
     And bells, and books, and mysteries."

The Wildgrave spurr'd his ardent steed,
     And, launching forward with a bound,
"Who, for thy drowsy priestlike rede,
     Would leave the jovial horn and hound?

"Hence, if our manly sport offend!
     With pious fools go chant and pray:
Well hast thou spoke, my dark-brow'd friend:
     Halloo, halloo! and hark away!"

The Wildgrave spurr'd his courser light,
     O'er moss and moor, o'er holt and hill;
And on the left and on the right,
     Each Stranger Horseman follow'd still.

Up springs, from yonder tangled thorn,
     A stag more white than mountain snow;
And louder rung the Wildgrave's horn,
     "Hark forward, forward! holla, ho!"

A heedless wretch has cross'd the way;
     He gasps the thundering hoofs below;—
But, live who can, or die who may,
     Still, "forward, forward!" on they go.

See, where yon simple fences meet,
     A field with Autumn's blessings crown'd:
See, prostrate at the Wildgrave's feet,
     A husbandman with toil embrown'd:

"O mercy, mercy, noble lord!
     Spare the poor's pittance," was his cry,
"Earn'd by the sweat these brows have pour'd,
     In scorching hour of fierce July."

Earnest the right-band Stranger pleads,
     The left still cheering to the prey;
The impetuous Earl no warning heeds,
     But furious holds the onward way.

"Away, thou hound! so basely born,
⠀⠀⠀⠀Or dread the scourge's echoing blow!"
Then loudly rung his bugle-horn,
⠀⠀⠀⠀"Hark forward, forward! holla, ho!"

So said, so done: A single bound
⠀⠀⠀⠀Clears the poor labourer's humble pale;
Wild follows man, and horse, and hound,
⠀⠀⠀⠀Like dark December's stormy gale.

And man and horse, and hound and horn,
⠀⠀⠀⠀Destructive sweep the field along;
While, joying o'er the wasted corn,
⠀⠀⠀⠀Fell Famine marks the maddening throng.

Again uproused, the timorous prey
⠀⠀⠀⠀Scours moss and moor, and holt and hill;
Hard run, he feels his strength decay,
⠀⠀⠀⠀And trusts for life his simple skill.

Too dangerous solitude appear'd;
⠀⠀⠀⠀He seeks the shelter of the crowd;
Amid the flock's domestic herd
⠀⠀⠀⠀His harmless head he hopes to shroud.

O'er moss and moor, and holt and hill,
⠀⠀⠀⠀His track the steady blood-hounds trace;
O'er moss and moor, unwearied still,
⠀⠀⠀⠀The furious Earl pursues the chase.

Full lowly did the herdsman fall;
⠀⠀⠀⠀"O spare, thou noble Baron, spare
These herds, a widow's little all;
⠀⠀⠀⠀These flocks, an orphan's fleecy care!"

Earnest the right-hand Stranger pleads,
⠀⠀⠀⠀The left still cheering to the prey;
The Earl nor prayer nor pity heeds,
⠀⠀⠀⠀But furious keeps the onward way.

"Unmanner'd dog! To stop my sport
⠀⠀⠀⠀Vain were thy cant and beggar whine,

Though human spirits, of thy sort,
    Were tenants of these carrion kine!"

Again he winds his bugle-horn,
    "Hark forward, forward! holla, ho!"
And through the herd, in ruthless scorn,
    He cheers his furious hounds to go.

In heaps the throttled victims fall;
    Down sinks their mangled herdsman near;
The murderous cries the stag appal,
    Again he starts, new-nerved by fear.

With blood besmear'd, and white with foam,
    While big the tears of anguish pour,
He seeks, amid the forest's gloom,
    The humble hermit's hallow'd bower.

But man and horse, and horn and hound,
    Fast rattling on his traces go;
The sacred chapel rung around
    With, "Hark away!" and "holla, ho!"

All mild, amid the rout profane,
    The holy hermit pour'd his prayer;
"Forbear with blood God's house to stain;
    Revere his altar, and forbear!

"The meanest brute has rights to plead,
    Which, wrong'd by cruelty, or pride,
Draw vengeance on the ruthless head:
    Be warn'd at length, and turn aside."

Still the Fair Horseman anxious pleads;
    The Black, wild whooping, points the prey:
Alas! the Earl no warning heeds,
    But frantic keeps the forward way.

"Holy or not, or right or wrong,
    Thy altar, and its rites, I spurn;
Not sainted martyrs' sacred song,
    Not God himself, shall make me turn!"

He spurs his horse, he winds his horn,
    "Hark forward, forward! holla, ho!"
But off, on whirlwind's pinions borne,
    The stag, the hut, the hermit, go.

And horse and man, and horn and hound,
    And clamour of the chase, was gone;
For hoofs, and howls, and bugle-sound,
    A deadly silence reign'd alone.

Wild gazed the affrighted Earl around;
    He strove in vain to wake his horn,
In vain to call: for not a sound
    Could from his anxious lips be borne.

He listens for his trusty hounds;
    No distant baying reach'd his ears:
His courser, rooted to the ground,
    The quickening spur unmindful bears.

Still dark and darker frown the shades,
    Dark as the darkness of the grave;
And not a sound the still invades,
    Save what a distant torrent gave.

High o'er the sinner's humbled head
    At length the solemn silence broke;
And, from a cloud of swarthy red,
    The awful voice of thunder spoke.

"Oppressor of creation fair!
    Apostate Spirits' harden'd tool!
Scorner of God! Scourge of the poor!
    The measure of thy cup is full.

"Be chased for ever through the wood;
    For ever roam the affrighted wild;
And let thy fate instruct the proud,
    God's meanest creature is his child."

'Twas hush'd: One flash, of sombre glare,
    With yellow tinged the forests brown;

Uprose the Wildgrave's bristling hair,
    And horror chill'd each nerve and bone.

Cold pour'd the sweat in freezing rill;
    A rising wind began to sing;
And louder, louder, louder still,
    Brought storm and tempest on its wing.

Earth heard the call; her entrails rend;
    From yawning rifts, with many a yell,
Mix'd with sulphureous flames, ascend
    The misbegotten dogs of hell.

What ghastly Huntsman next arose,
    Well may I guess, but dare not tell;
His eye like midnight lightning glows,
    His steed the swarthy hue of hell.

The Wildgrave flies o'er bush and thorn,
    With many a shriek of helpless woe;
Behind him hound, and horse, and horn,
    And "Hark away!" and "Holla, ho!"

With wild despair's reverted eye,
    Close, close behind, he marks the throng.
With bloody flings and eager cry;
    In frantic fear he scours along.

Still, still shall last the dreadful chase,
    Till time itself shall have an end;
By day, they scour earth's cavern'd space,
    At midnight's witching hour, ascend.

This is the horn, and hound, and horse,
    That oft the lated peasant hears;
Appall'd, he signs the frequent cross,
    When the wild din invades his ears.

The wakeful priest oft drops a tear
    For human pride, for human woe,
When, at his midnight mass, he hears
    The infernal cry of "Holla, ho!"

Samuel Taylor Coleridge (1772–1834)

From youth British author Samuel Taylor Coleridge was fascinated by works of imagination, speculative philosophy, comparative religion, and mythology. *Lyrical Ballads* (1798)—said to mark the beginning of the English Romantic movement—offered contributions by both William Wordsworth and Coleridge, including the first version of the latter's *Rime of the Ancient Mariner.* Coleridge's style is marked by both his neurotic temperament and the narcotics he used to medicate himself. He struggled with a progressively debilitating addiction to opium and ultimately fell out with Wordsworth. By 1811, however, he had aligned himself with the Anglican church and recovered enough to become a popular lecturer. In 1817 he published the drama *Zapolya* and the verse collection *Sibylline Leaves* and wrote *Biographia Literaria,* a rambling work in which he outlined the evolution of his thought. A third edition of Coleridge's *Poetical Works* appeared before his final illness and death in 1834. "Kubla Khan," written in 1798, was the product of a dream, although upon waking Coleridge could only remember about 50 of the 200 to 300 lines that had come to him in the dream. It was first published in *Christabel* (1816).

The Rime of the Ancient Mariner

Facile credo, plures esse Naturas invisibiles quam visibiles in rerum universitate. Sed horum omnium familiam quis nobis enarrabit? et gradus et cognationes et discrimina et singulorum munera? Quid agunt? quae loca habitant? Harum rerum notitiam semper ambivit ingenium humanum, nunquam attigit. Juvat, interea, non diffiteor, quandoque in animo, tanquam in tabulâ, majoris et melioris mundi imaginem contemplari: ne mens assuefacta hodiernae vitae minutiis se contrahat nimis, et tota subsidat in pusillas cogitationes. Sed veritati interea invigilandum est, modusque servandus, ut certa ab incertis, diem a nocte, distinguamus.—T. BURNET, *Archaeol. Phil.* p. 68.

ARGUMENT

How a Ship having passed the Line was driven by storms to the
cold Country towards the South Pole; and how from thence she
made her course to the tropical Latitude of the Great Pacific
Ocean; and of the strange things that befell; and in what manner
the Ancyent Marinere came back to his own Country.

Part I

It is an ancient Mariner,
And he stoppeth one of three.
"By thy long grey beard and glittering eye,
Now wherefore stopp'st thou me?

The Bridegroom's doors are opened wide,
And I am next of kin;
The guests are met, the feast is set:
May'st hear the merry din."

He holds him with his skinny hand,
"There was a ship," quoth he.
"Hold off! unhand me, grey-beard loon!"
Eftsoons his hand dropt he.

He holds him with his glittering eye—
The Wedding-Guest stood still,
And listens like a three years' child:
The Mariner hath his will.

The Wedding-Guest sat on a stone:
He cannot choose but hear;
And thus spake on that ancient man,
The bright-eyed Mariner.

"The ship was cheered, the harbour cleared,
Merrily did we drop
Below the kirk, below the hill,
Below the lighthouse top.

The Sun came up upon the left,

Out of the sea came he!
And he shone bright, and on the right
Went down into the sea.

Higher and higher every day,
Till over the mast at noon—"
The Wedding-Guest here beat his breast,
For he heard the loud bassoon.

The bride hath paced into the hall,
Red as a rose is she;
Nodding their heads before her goes
The merry minstrelsy.

The Wedding-Guest he beat his breast,
Yet he cannot choose but hear;
And thus spake on that ancient man,
The bright-eyed Mariner.

"And now the STORM-BLAST came, and he
Was tyrannous and strong:
He struck with his o'ertaking wings,
And chased us south along.

With sloping masts and dipping prow,
As who pursued with yell and blow
Still treads the shadow of his foe,
And forward bends his head,
The ship drove fast, loud roared the blast,
And southward aye we fled.

And now there came both mist and snow,
And it grew wondrous cold:
And ice, mast-high, came floating by,
As green as emerald.

And through the drifts the snowy clifts
Did send a dismal sheen:
Nor shapes of men nor beasts we ken—
The ice was all between.

The ice was here, the ice was there,
The ice was all around:

It cracked and growled, and roared and howled,
Like noises in a swound!

At length did cross an Albatross,
Thorough the fog it came;
As if it had been a Christian soul,
We hailed it in God's name.

It ate the food it ne'er had eat,
And round and round it flew.
The ice did split with a thunder-fit;
The helmsman steered us through!

And a good south wind sprung up behind;
The Albatross did follow,
And every day, for food or play,
Came to the mariner's hollo!

In mist or cloud, on mast or shroud,
It perched for vespers nine;
Whiles all the night, through fog-smoke white,
Glimmered the white Moon-shine."

"God save thee, ancient Mariner!
From the fiends, that plague thee thus!—
Why look'st thou so?"—With my cross-bow
I shot the ALBATROSS.

Part II

The Sun now rose upon the right:
Out of the sea came he,
Still hid in mist, and on the left
Went down into the sea.

And the good south wind still blew behind,
But no sweet bird did follow,
Nor any day for food or play
Came to the mariners' hollo!

And I had done a hellish thing,
And it would work 'em woe:
For all averred, I had killed the bird

That made the breeze to blow.
Ah wretch! said they, the bird to slay,
That made the breeze to blow!

Nor dim nor red, like God's own head,
The glorious Sun uprist:
Then all averred, I had killed the bird
That brought the fog and mist.
'Twas right, said they, such birds to slay,
That bring the fog and mist.

The fair breeze blew, the white foam flew,
The furrow followed free;
We were the first that ever burst
Into that silent sea.

Down dropt the breeze, the sails dropt down,
'Twas sad as sad could be;
And we did speak only to break
The silence of the sea!

All in a hot and copper sky,
The bloody Sun, at noon,
Right up above the mast did stand,
No bigger than the Moon.

Day after day, day after day,
We stuck, nor breath nor motion;
As idle as a painted ship
Upon a painted ocean.

Water, water, every where,
And all the boards did shrink;
Water, water, every where,
Nor any drop to drink.

The very deep did rot: O Christ!
That ever this should be!
Yea, slimy things did crawl with legs
Upon the slimy sea.

About, about, in reel and rout
The death-fires danced at night;

The water, like a witch's oils,
Burnt green, and blue and white.

And some in dreams assuréd were
Of the Spirit that plagued us so;
Nine fathom deep he had followed us
From the land of mist and snow.

And every tongue, through utter drought,
Was withered at the root;
We could not speak, no more than if
We had been choked with soot.

Ah! well a-day! what evil looks
Had I from old and young!
Instead of the cross, the Albatross
About my neck was hung.

Part III

There passed a weary time. Each throat
Was parched, and glazed each eye.
A weary time! a weary time!
How glazed each weary eye,
When looking westward, I beheld
A something in the sky.

At first it seemed a little speck,
And then it seemed a mist;
It moved and moved, and took at last
A certain shape, I wist.

A speck, a mist, a shape, I wist!
And still it neared and neared:
As if it dodged a water-sprite,
It plunged and tacked and veered.

With throats unslaked, with black lips baked,
We could nor laugh nor wail;
Through utter drought all dumb we stood!
I bit my arm, I sucked the blood,
And cried, A sail! a sail!

With throats unslaked, with black lips baked,
Agape they heard me call:
Gramercy! they for joy did grin,
And all at once their breath drew in,
As they were drinking all.

See! see! (I cried) she tacks no more!
Hither to work us weal;
Without a breeze, without a tide,
She steadies with upright keel!

The western wave was all a-flame.
The day was well nigh done!
Almost upon the western wave
Rested the broad bright Sun;
When that strange shape drove suddenly
Betwixt us and the Sun.

And straight the Sun was flecked with bars,
(Heaven's Mother send us grace!)
As if through a dungeon-grate he peered
With broad and burning face.

Alas! (thought I, and my heart beat loud)
How fast she nears and nears!
Are those *her* sails that glance in the Sun,
Like restless gossameres?

Are those *her* ribs through which the Sun
Did peer, as through a grate?
And is that Woman all her crew?
Is that a DEATH? and are there two?
Is DEATH that woman's mate?

Her lips were red, *her* looks were free,
Her locks were yellow as gold:
Her skin was as white as leprosy,
The Night-mare LIFE-IN-DEATH was she,
Who thicks man's blood with cold.

The naked hulk alongside came,
And the twain were casting dice;

"The game is done! I've won! I've won!"
Quoth she, and whistles thrice.

The Sun's rim dips; the stars rush out:
At one stride comes the dark;
With far-heard whisper, o'er the sea,
Off shot the spectre-bark.

We listened and looked sideways up!
Fear at my heart, as at a cup,
My life-blood seemed to sip!
The stars were dim, and thick the night,
The steersman's face by his lamp gleamed white;
From the sails the dew did drip—
Till clomb above the eastern bar
The hornéd Moon, with one bright star
Within the nether tip.

One after one, by the star-dogged Moon,
Too quick for groan or sigh,
Each turned his face with a ghastly pang,
And cursed me with his eye.

Four times fifty living men,
(And I heard nor sigh nor groan)
With heavy thump, a lifeless lump,
They dropped down one by one.

The souls did from their bodies fly,—
They fled to bliss or woe!
And every soul, it passed me by,
Like the whizz of my cross-bow!

Part IV

"I fear thee, ancient Mariner!
I fear thy skinny hand!
And thou art long, and lank, and brown,
As is the ribbed sea-sand.

I fear thee and thy glittering eye,
And thy skinny hand, so brown."—

Fear not, fear not, thou Wedding-Guest!
This body dropt not down.

Alone, alone, all, all alone,
Alone on a wide wide sea!
And never a saint took pity on
My soul in agony.

The many men, so beautiful!
And they all dead did lie:
And a thousand thousand slimy things
Lived on; and so did I.

I looked upon the rotting sea,
And drew my eyes away;
I looked upon the rotting deck,
And there the dead men lay.

I looked to heaven, and tried to pray;
But or ever a prayer had gusht,
A wicked whisper came, and made
My heart as dry as dust.

I closed my lids, and kept them close,
And the balls like pulses beat;
For the sky and the sea, and the sea and the sky
Lay like a load on my weary eye,
And the dead were at my feet.

The cold sweat melted from their limbs,
Nor rot nor reek did they:
The look with which they looked on me
Had never passed away.

An orphan's curse would drag to hell
A spirit from on high;
But oh! more horrible than that
Is the curse in a dead man's eye!
Seven days, seven nights, I saw that curse,
And yet I could not die.

The moving Moon went up the sky.
And no where did abide:

Softly she was going up,
And a star or two beside—

Her beams bemocked the sultry main,
Like April hoar-frost spread;
But where the ship's huge shadow lay,
The charméd water burnt alway
A still and awful red.

Beyond the shadow of the ship,
I watched the water-snakes:
They moved in tracks of shining white,
And when they reared, the elfish light
Fell off in hoary flakes.

Within the shadow of the ship
I watched their rich attire:
Blue, glossy green, and velvet black,
They coiled and swam; and every track
Was a flash of golden fire.

O happy living things! no tongue
Their beauty might declare:
A spring of love gushed from my heart,
And I blessed them unaware:
Sure my kind saint took pity on me,
And I blessed them unaware.

The self-same moment I could pray;
And from my neck so free
The Albatross fell off, and sank
Like lead into the sea.

Part V

Oh sleep! it is a gentle thing,
Beloved from pole to pole!
To Mary Queen the praise be given!
She sent the gentle sleep from Heaven,
That slid into my soul.

The silly buckets on the deck,
That had so long remained,

I dreamt that they were filled with dew;
And when I awoke, it rained.

My lips were wet, my throat was cold,
My garments all were dank;
Sure I had drunken in my dreams,
And still my body drank.

I moved, and could not feel my limbs:
I was so light—almost
I thought that I had died in sleep,
And was a blessèd ghost.

And soon I heard a roaring wind:
It did not come anear;
But with its sound it shook the sails,
That were so thin and sere.

The upper air burst into life!
And a hundred fire-flags sheen,
To and fro they were hurried about!
And to and fro, and in and out,
The wan stars danced between.

And the coming wind did roar more loud,
And the sails did sigh like sedge;
And the rain poured down from one black cloud;
The Moon was at its edge.

The thick black cloud was cleft, and still
The Moon was at its side:
Like waters shot from some high crag,
The lightning fell with never a jag,
A river steep and wide.

The loud wind never reached the ship,
Yet now the ship moved on!
Beneath the lightning and the Moon
The dead men gave a groan.

They groaned, they stirred, they all uprose,
Nor spake, nor moved their eyes;

It had been strange, even in a dream,
To have seen those dead men rise.

The helmsman steered, the ship moved on;
Yet never a breeze up-blew;
The mariners all 'gan work the ropes,
Where they were wont to do;
They raised their limbs like lifeless tools—
We were a ghastly crew.

The body of my brother's son
Stood by me, knee to knee:
The body and I pulled at one rope,
But he said nought to me.

"I fear thee, ancient Mariner!"
Be calm, thou Wedding-Guest!
'Twas not those souls that fled in pain,
Which to their corses came again,
But a troop of spirits blest:

For when it dawned—they dropped their arms,
And clustered round the mast;
Sweet sounds rose slowly through their mouths,
And from their bodies passed.

Around, around, flew each sweet sound,
Then darted to the Sun;
Slowly the sounds came back again,
Now mixed, now one by one.

Sometimes a-dropping from the sky
I heard the sky-lark sing;
Sometimes all little birds that are,
How they seemed to fill the sea and air
With their sweet jargoning!

And now 'twas like all instruments,
Now like a lonely flute;
And now it is an angel's song,
That makes the heavens be mute.

It ceased; yet still the sails made on
A pleasant noise till noon,
A noise like of a hidden brook
In the leafy month of June,
That to the sleeping woods all night
Singeth a quiet tune.

Till noon we quietly sailed on,
Yet never a breeze did breathe:
Slowly and smoothly went the ship,
Moved onward from beneath.

Under the keel nine fathom deep,
From the land of mist and snow,
The spirit slid: and it was he
That made the ship to go.
The sails at noon left off their tune,
And the ship stood still also.

The Sun, right up above the mast,
Had fixed her to the ocean:
But in a minute she 'gan stir,
With a short uneasy motion—
Backwards and forwards half her length
With a short uneasy motion.

Then like a pawing horse let go,
She made a sudden bound;
It flung the blood into my head,
And I fell down in a swound.

How long in that same fit I lay,
I have not to declare;
But ere my living life returned,
I heard and in my soul discerned
Two voices in the air.

"Is it he?" quoth one, "Is this the man?
By him who died on cross,
With his cruel bow he laid full low
The harmless Albatross.

The spirit who bideth by himself
In the land of mist and snow,
He loved the bird that loved the man
Who shot him with his bow."

The other was a softer voice,
As soft as honey-dew:
Quoth he, "The man hath penance done,
And penance more will do."

Part VI

FIRST VOICE
"But tell me, tell me! speak again,
Thy soft response renewing—
What makes that ship drive on so fast?
What is the ocean doing?"

SECOND VOICE
"Still as a slave before his lord,
The ocean hath no blast;
His great bright eye most silently
Up to the Moon is cast—

If he may know which way to go;
For she guides him smooth or grim.
See, brother, see! how graciously
She looketh down on him."

FIRST VOICE
"But why drives on that ship so fast,
Without or wave or wind?"

SECOND VOICE
"The air is cut away before,
And closes from behind.

Fly, brother, fly! more high, more high!
Or we shall be belated:
For slow and slow that ship will go,
When the Mariner's trance is abated."

I woke, and we were sailing on
As in a gentle weather:
'Twas night, calm night, the moon was high;
The dead men stood together.

All stood together on the deck,
For a charnel-dungeon fitter:
All fixed on me their stony eyes,
That in the Moon did glitter.

The pang, the curse, with which they died,
Had never passed away:
I could not draw my eyes from theirs,
Nor turn them up to pray.

And now this spell was snapt: once more
I viewed the ocean green,
And looked far forth, yet little saw
Of what had else been seen—

Like one, that on a lonesome road
Doth walk in fear and dread,
And having once turned round walks on,
And turns no more his head;
Because he knows, a frightful fiend
Doth close behind him tread.

But soon there breathed a wind on me,
Nor sound nor motion made:
Its path was not upon the sea,
In ripple or in shade.

It raised my hair, it fanned my cheek
Like a meadow-gale of spring—
It mingled strangely with my fears,
Yet it felt like a welcoming.

Swiftly, swiftly flew the ship,
Yet she sailed softly too:
Sweetly, sweetly blew the breeze—
On me alone it blew.

Oh! dream of joy! is this indeed
The light-house top I see?
Is this the hill? is this the kirk?
Is this mine own countree?

We drifted o'er the harbour-bar,
And I with sobs did pray—
O let me be awake, my God!
Or let me sleep alway.

The harbour-bay was clear as glass,
So smoothly it was strewn!
And on the bay the moonlight lay,
And the shadow of the Moon.

The rock shone bright, the kirk no less,
That stands above the rock:
The moonlight steeped in silentness
The steady weathercock.

And the bay was white with silent light,
Till rising from the same,
Full many shapes, that shadows were,
In crimson colours came.

A little distance from the prow
Those crimson shadows were:
I turned my eyes upon the deck—
Oh, Christ? what saw I there!

Each corse lay flat, lifeless and flat,
And, by the holy rood!
A man all light, a seraph-man,
On every corse there stood.

This seraph-band, each waved his hand:
It was a heavenly sight!
They stood as signals to the land,
Each one a lovely light;

This seraph-band, each waved his hand,
No voice did they impart—

No voice; but oh! the silence sank
Like music on my heart.

But soon I heard the dash of oars,
I heard the Pilot's cheer;
My head was turned perforce away,
And I saw a boat appear.

The Pilot and the Pilot's boy,
I heard them coming fast:
Dear Lord in Heaven! it was a joy
The dead men could not blast.

I saw a third—I heard his voice:
It is the Hermit good!
He singeth loud his godly hymns
That he makes in the wood.
He'll shrieve my soul, he'll wash away
The Albatross's blood.

Part VII

This Hermit good lives in that wood
Which slopes down to the sea.
How loudly his sweet voice he rears!
He loves to talk with marineres
That come from a far countree.

He kneels at morn, and noon, and eve—
He hath a cushion plump:
It is the moss that wholly hides
The rotted old oak-stump.

The skiff-boat neared: I heard them talk,
"Why, this is strange, I trow!
Where are those lights so many and fair,
That signal made but now?"

"Strange, by my faith!" the Hermit said—
"And they answered not our cheer!
The planks looked warped! and see those sails,
How thin they are and sere!

I never saw aught like to them,
Unless perchance it were

Brown skeletons of leaves that lag
My forest-brook along;
When the ivy-tod is heavy with snow,
And the owlet whoops to the wolf below,
That eats the she-wolf's young."

"Dear Lord! it hath a fiendish look—
(The Pilot made reply)
I am a-feared"—"Push on, push on!"
Said the Hermit cheerily.

The boat came closer to the ship,
But I nor spake nor stirred;
The boat came close beneath the ship,
And straight a sound was heard.

Under the water it rumbled on,
Still louder and more dread:
It reached the ship, it split the bay:
The ship went down like lead.

Stunned by that loud and dreadful sound,
Which sky and ocean smote,
Like one that hath been seven days drowned
My body lay afloat;
But swift as dreams, myself I found
Within the Pilot's boat.

Upon the whirl, where sank the ship,
The boat spun round and round;
And all was still, save that the hill
Was telling of the sound.

I moved my lips—the Pilot shrieked
And fell down in a fit;
The holy Hermit raised his eyes,
And prayed where he did sit.

I took the oars: the Pilot's boy,
Who now doth crazy go,

Laughed loud and long, and all the while
His eyes went to and fro.
"Ha! ha!" quoth he, "full plain I see,
The Devil knows how to row."

And now, all in my own countree,
I stood on the firm land!
The Hermit stopped forth from the boat,
And scarcely he could stand.

"O shrieve me, shrieve me, holy man!"
The Hermit crossed his brow.
"Say quick," quoth he, "I bid thee say—
What manner of man art thou?"

Forthwith this frame of mine was wrenched
With a woful agony,
Which forced me to begin my tale;
And then it left me free.

Since then, at an uncertain hour,
That agony returns:
And till my ghastly tale is told,
This heart within me burns.

I pass, like night, from land to land;
I have strange power of speech;
That moment that his face I see,
I know the man that must hear me:
To him my tale I teach.

What loud uproar bursts from that door!
The wedding-guests are there:
But in the garden-bower the bride
And bride-maids singing are:
And hark the little vesper bell,
Which biddeth me to prayer!

O Wedding-Guest! this soul hath been
Alone on a wide wide sea:
So lonely 'twas, that God himself
Scarce seeméd there to be.

O sweeter than the marriage-feast,
'Tis sweeter far to me,
To walk together to the kirk
With a goodly company!—

To walk together to the kirk,
And all together pray,
While each to his great Father bends,
Old men, and babes, and loving friends
And youths and maidens gay!

Farewell, farewell! but this I tell
To thee, thou Wedding-Guest!
He prayeth well, who loveth well
Both man and bird and beast.

He prayeth best, who loveth best
All things both great and small;
For the dear God who loveth us,
He made and loveth all.

The Mariner, whose eye is bright,
Whose beard with age is hoar,
Is gone: and now the Wedding-Guest
Turned from the bridegroom's door.

He went like one that hath been stunned,
And is of sense forlorn:
A sadder and a wiser man,
He rose the morrow morn.

Kubla Khan

In Xanadu did Kubla Khan
A stately pleasure-dome decree:
Where Alph, the sacred river, ran
Through caverns measureless to man
      Down to a sunless sea.
So twice five miles of fertile ground
With walls and towers were girdled round:
And there were gardens bright with sinuous rills,

Where blossomed many an incense-bearing tree;
And here were forests ancient as the hills,
Enfolding sunny spots of greenery.

But oh! that deep romantic chasm which slanted
Down the green hill athwart a cedarn cover!
A savage place! as holy and enchanted
As e'er beneath a waning moon was haunted
By woman wailing for her demon-lover!
And from this chasm, with ceaseless turmoil seething,
As if this earth in fast thick pants were breathing,
A mighty fountain momently was forced:
Amid whose swift half-intermitted burst
Huge fragments vaulted like rebounding hail,
Or chaffy grain beneath the thresher's flail:
And 'mid these dancing rocks at once and ever
It flung up momently the sacred river.
Five miles meandering with a mazy motion
Through wood and dale the sacred river ran,
Then reached the caverns measureless to man,
And sank in tumult to a lifeless ocean:
And 'mid this tumult Kubla heard from far
Ancestral voices prophesying war!
        The shadow of the dome of pleasure
        Floated midway on the waves;
        Where was heard the mingled measure
        From the fountain and the caves.
It was a miracle of rare device,
A sunny pleasure-dome with eaves of ice!

            A damsel with a dulcimer
            In a vision once I saw:
            It was an Abyssinian maid,
            And on her dulcimer she played,
            Singing of Mount Abora.
            Could I revive within me
            Her symphony and song,
            To such a deep delight 'twould win me,
That with music loud and long,
I would build that dome in air,
That sunny dome! those caves of ice!

And all who heard should see them there,
And all should cry, Beware! Beware!
His flashing eyes, his floating hair!
Weave a circle round him thrice,
And close your eyes with holy dread,
For he on honey-dew hath fed,
And drunk the milk of Paradise.

Robert Southey (1774–1843)

British author Robert Southey is largely remembered today for his association with Wordsworth and Coleridge. With the latter he created an abortive plan for a utopian agricultural community in America. Starting with *Joan of Arc: An Epic Poem* (1796), Southey pursued poetry as his primary artistic focus, but was forced to produce literary material unremittingly—criticism, history, biography, journalism, translations, and editions of earlier writers—to support his family. Of primary relevance to poetry of the imagination are two highly colored "Oriental" epic poems: *Thalaba the Destroyer* (1801)—about a hero's mission to avenge the death of his family amidst magic and superstition—and *The Curse of Kehama* (1810), about a Hindu rajah with supernatural powers. Southey was Poet Laureate for thirty years prior to his death in 1843. "To Horror" appeared in Southey's *Poems* (1797). It is frequently omitted from editions of his collected poems.

To Horror

Dark Horror, hear my call!
    Stern Genius hear from thy retreat
    On some old sepulchre's moss-cankered seat,
Beneath the Abbey's ivied wall
    That trembles o'er its shade;
Where wrapt in midnight gloom, alone,
    Thou lovest to lie and hear
    The roar of waters near,
And listen to the deep dull groan

Of some perturbed sprite
Borne fitful on the heavy gales of night.

Or whether o'er some wide waste hill
    Thou mark'st the traveller stray,
    Bewilder'd on his lonely way,
When, loud and keen and chill,
The evening winds of winter blow
Drifting deep the dismal snow.

Or if thou followest now on Groenland's shore,
    With all thy terrors, on the lonely way
Of some wrecked mariner, when to the roar
    Of herded bears the floating ice-hills round
    Pour their deep echoing sound,
    And by the dim drear Boreal light
Givest half his dangers to the wreches sight.

Or if thy fury form,
    When o'er the midnight deep
    The dark-wing'd tempests sweep
Watches from some high cliff the encreasing storm,
    Listening with strange delight
As the black billows to the thunder rave
    When by the lightnings light
Thou seest the tall ship sink beneath the wave.

Dark Horror! bear me where the field of sight
    Scatters contagion on the tainted gale,
    When to the Moon's faint beam,
On many a carcase shine the dews of night
    And a dead silence stills the vale
Save when at times is heard the glutted Raven's scream.

Where some wreck'd army from the Conquerors might
Speed their disastrous flight,
    With thee fierce Genius! let me trace their way,
And hear at times the deep heart-groan
Of some poor sufferer left to die alone,
    His sore wounds smarting with the winds of night;
And we will pause, where, on the wild,
    The Mother to her frozen breast,

On the heap'd snows reclining clasps her child
    And with him sleeps, chill'd to eternal rest!

Black Horror! speed we to the bed of Death,
    Where he whose murderous power afar
    Blasts with the myriad plagues of war,
Struggles with his last breath,
    Then to his wildly-starting eyes
    The phantoms of the murder'd rise,
    Then on his frenzied ear
Their groans for vengeance and the Demon's yell
In one heart-maddening chorus swell.
Cold on his brow convulsing stands the dew,
And night eternal darkens on his view.

Horror! I call thee yet once more!
Bear me to that accursed shore
Where round the stake the impaled Negro writhes.
Assume thy sacred terrors then! dispense
The blasting gales of Pestilence!
Arouse the race of Afric! holy Power,
Lead them to vengeance! and in that dread hour
When Ruin rages wide
I will behold and smile by Mercy's side.

Matthew Gregory Lewis (1775–1818)

British novelist and playwright Matthew Gregory Lewis gained celebrity and notoriety with the publication of the Gothic novel *The Monk* (1796), which was condemned in its day for lasciviousness and other perceived moral defects. Included in the novel were bits of verse, including "Alonzo the Brave and Fair Imogene," later included in Lewis's anthology of weird balladry, *Tales of Wonder* (1801; published 1800), a volume that was considered so extravagant that it led to a parody, *Tales of Terror* (1801), which many subsequent readers and scholars believed was also the work of Lewis. Lewis wrote no more Gothic novels, but much supernaturalism is incorporated in his various stage plays.

Alonzo the Brave and Fair Imogene

A warrior so bold and a virgin so bright
        Conversed, as they sat on the green;
They gazed on each other with tender delight:
Alonzo the Brave was the name of the knight,
        The maid's was the Fair Imogene.

"And, oh!" said the youth, "since to-morrow I go
        To fight in a far distant land,
Your tears for my absence soon leaving to flow,
Some other will court you, and you will bestow
        On a wealthier suitor your hand."

"Oh! hush these suspicions," Fair Imogene said,
        "Offensive to love and to me!
For, if you be living, or if you be dead,
I swear by the Virgin, that none in your stead
        Shall husband of Imogene be.

"And if e'er for another my heart should decide,
        Forgetting Alonzo the Brave,
God grant, that, to punish my falsehood and pride,
Your ghost at the marriage may sit by my side,
May tax me with perjury, claim me as bride,
        And bear me away to the grave!"

To Palestine hastened the hero so bold;
        His love she lamented him sore:
But scarce had a twelvemonth elapsed, when behold,
A Baron all covered with jewels and gold
        Arrived at Fair Imogene's door.

His treasure, his presents, his spacious domain,
        Soon made her untrue to her vows:
He dazzled her eyes; he bewildered her brain;
He caught her affections so light and so vain,
        And carried her home as his spouse.

And now had the marriage been blessed by the priest;
        The revelry now was begun:
The tables they groaned with the weight of the feast;

Nor yet had the laughter and merriment ceased,
 When the bell of the castle tolled—"one!"

Then first with amazement Fair Imogene found
 That a stranger was placed by her side:
His air was terrific; he uttered no sound;
He spoke not, he moved not, he looked not around,
 But earnestly gazed on the bride.

His vizor was closed, and gigantic his height;
 His armour was sable to view;
All pleasure and laughter were hushed at his sight;
The dogs, as they eyed him, drew back in affright;
 The lights in the chamber burnt blue!

His presence all bosoms appeared to dismay;
 The guests sat in silence and fear:
At length spoke the bride, while she trembled—"I pray,
Sir Knight, that your helmet aside you would lay,
 And deign to partake of our cheer."

The lady is silent: the stranger complies,
 His vizor he slowly unclosed;
Oh! then what a sight met Fair Imogene's eyes!
What words can express her dismay and surprise,
 When a skeleton's head was exposed!

All present then uttered a terrified shout;
 All turned with disgust from the scene.
The worms they crept in, and the worms they crept out,
And sported his eyes and his temples about,
 While the spectre addressed Imogene:

"Behold me, thou false one! behold me!" he cried;
 "Remember Alonzo the Brave!
God grants, that, to punish thy falsehood and pride,
My ghost at thy marriage should sit by thy side,
Should tax thee with perjury, claim thee as bride,
 And bear thee away to the grave!"

Thus saying, his arms round the lady he wound,
 While loudly she shrieked in dismay;

Then sank with his prey through the wide-yawning ground:
Nor ever again was Fair Imogene found,
    Or the spectre who bore her away.

Not long lived the Baron: and none since that time
    To inhabit the castle presume;
For chronicles tell, that, by order sublime,
There Imogene suffers the pain of her crime,
    And mourns her deplorable doom.

At midnight four times in each year does her sprite,
    When mortals in slumber are bound,
Arrayed in her bridal apparel of white,
Appear in the hall with the skeleton-knight,
    And shriek as he whirls her around.

While they drink out of skulls newly torn from the grave,
    Dancing round them pale spectres are seen:
Their liquor is blood, and this horrible stave
They howl: "To the health of Alonzo the Brave,
    And his consort the False Imogene!"

Thomas Moore (1779–1852)

Irish poet and memoirist Thomas Moore began writing ballads and other poems while attending Trinity College, Dublin. His first book was *Odes of Anacreon* (1800). He became friends with Lord Byron, Samuel Taylor Coleridge, and other leading figures of the British Romantic movement; he would later edit Byron's *Letters and Journals* (1830). Of his own work, the best-known are *Lalla Rookh* (1817), an Oriental romance in verse; *The Epicurean* (1827), a short novel based on the unfinished poem "Alciphron"; and *Irish Melodies* (1820). His own journal has been published in 6 volumes (1983–91). "The Lake of the Dismal Swamp" was first published in Moore's late collection *Songs, Ballads, and Sacred Songs* (1849).

The Lake of the Dismal Swamp

"They tell of a young man, who lost his mind upon the death of a girl he loved, and who, suddenly disappearing from his friends, was never afterwards heard of. As he had frequently said, in his ravings, that the girl was not dead, but gone to the Dismal Swamp, it is supposed he had wandered into that dreary wilderness, and had died of hunger, or been lost in some of its dreadful morasses."—*Anon.*

"La Poésie a ses monstres comme la nature."—D'ALEMBERT.

"They made her a grave, too cold and damp
    For a soul so warm and true;
And she's gone to the Lake of the Dismal Swamp,
Where, all night long, by a fire-fly lamp,
    She paddles her white canoe.

"And her firefly lamp I soon shall see,
    And her paddle I soon shall hear;
Long and loving our life shall be,
And I'll hide the maid in a cypress tree,
    When the footstep of death is near."

Away to the Dismal Swamp he speeds—
    His path was rugged and sore,
Through tangled juniper, beds of reeds,
Through many a fen, where the serpent feeds,
    And man never trod before.

And, when on the earth he sunk to sleep,
    If slumber his eyelids knew,
He lay, where the deadly vine doth weep
Its venomous tear and nightly steep
    The flesh with blistering dew!

And near him the she-wolf stirr'd the brake,
    And the copper-snake breath'd in his ear,
Till he starting cried, from his dream awake,
"Oh! when shall I see the dusky Lake,
    And the white canoe of my dear?"

He saw the Lake, and a meteor bright
    Quick over its surface play'd—
"Welcome," he said, "my dear one's light!"
And the dim shore echoed, for many a night,
    The name of the death-cold maid.

He hollow'd a boat of the birchen bark,
    Which carried him off from shore;
Far, far he follow'd the meteor spark,
The wind was high and the clouds were dark,
    And the boat return'd no more.

But oft, from the Indian hunter's camp
    This lover and maid so true
Are seen at the hour of midnight damp
To cross the Lake by a fire-fly lamp,
    And paddle their white canoe!

George Gordon, Lord Byron (1788–1824)

George Gordon Byron was born club-footed and impoverished, but at the age of ten he unexpectedly inherited from a great-uncle a title and a ruined abbey, becoming the 6th Lord Byron. He went on to live an adventurous life, characterized by the extremes of melancholy and mirth that tint his literary creations. In 1806 his early poems were privately printed as *Fugitive Pieces*. *Hours of Idleness* appeared in 1807; a negative review of the book drew from Byron the versified satire *English Bards and Scotch Reviewers* (1809), which gained him his first recognition. Wider acknowledgment came with *Childe Harold's Pilgrimage* (1812–18) and a series of gloomy Oriental verse tales beginning with *The Giaour* (1813). These were followed by the Faustian poetic drama *Manfred* (1817) and the satiric realism of *Don Juan* (1819–24). Byron went to Greece to support the struggle for independence from the Turks; he died from fever there in 1824. "Darkness" was first published in *The Prisoner of Chillon and Other Poems* (1816).

Darkness

I had a dream, which was not all a dream.
The bright sun was extinguish'd, and the stars
Did wander darkling in the eternal space,
Rayless, and pathless, and the icy earth
Swung blind and blackening in the moonless air;
Morn came and went—and came, and brought no day,
And men forgot their passions in the dread
Of this their desolation; and all hearts
Were chill'd into a selfish prayer for light:
And they did live by watchfires—and the thrones,
The palaces of crowned kings—the huts,
The habitations of all things which dwell,
Were burnt for beacons; cities were consumed,
And men were gather'd round their blazing homes
To look once more into each other's face;
Happy were those who dwelt within the eye
Of the volcanos, and their mountain-torch:
A fearful hope was all the world contain'd;
Forests were set on fire—but hour by hour
They fell and faded—and the crackling trunks
Extinguish'd with a crash—and all was black.
The brows of men by the despairing light
Wore an unearthly aspect, as by fits
The flashes fell upon them; some lay down
And hid their eyes and wept; and some did rest
Their chins upon their clenched hands, and smiled;
And others hurried to and fro, and fed
Their funeral piles with fuel, and look'd up
With mad disquietude on the dull sky,
The pall of a past world; and then again
With curses cast them down upon the dust,
And gnash'd their teeth and howl'd: the wild birds shriek'd
And, terrified, did flutter on the ground,
And flap their useless wings; the wildest brutes
Came tame and tremulous; and vipers crawl'd
And twined themselves among the multitude,
Hissing, but stingless—they were slain for food.
And War, which for a moment was no more,

Did glut himself again:—a meal was bought
With blood, and each sate sullenly apart
Gorging himself in gloom: no love was left;
All earth was but one thought—and that was death
Immediate and inglorious; and the pang
Of famine fed upon all entrails—men
Died, and their bones were tombless as their flesh;
The meagre by the meagre were devour'd,
Even dogs assail'd their masters, all save one,
And he was faithful to a corse, and kept
The birds and beasts and famish'd men at bay,
Till hunger clung them, or the dropping dead
Lured their lank jaws; himself sought out no food,
But with a piteous and perpetual moan,
And a quick desolate cry, licking the hand
Which answer'd not with a caress—he died.
The crowd was famish'd by degrees; but two
Of an enormous city did survive,
And they were enemies: they met beside
The dying embers of an altar-place
Where had been heap'd a mass of holy things
For an unholy usage; they raked up,
And shivering scraped with their cold skeleton hands
The feeble ashes, and their feeble breath
Blew for a little life, and made a flame
Which was a mockery; then they lifted up
Their eyes as it grew lighter, and beheld
Each other's aspects—saw, and shriek'd, and died—
Even of their mutual hideousness they died,
Unknowing who he was upon whose brow
Famine had written Fiend. The world was void,
The populous and the powerful was a lump,
Seasonless, herbless, treeless, manless, lifeless,
A lump of death—a chaos of hard clay.
The rivers, lakes, and ocean all stood still,
And nothing stirr'd within their silent depths;
Ships sailorless lay rotting on the sea,
And their masts fell down piecemeal: as they dropp'd
They slept on the abyss without a surge—
The waves were dead; the tides were in their grave,

The moon, their mistress, had expired before;
The winds were wither'd in the stagnant air,
And the clouds perish'd; Darkness had no need
Of aid from them—She was the Universe.

Percy Bysshe Shelley (1792–1822)

Percy Bysshe Shelley was a major Romantic poet and ranks among the finest lyric poets of the English language. He is best known both for short lyrics such as "Ozymandias" and "Ode to a Skylark" and for long, visionary poems such as *Alastor* (1815), *The Revolt of Islam* (1817), *Prometheus Unbound* (1820), and *Adonaïs* (1821). At Eton, Shelley developed a keen interest in science and began reading Gothic mysteries; the influence of the latter is seen in the early prose romances *Zastrozzi* (1810) and *St. Irvyne* (1811). A nonconformist born into a conservative aristocratic family, Shelley's work contains a vein of political radicalism that has made him something of an icon among socialists and the labor movement. He eloped with the daughter of the radical William Godwin, fellow author Mary Wollstonecraft, who later wrote *Frankenstein* (1818). Their life was marred by tragedy, as Shelley drowned in July 1822 when his boat capsized in bad weather off the Italian coast. "Sister Rosa: A Ballad" was included in *St. Irvyne*.

Sister Rosa: A Ballad

> The death-bell beats!—
> The mountain repeats
> The echoing sound of the knell;
> And the dark Monk now
> Wraps the cowl round his brow,
> As he sits in his lonely cell.

> And the cold hand of death
> Chills his shuddering breath,
> As he lists to the fearful lay
> Which the ghosts of the sky,
> As they sweep wildly by,

Sing to departed day.
  And they sing of the hour
  When the stern fates had power
To resolve Rosa's form to its clay.

  But that hour is past;
  And that hour was the last
Of peace to the dark Monk's brain.
  Bitter tears, from his eyes, gushed silent and fast;
And he strove to suppress them in vain.

Then his fair cross of gold he dashed on the floor,
When the death-knell struck on his ear.—
  "Delight is in store
  For her evermore;
But for me is fate, horror, and fear."

  Then his eyes wildly rolled,
  When the death-bell tolled,
And he raged in terrific woe.
  And he stamped on the ground,—
  But when ceased the sound,
Tears again began to flow.

  And the ice of despair
  Chilled the wild throb of care,
And he sate in mute agony still;
  Till the night-stars shone through the cloudless air,
And the pale moonbeam slept on the hill.

  Then he knelt in his cell:—
  And the horrors of hell
Were delights to his agonized pain,
  And he prayed to God to dissolve the spell,
Which else must for ever remain.

And in fervent pray'r he knelt on the ground,
  Till the abbey bell struck One:
His feverish blood ran chill at the sound:
A voice hollow and horrible murmured around—
  "The term of thy penance is done!"

Grew dark the night;
The moonbeam bright
Waxed faint on the mountain high;
And, from the black hill,
Went a voice cold and still,—
"Monk! Thou art free to die."

Then he rose on his feet,
And his heart loud did beat,
And his limbs they were palsied with dread;
Whilst the grave's clammy dew
O'er his pale forehead grew;
And he shuddered to sleep with the dead.

And the wild midnight storm
Raved around his tall form,
As he sought the chapel's gloom:
And the sunk grass did sigh
To the wind, bleak and high,
As he searched for the new-made tomb.

And forms, dark and high,
Seemed around him to fly,
And mingle their yells with the blast:
And on the dark wall
Half-seen shadows did fall,
As enhorrored he onward passed.

And the storm-fiends wild rave
O'er the new-made grave,
And dread shadows linger around.
The Monk called on God his soul to save,
And, in horror, sank on the ground.

Then despair nerved his arm
To dispel the charm,
And he burst Rosa's coffin asunder.
And the fierce storm did swell
More terrific and fell,
And louder pealed the thunder.

And laughed, in joy, the fiendish throng,

Mixed with ghosts of the mouldering dead:
And their grisly wings, as they floated along,
    Whistled in murmurs dread.

And her skeleton form the dead Nun reared
    Which dripped with the chill dew of hell.
In her half-eaten eyeballs two pale flames appeared,
And triumphant their gleam on the dark Monk glared,
    As he stood within the cell.

And her lank hand lay on his shuddering brain;
    But each power was nerved by fear.—
"I never, henceforth, may breathe again;
Death now ends mine anguished pain.—
    The grave yawns,—we meet there."

And her skeleton lungs did utter the sound,
    So deadly so lone and so fell,
That in long vibrations shuddered the ground;
And as the stern notes floated around,
    A deep groan was answered from hell.

John Clare (1793–1864)

British poet John Clare was the son of a farm laborer and himself became an agricultural laborer. With little formal education, he began writing poetry after he obtained a copy of James Thomson's *The Seasons*. He published *The Shepherd's Calendar* in 1827, but it was not a commercial or critical success. A later volume, *The Rural Muse* (1835), was well received by critics, but by this time Clare was exhibiting the signs of depression and other mental illnesses that led to his entering two different mental institutions, where he spent the last twenty-seven years of his life. Much of his poetry, now celebrated for its evocation of the British countryside, was published posthumously. "The Nightmare," probably written in the years 1821–24, first appeaed in J. W. Tribble's edition of *The Poems of John Clare* (1935).

The Nightmare

Her steps take hold of hell.—*Solomon*.

My dream began in bliss and lifted high
My sleeping feelings into fancy's joy;
Though like one wandering in a sweet far land
I seemed to hear and could not understand
Among the many voices humming by,
Nor knew one face where many met my eye.
That dim-seen mystery which in dreams appears
Was mine, a feeling of joy, hopes, and fears,
Mingling together; yet I knew not why,
Where all was beauty, trouble should be by.
The place was light—and yet no sun was there
To cause it—pale and beautifully fair,
Nor glare nor gloom but like eternity
Mild, like what spirits may expect to see;
But there was earth and sky and trees and flowers,
Different in kind and yet resembling ours;
And mightiest objects that the eye surveyed,
No light they clouded and they cast no shade;
But in that sky no cloud crossed east and west,
No storm crept frowning o'er its crystal rest.

At length a mighty mansion gathered high,
Whose bounds seemed almost boundless to the eye,
A place that wakened fancy's wonders there,
As mystery's mask left half her shadow bare;
A shapeless shape and semblance faint of things
That earth calls palaces, the place of kings.
Here all seemed entering; yet there was no crowd,
No anxious rushing, and no noises loud.
All seemed intent on matters yet unknown,
And every other's interest seemed their own,
Like as a brook pursues its gliding way,
Urged by an impulse which they could not stay.
Fear shrank to silence now and hovered round,
Till wandering steps seemed listening for their sound.
Restless as waves in their eternal race,

Where one crowd passed another took its place.
The gathering throngs that seemed to make one spot,
I seemed to know some and then knew them not;
Some more familiar seemed; I turned again
And they were strange and left a lonely pain;
And other eyes on my inquiries came
And seemed they knew me, but to feel the same;
As birds seek nests which idle boys have got,
They sought what had been and they found it not;
What memory's shadows dimly might display—
Friends, loves, and kin—found none and turned away.
At length one singled from the mighty throng
Where I had gazed on vacant looks so long,
With flowing robes, blue eyes, and face divine,
Came forth and fixed her tender gaze on mine.
It looked familiar as I'd seen the same;
But recollections of her earthly name
Were lost, if e'er she had a claim to one;
She joined my steps and seemed to lead me on.
We entered with the rest, and by my side
She stood, my all companion, friend, and guide.
Arches empillared like the rainbow's height
Went sweeping up and almost left the sight;
And yet o'er them a covering met the eye,
As earth seems covered with surrounding sky.
At last the silence with a murmur broke
Like the first hum when organs are awoke,
And every face seemed turned towards the sound
Where hope would soothe and mystery would confound;
Fate seemed as writing upon every brow
A fearful question, "Who'll be summoned now?"
Yet woman seemed (though beauty's face beguiles
One's heart to favour) checking fears with smiles;
And my companion seated by my side
Seemed checking mine and strove her own to hide;
Her long white hand pressed mine with cheering power
As offering safety in a dangerous hour;
She looked and spake not yet, her lips the while
Closed mid the tumult in a timid smile;
And as the mystery waking gathered near,

Looked as one dares a danger, "Never fear."
More loud the music rose and yet more loud
Chorused with humming of a mighty crowd;
And through the mild light that at first clothed all
A brighter streamed, like sunbeams on a wall,
Growing more bright and losing it away
Like creeping sunrise on a summer's day;
A light that dazzled not, and yet it threw
Around o'erpowering splendour as it grew;
More high the music seemed, more strong the fear,
And awful symptoms rousing gathered near;
Voices awoke from many a troubling tongue,
But no words came distinctly from the throng;
Fears grew within me, and I fain had tried
To search the purpose of my angel guide.
Anxiety turned on her quiet face,
And recollections would [old] memories trace,
As one I'd witnessed once or else the same,
The looks of one I had not power to name;
She seemed at first as living beauty seems,
Then changed more lovely in the shade of dreams;
Then faded dim, confused, and hurrying by
Like memory waning into vacancy.
The music rose in terror's ecstasies,
In gradual swells like winds in summer trees,
Gathering and gathering to its highest bound,
And burst at last in mystery's mightiest sound.

     Millions of hopes, hung on a spider's tie
'Tween time's suspense and fate's eternity,
Seemed cut at once, and all around the host
Felt at that moment if his own was lost;
And in a moment sudden changes rang
Confusion's uproar—discord's jarring clang,
Harsh noises, stunning crush, and thrilling yell,
As the whole mansion on their shoulders fell.
A light glowed round with horror's staggering sound,
And all seemed giddy, reeling, sinking round;
A weight plopt on me with a sudden crush,
A noise like waters that for freedom rush;

I could not move, nor speak; yet reason's power
Seemed wide awake in that spell-prisoning hour;
I felt as tried, whate'er the lot might be,
And strove and struggled with my destiny;
And then my eyes in hopeless wandering spied
That lovely shadow which had been my guide,
Seemly bent o'er me, offering mercy's plea,
'Tween death's dark hell and life's eternity.
Her face grew pale and awful, yet a shade
Of beauty hung in every change it made.
Her eyes o'er mine hung beautiful and bright,
Like the sun setting upon deepening night;
And love, fear, hope—all mortals can recall—
I felt none separate, but I felt them all.
Her white round arms threw back her streaming hair,
And smiles hung o'er me as in death's despair.

      Something drew near me and my guide withdrew,
Beauteous as ever but in terror too;
Her bright eyes lessened dim but not with tears,
Heavy with sorrows and the gloom of fears;
And scarce I turned her desert flight to trace
Ere a foul fiend seemed standing in her place.
'Twas Mary's voice that hung in her farewell;
The sound that moment on my memory fell—
A sound that held the music of the past;
But she was blest and I alone was cast;
My dangers dimmed the glory of her eyes,
And turned her smiling and her hopes to sighs.
The gloomiest pictures fear could ever make,
The fiend drew near to make my terrors ache—
Huge circles lost to eyes, and rotten hulls
Raised with dead groans from the dread "place of skulls",—
Then turned with horrid laugh its haggard head
To where the earth-loved shadow dimly fled,
As mockery—waking hell with horrid sound
Like many murmurs moving underground,
I shuddering struggled from his horrid glare
And snapped my bonds and ended my despair,
And—as woke reason from the vision crept,

She seemed to start as one that ne'er had slept;
Horror and joy and mystery when by
Seemed less of vision than reality,
A nightmare mystery of a sealing doom,
A feeble picture of the dread to come.

Note. I wish to acknowledge that whatsoever merit this and "The Dream" may be thought to possess they owe it in part to the *English Opium Eater,* as they were written after (though actual dreams) the perusal of that singular and interesting production.

John Keats (1795–1821)

British poet John Keats was born of working-class parents in London. He was educated at Clarke's School in Enfield and was apprenticed to an apothecary-surgeon. His first poems date to 1814 and betray the influence of classical poets as well as Edmund Spenser. His first volume of poems appeared in 1817, followed by the long poem *Endymion* (1817), which was viciously attacked by some reviewers as an example of "Cockney Poetry," or poetry written by lower-class poets. Undeterred, and bolstered by the friendship of Percy Bysshe Shelley as well as the critics Leigh Hunt and William Hazlitt, Keats went on to publish *Lamia, Isabella, The Eve of St. Agnes, and Other Poems* (1820). *Lamia* is a long poem about a shape-changer, who appears alternately as a woman and a snake. *The Eve of St. Agnes* also has elements of weirdness. Keats, afflicted with increasingly worsening tuberculosis, moved to Italy in 1820 but died there in early 1821. "La Belle Dame sans Merci" was written on April 21, 1819, and first published in the *Indicator* (May 10, 1820).

La Belle Dame sans Merci: A Ballad

O what can ail thee, knight-at-arms,
    Alone and palely loitering?
The sedge has withered from the lake,
    And no birds sing.

O what can ail thee, knight-at-arms,
    So haggard and so woe-begone?
The squirrel's granary is full,
    And the harvest's done.

I see a lily on thy brow,
    With anguish moist and fever-dew,
And on thy cheeks a fading rose
    Fast withereth too.

I met a lady in the meads,
    Full beautiful—a faery's child,
Her hair was long, her foot was light,
    And her eyes were wild.

I made a garland for her head,
    And bracelets too, and fragrant zone;
She looked at me as she did love,
    And made sweet moan.

I set her on my pacing steed,
    And nothing else saw all day long,
For sidelong would she bend, and sing
    A faery's song.

She found me roots of relish sweet,
    And honey wild, and manna-dew,
And sure in language strange she said—
    "I love thee true."

She took me to her elfin grot,
    And there she wept and sighed full sore,
And there I shut her wild wild eyes
    With kisses four.

And there she lulled me asleep
    And there I dreamed—Ah! woe betide!—
The latest dream I ever dreamt
    On the cold hill side.

I saw pale kings and princes too,
    Pale warriors, death-pale were they all;

They cried—"La Belle Dame sans Merci
    Thee hath in thrall!"

I saw their starved lips in the gloam,
    With horrid warning gapèd wide,
And I awoke and found me here,
    On the cold hill's side.

And this is why I sojourn here
    Alone and palely loitering,
Though the sedge is withered from the lake,
    And no birds sing.

Heinrich Heine (1797–1856)

German poet Heinrich (Christian Johann) Heine's first volume of verse, *Gedichte* (Poems), appeared in 1821, followed by *Lyrisches Intermezzo* (1823). Four years later *Das Buch der Lieder* (The Book of Songs) was an immense success and would go through thirteen editions in his lifetime. Heine, born Jewish in the area of Germany that was to become Prussia, became disillusioned by undercurrents of anti-Semitism there. He severed his ties with Germany and, after visiting London, Munich, and Italy, settled in Paris. He was initially best known for his lyric poetry, which contemporary composers sometimes set to music. In Paris he associated with a group of utopian socialists and began to focus more on contemporary topics, often in prose form—a whimsical amalgam of fact, fiction, social criticism, political comment, and polemic. *Atta Troll* (1843–45) is a long poetic spoof that reflects his interest in contemporary politics. *Neue Gedichte* (New Poems) appeared in 1844 and included not only love poems but ballads, satiric poetry, and items on current social issues. He was bedridden with ill-health in the final years of life, when he returned to poetry. His final volume of poems, *Romanzero* (1851), which contains what many consider his finest poems, is a bleak commentary on his personal circumstances and the human condition. "The Lorelei" ("Die Lorelei") was first collected in *Reisebilder* (1826–27).

The Lorelei

I know not what sorrow is o'er me,
  What spell is upon my heart;
But a tale of old times is before me—
  A legend that will not depart.

Night falls as I linger, dreaming,
  And calmly flows the Rhine;
The peaks of the mountains gleaming
  In the golden sunset shine.

A wondrous lovely maiden
  Sits high in glory there;
Her robe with gems is laden,
  And she combs out her golden hair.

And she spreads out the golden treasure,
  Still singing in harmony;
And the song has a mystical measure,
  And a wonderful melody.

The boatman, when once she has bound him,
  Is lost in a wild sad love;
He sees not the black rocks around him,
  He sees but the beauty above.

I believe that the billows springing
  The boat and the boatman drown;
And that this, with her magical singing,
  The Lorelei has done.

        [tr. Charles Godfrey Leland (1898)]

Thomas Hood (1799–1845)

British writer Thomas Hood is chiefly known as the editor of numer-
ous British periodicals of the 1820s–1840s and as a comic and satirical
poet; but in his bountiful poetic work there are a number of grimly
serious and fantastic poems, including "The Dream of Eugene Aram,"

a celebrated poem about a murderer. Hood's son, Thomas Hood the Younger (1835–1874), was also a poet and editor. "The Demon Ship" was first published in the *Literary Gazette* (30 June 1827) and collected in *Whims and Oddities: Second Series* (1827).

The Demon-Ship

'Twas off the Wash—the sun went down—the sea look'd black and
    grim,
For stormy clouds, with murky fleece, were mustering at the brim;
Titanic shades! enormous gloom!—as if the solid night
Of Erebus rose suddenly to seize upon the light!
It was a time for mariners to bear a wary eye,
With such a dark conspiracy between the sea and sky!

Down went my helm—close reef'd—the tack held freely in my
    hand—
With ballast snug—I put about, and scudded for the land.
Loud hiss'd the sea beneath her lee—my little boat flew fast,
But faster still the rushing storm came borne upon the blast.
Lord! what a roaring hurricane beset the straining sail!
What furious sleet, with level drift, and fierce assaults of hail!
What darksome caverns yawn'd before! what jagged steeps behind!
Like battle-steeds, with foamy manes, wild tossing in the wind.
Each after each sank down astern, exhausted in the chase,
But where it sank another rose and gallop'd in its place;
As black as night—they turned to white, and cast against the cloud
A snowy sheet, as if each surge upturn'd a sailor's shroud:—
Still flew my boat; alas! alas! her course was nearly run!
Behold yon fatal billow rise—ten billows heap'd in one!
With fearful speed the dreary mass came rolling, rolling, fast,
As if the scooping sea contain'd one only wave at last!
Still on it came, with horrid roar, a swift pursuing grave;
It seem'd as though some cloud had turn'd its hugeness to a wave!
Its briny sleet began to beat beforehand in my face—
I felt the rearward keel begin to climb its swelling base!
I saw its alpine hoary head impending over mine!
Another pulse—and down it rush'd—an avalanche of brine!
Brief pause had I, on God to cry, or think of wife and home;
The waters clos'd—and when I shriek'd, I shriek'd below the foam!

Beyond that rush I have no hint of any after deed—
For I was tossing on the waste, as senseless as a weed.

"Where am I? in the breathing world, or in the world of death?"
With sharp and sudden pang I drew another birth of breath;
My eyes drank in a doubtful light, my ears a doubtful sound—
And was that ship a *real* ship whose tackle seem'd around?
A moon, as if the earthly moon, was shining up aloft;
But were those beams the very beams that I had seen so oft?
A face, that mock'd the human face, before me watch'd alone;
But were those eyes the eyes of man that look'd against my own?

Oh! never may the moon again disclose me such a sight
As met my gaze, when first I look'd, on that accursed night!
I've seen a thousand horrid shapes begot of fierce extremes
Of fever; and most frightful things have haunted in my dreams—
Hyenas—cats—blood-loving bats—and apes with hateful stare,—
Pernicious snakes, and shaggy bulls—the lion, and she-bear—
Strong enemies, with Judas looks, of treachery and spite—
Detected features, hardly dimm'd and banish'd by the light!
Pale-sheeted ghosts, with gory locks, upstarting from their tombs—
All phantasies and images that flit in midnight glooms—
Hags, goblins, demons, lemures, have made me all aghast,—
But nothing like that GRIMLY ONE who stood beside the mast!

His cheek was black—his brow was black—his eyes and hair as dark:
His hand was black, and where it touch'd, it left a sable mark;
His throat was black, his vest the same, and when I look'd beneath,
His breast was black—all, all, was black except his grinning teeth.
His sooty crew were like in hue, as black as Afric slaves!
Oh, horror! e'en the ship was black that plough'd the inky waves!

"Alas!" I cried, "for love of truth and blessed mercy's sake,
Where am I? in what dreadful ship? upon what dreadful lake?
What shape is that, so very grim, and black as any coal?
It is Mahound, the Evil One, and he has gain'd my soul!
Oh, mother dear! my tender nurse! dear meadows that beguil'd
My happy days, when I was yet a little sinless child,—
My mother dear—my native fields, I never more shall see:
I'm sailing in the Devil's Ship, upon the Devil's Sea!"

Loud laugh'd that SABLE MARINER, and loudly in return

His sooty crew sent forth a laugh that rang from stem to stern—
A dozen pair of grimly cheeks were crumpled on the nonce—
As many sets of grinning teeth came shining out at once:
A dozen gloomy shapes at once enjoy'd the merry fit,
With shriek and yell, and oaths as well, like Demons of the Pit.
They crow'd their fill, and then the Chief made answer for the
    whole:—
"Our skins," said he, "are black ye see, because we carry coal;
You'll find your mother sure enough, and see your native fields—
For this here ship has pick'd you up—the Mary Ann of Shields!"

IV. The Later Nineteenth Century

Victor Hugo (1802–1885)

French novelist, dramatist, and poet Victor Hugo, one of the giants of world literature, is chiefly known outside France for the novels *Les Misérables* (1862) and *Nôtre Dame de Paris* (1831); but in his own country he is revered for his contributions as a Romantic poet, dramatist, and public figure. Schooled in Spain and France, he went on to launch several magazines beginning with *Le Conservateur Littéraire* in 1819. He began a successful political career in 1845 and, following the formation of the Second Republic, was elected to the Constitutional Assembly and the Legislative Assembly. Positioning himself against Napoleon III, he lived in exile from 1851 to 1870 in Brussels and later the British Isles of Jersey and Guernsey. During his exile Hugo became interested in the supernatural, participating in numerous séances. He transcribed spirit communications from family, fellow political exiles, and the famous—including Shakespeare, Plato, and Galileo—as well as less familiar entities including Balaam's Ass, the Lion of Androcles, "the Shadow of the Sepulcher," "Metempsychosis," "Ocean," and even aliens from Mercury and Jupiter. He returned to France a hero, where he spent his remaining years. "The Vanished City" ("La Ville disparue") was collected in *La Légende des siècles: Nouvelle série* (1877).

The Vanished City

Water is never idle. Thousand years,
Ere Adam was, that spectre with white hairs,
Our ancestor—so your descent you trace—
When giants still mixed with the human race—
In times whereof tradition speaketh not,
A brick-built city stood upon the spot
Where now the north wind stirs the ocean foam.
That city was of mad excess the home:
Pale lightnings did at times its riot threat;
What now is sea was a wide plain as yet;

Ships voyage now where chariots rolled before,
And hurricanes replace the kings of yore.
For, to make deserts, God, who rules mankind,
Begins with kings, and ends the work by wind.
This folk, this ant-hill, rumor, gossip, noise,
This troop of souls, by sorrow moved, and joys,
Sounded as in a tempest hums a swarm—
The neighboring ocean caused them no alarm.

This city had its kings: kings proud and great,
Who heads had 'neath them, as the reapers wheat.
Were they bad?—No!—But they were kings. And kings
Are men o'er-high, whom a vague terror wrings.
In wrong they pleasure seek, and fears allay,
And are, 'mid beasts of burden, beasts of prey.
"'Tis not their fault!" the sage, with pity, cries,
"They would be better if born otherwise."
Men still are men. The despot's wickedness
Comes of ill teaching, and of power's excess—
Comes of the purple he from childhood wears:
Slaves would be tyrants if the chance were theirs.
This ancient city, then, was built of brick,
With ships, bazaars, and lofty towers thick;
Arches, and palaces for music famed,
And brazen monsters which their gods they named.
Cruel, and gay, this town whose squares and streets
Showed gibbets which the crowd with laughter greets;
Hymns of forgetfulness they sing, for man
Is but a breath, and only lasts a span—
The avenues of sparkling lakes were closed;
The king's wives bathed, their naked charms exposed
In parks where peacocks all their stars display.
Hammers that drive the sleeper's rest away
Pounded on anvils black, from dawn to night,
And vultures preened their feathers, and alight
Upon the temples, by no fears deterred,
For savage idols love the cruel bird;
Tigers with hydras suit—the eagles know
That they no ancient customs overthrow
If, when blood flows from th' altar to the sod,
They come, and share the slaughter with the god.

Pure gold the altar of that fane august;
The cedar roof was clenched, for fear of rust,
With wooden pegs for nails, and night and day
Did hautboys, clarions, cymbals loudly play
For fear their savage god should fall asleep;
Such life, such deeds that mighty city steep,
There women flock for riot vile, and pelf.

One day the ocean 'gan to stir itself
Gently, devoid of rage, beside the town:
It silently gnawed through the rocks, and down
Without noise, shock, or the least movement rough,
Like a grave workman who has time enough.
In vain a man his ear fixed to the ground
Had closely listened; he had heard no sound;
The water dumbly, softly wears, destroys;
Over deep silence raves the city's noise,
So that at eve, at Nature's shuddering hour,
When (like an emir of tyrannic power)
Sirius appears, and on the horizon black,
Bids countless stars pursue their mighty track,
The clouds the only birds that never sleep,
Collected by the winds through heaven's steep—
The moon, the stars, the white-capped hills descry
Houses, domes, pillars, arches, suddenly
With the whole city, people, army all,
Their king who sang and feasted in his hall,
And had not time to rise up from the board—
Sink into nameless depth of darkness poured,
And whilst at once, heaped up from top to base,
Towers, palaces are gulfed without a trace,
A hoarse, a savage murmuring arose,
And you behold like a vast mouth unclose,
A hole, whence spouts a stream of foaming wrath,
Gulf where the town falls in, the sea comes forth.

And then all vanished!—waves roll o'er the plain.—
Now you see nothing but the deep, wide main,
Stirred by the winds, alone beneath the skies.

Such is the shock of ocean's mysteries!

                          [tr. Henry Carrington (1887)]

Thomas Lovell Beddoes (1803–1849)

British poet and dramatist Thomas Lovell Beddoes began his career by studying medicine, but later took to writing. Among his plays are *The Improvvisatore* (1821) and *The Brides' Tragedy* (1822), both of which reveal his devotion to Elizabethan and Jacobean poetry, as does his most celebrated work, *Death's Jest-Book,* a work begun as early as 1825 but not published until after his death, in 1850. "The Ghosts' Moonshine," "The Boding Dreams," and "Doomsday" were all written for inclusion in *Death's Jest-Book,* the first in 1825–29 and the other two in 1829–44.

The Ghosts' Moonshine

I.

It is midnight, my wedded;
    Let us lie under
The tempest bright undreaded,
    In the warm thunder:
(Tremble and weep not! What can you fear?)
    My heart's best wish is thine,—
That thou wert white, and bedded,
    On the softest bier,
        In the ghosts' moonshine.
    Is that the wind? No, no;
    Only two devils, that blow
Through the murderer's ribs to and fro,
        In the ghosts' moonshine.

II.

Who is there, she said afraid, yet
    Stirring and awaking
The poor old dead? His spade, it
    Is only making,—
(Tremble and weep not! What do you crave?)
    Where yonder grasses twine,
A pleasant bed, my maid, that
    Children call a grave,
        In the cold moonshine.
    Is that the wind? No, no;

Only two devils, that blow
        Through the murderer's ribs to and fro,
                In the ghosts' moonshine.

III.

What dost thou strain above her
        Lovely throat's whiteness?
A silken chain, to cover
        Her bosom's brightness?
(Tremble and weep not: what dost thou fear?)
        —My blood is spilt like wine,
Thou hast strangled and slain me, lover,
        Thou hast stabbed me dear,
                In the ghosts' moonshine.
        Is that the wind? No, no;
        Only her goblin doth blow
        Through the murderer's ribs to and fro,
                In its own moonshine.

The Boding Dreams

I.

In lover's ear a wild voice cried:
        "Sleeper, awake and rise!"
A pale form stood by his bed-side,
        With heavy tears in her sad eyes.
"A beckoning hand, a meaning sound,
A new-dug grave in weedy ground
For her who sleeps in dreams of thee.
Awake! Let not the murder be!"
Unheard the faithful dream did pray,
And sadly sighed itself away.
        "Sleep on," sung Sleep, "to-morrow
        'Tis time to know thy sorrow."
        "Sleep on," sung Death, "to-morrow
        From me thy sleep thou'lt borrow."
                Sleep on, lover, sleep on,
                The tedious dream, is gone:
                        The bell tolls one.

II.

Another hour, another dream:
    "Awake! awake!" it wailed,
"Arise, ere with the moon's last beam
    Her rosy life hath paled."
A hidden light, a muffled tread,
A daggered hand beside the bed
Of her who sleeps in dreams of thee.
Thou wak'st not: let the murder be.
In vain the faithful dream did pray,
And sadly sighed itself away.
    "Sleep on," sung Sleep, "to-morrow
    'Tis time to know thy sorrow."
    "Sleep on," sung Death, "to-morrow
    From me thy sleep thou'lt borrow."
        Sleep on, lover, sleep on,
        The tedious dream is gone;
            Soon comes the sun.

III.

Another hour, another dream:
    A red wound on a snowy breast,
A rude hand stifling the last scream,
    On rosy lips a death-kiss pressed.
Blood on the sheets, blood on the floor,
The murderer stealing through the door.
"Now," said the voice, with comfort deep,
"She sleeps indeed, and thou may'st sleep."
The scornful dream then turned away
To the first, bleeding cloud of day.
    "Sleep on," sung Sleep, "to-morrow
    'Tis time to know thy sorrow."
    "Sleep on," sung Death, "to-morrow
    From me thy sleep thou'lt borrow."
        Sleep on, lover, sleep on,
        The tedious dream is gone;
            The murder's done.

Doomsday

If I can raise one ghost, why I will raise
And call up doomsday from behind the east.
Awake then, ghostly doomsday!
Throw up your monuments, ye buried men
That lie in ruined cities of the wastes!
Ye battle fields, and woody mountain sides,
Ye lakes and oceans, and ye lava floods
That have o'erwhelmed great cities, now roll back!
And let the sceptred break their pyramids,
An earthquake of the buried shake the domes
Of arched cathedrals, and o'erturn the forests,
Until the grassy mounds and sculptured floors,
The monumental statues, hollow rocks,
The paved churchyard, and the flowery mead,
And ocean's billowy sarchophagi,
Pass from the bosoms of the rising people
Like clouds! Enough of stars and suns immortal
Have risen in heaven: to-day, in earth and sea
Riseth mankind. And first, yawn deep and wide,
Ye marble palace-floors,
And let the uncoffined bones, which ye conceal,
Ascend, and dig their purple murderers up,
Out of their crowned death. Ye catacombs
Open your gates, and overwhelm the sands
With an eruption of the naked millions,
Out of old centuries! The buried navies
Shall hear the call, and shoot up from the sea,
Whose wrecks shall knock against the hollow mountains,
And wake the swallowed cities in their hearts.
Forgotten armies rattle with their spears
Against the rocky walls of their sepulchres:
An earthquake of the buried shakes the pillars
Of the thick-sown cathedrals; guilty forests,
Where bloody spades have dug 'mid nightly storms;
The muddy drowning-places of the babes;
The pyramids, and bony hiding places.

*   *   *

"Thou rainbow on the tearful lash of doomsday's morning star
Rise quick, and let me gaze into that planet deep and far,
        As into a loved eye;
Or I must, like the fiery child of the Vesuvian womb,
Burst with my flickering ghost abroad, before the sun of doom
        Rolls up the spectre sky."
A lowly mound, at stormy night, sent up this ardent prayer
        Out of a murderer's grave, a traitor's nettly bed,
And the deeds of him, more dread than Cain, whose wickedness lay
    there,
        All mankind hath heard or read.

"Oh doomsday, doomsday come! thou creative morn
Of graves in earth, and under sea, all teeming at the horn
        Of angels fair and dread.
As thou the ghosts shalt waken, so I, the ghost, wake thee;
For thy rising sun and I shall rise together from the sea,
        The eldest of the dead."

So crying, o'er the billowy main, an old ghost strode
        To a churchyard on the shore,
O'er whose ancient corpse the billowy main of ships had ebbed and
    flowed,
        Four thousand years or more.

"World, wilt thou yield thy spirits up, and be convulsed and die?
And, as I haunt the billowy main, thy ghost shall haunt the sky,
        A pale unheeded star.
Oh doomsday, doomsday, when wilt thou dawn at length for me?"
So having prayed in moonlight waves, beneath the shipwrecked sea,
        In spectral caverns far.

Henry Wadsworth Longfellow (1807–1822)

Although American writer Henry Wadsworth Longfellow was edu-
cated in New England, he spent much of his early years teaching and
traveling in Europe, where he fell under the influence of German
Romanticism. Outshone critically by other exponents of the "Ameri-
can Renaissance," he was yet the most popular American poet in the

nineteenth century. In 1839 he published the verses *Voices of the Night* and novel *Hyperion*, which were followed by *Ballads and Other Poems* (1841), *Poems on Slavery* (1842), and *Evangeline* (1847). Later came more narrative poetry such as *The Song of Hiawatha* (1855), *The Courtship of Miles Standish* (1858), and *The Tales of a Wayside Inn* (1863). "Haunted Houses" and "The Haunted Chamber" both appeared in *Birds of Passage*, the first in the "first flight" (published 1858), the second in the "third flight" (published 1873).

Haunted Houses

All houses wherein men have lived and died
    Are haunted houses. Through the open doors
The harmless phantoms on their errands glide,
    With feet that make no sound upon the floors.

We meet them at the doorway, on the stair,
    Along the passages they come and go,
Impalpable impressions on the air,
    A sense of something moving to and fro.

There are more guests at table than the hosts
    Invited; the illuminated hall
Is thronged with quiet, inoffensive ghosts,
    As silent as the pictures on the wall.

The stranger at my fireside cannot see
    The forms I see, nor hear the sounds I hear;
He but perceives what is; while unto me
    All that has been is visible and clear.

We have no title-deeds to house or lands;
    Owners and occupants of earlier dates
From graves forgotten stretch their dusty hands,
    And hold in mortmain still their old estates.

The spirit-world around this world of sense
    Floats like an atmosphere, and everywhere
Wafts through these earthly mists and vapors dense
    A vital breath of more ethereal air.

Our little lives are kept in equipoise
        By opposite attractions and desires:
The struggle of the instinct that enjoys,
        And the more noble instinct that aspires.

These perturbations, this perpetual jar
        Of earthly wants and aspirations high,
Come from the influence of an unseen star,
        An undiscovered planet in our sky.

And as the moon from some dark gate of cloud
        Throws o'er the sea a floating bridge of light,
Across whose trembling planks our fancies crowd
        Into the realm of mystery and night,—

So from the world of spirits ther descends,
        A bridge of light, connecting it with this,
O'er whose unsteady floor, that sways and bends,
        Wander our thoughts above the dark abyss.

The Haunted Chamber

Each heart has its haunted chamber,
        Where the silent moonlight falls!
On the floor are mysterious footsteps,
        There are whispers along the walls!

And mine at times is haunted
        By phantoms of the Past,
As motionless as shadows
        By the silent moonlight cast.

A form sits by the window,
        That is not seen by day,
For as soon as the dawn approaches
        It vanishes away.

It sits there in the moonlight,
        Itself as pale and still,
And points with its airy finger
        Across the window-sill.

Without, before the window,
    There stands a gloomy pine,
Whose boughs wave upward and downward
    As wave these thoughts of mine.

And underneath its branches
    Is the grave of a little child,
Who died upon life's threshold,
    And never wept nor smiled.

What are ye, O pallid phantoms!
    That haunt my troubled brain?
That vanish when day approaches
    And at night return again?

What are ye, O pallid phantoms!
    But the statues without breath,
That stand on the bridge overarching
    The silent river of death?

Edgar Allan Poe (1809–1849)

American poet and short story writer Edgar Allan Poe's earliest publications were volumes of poetry: the fabulously rare *Tamerlane and Other Poems* (1827), *Al Aaraaf, Tamerlane, and Minor Poems* (1829), and *Poems* (1831). Many of his later poems were collected in *The Raven and Other Poems* (1845). His tales of horror and the supernatural—collected in *Tales of the Grotesque and Arabesque* (1840), *Tales* (1845), and other volumes—revolutionized the field. "The City in the Sea" was first published (as "The Doomed City") in *Poems* (1831); a revised version appeared in the *Broadway Journal* (30 August 1845) and in *The Raven and Other Poems*. "The Haunted Palace" was first published in the *American Museum of Science, Literature and the Arts* (April 1839) and subsequently included in all editions of the story "The Fall of the House of Usher" (*Burton's Gentleman's Magazine,* September 1839). "The Conqueror Worm" first appeared in *Graham's Magazine* (January 1843) and was subsequently incorporated in all editions of the story "Ligeia" (*Broadway Journal,* 27 September 1845). "Dream-Land" was first published in

Graham's Magazine (June 1844) and included in *The Raven and Other Poems.* "Ulalume" was first published in the *American Review* (December 1847).

The City in the Sea

Lo! Death has reared himself a throne
In a strange city lying alone
Far down within the dim West,
Where the good and the bad and the worst and the best
Have gone to their eternal rest.
There shrines and palaces and towers
(Time-eaten towers that tremble not!)
Resemble nothing that is ours.
Around, by lifting winds forgot,
Resignedly beneath the sky
The melancholy waters lie.

No rays from the holy heaven come down
On the long night-time of that town;
But light from out the lurid sea
Streams up the turrets silently—
Gleams up the pinnacles far and free
Up domes—up sires—up kingly halls—
Up fanes—up Bablyon-like walls—
Up shadowy long-forgotten bowers
Of sculptured ivy and stone flowers—
Up many and many a marvellous shrine
Whose wreathéd friezes intertwine
The viol, the violet, and the vine.

Resignedly beneath the sky
The melancholy waters lie.
So blend the turrets and shadows there
That all seem pendulous in air,
While from a proud tower in the town
Death looks gigantically down.

There open fanes and gaping graves
Yawn level with the luminous waves;
But not the riches there that lie

In each idol's diamond eye—
Not the gaily-jewelled dead
Tempt the waters from their bed;
For no ripples curl, alas!
Along that wilderness of glass—
No swellings tell that winds may be
Upon some far-off happier sea—
No heavings hint that winds have been
On seas less hideously serene.

But lo, a stir is in the air!
The wave—there is a movement there!
As if the towers had thrust aside,
In slightly sinking, the dull tide—
As if their tops had feebly given
A void within the filmy Heaven.
The waves have now a redder glow—
The hours are breathing faint and low—
And when, amid no earthly moans,
Down, down that town shall settle hence,
Hell, rising from a thousand thrones,
Shall do it reverence.

The Haunted Palace

In the greenest of our valleys
    By good angels tenanted,
Once a fair and stately palace—
    Radiant palace—reared its head.
In the monarch Thought's dominion—
    It stood there!
Never seraph spread his pinion
    Over fabric half so fair!

Banners yellow, glorious, golden,
    On its roof did float and flow—
(This—all this— was in the olden
    Time long ago)
And every gentle air that dallied,
    In that sweet day,

Along the ramparts plumed and pallid,
    A wingéd odor went away.

All wanderers in that happy valley,
    Through two luminous windows, saw
Spirits moving musically,
    To a lute's well tunéd law,
Round about a throne where, sitting,
    Porphyrogene,
In state his glory well befitting
    The ruler of the realm was seen.

And all with pearl and ruby glowing
    Was the fair palace door,
Through which came flowing, flowing, flowing,
    And sparkling evermore,
A troop of Echoes whose sweet duty
    Was but to sing,
In voices of surpassing beauty,
    The wit and wisdom of their king.

But evil things, in robes of sorrow,
    Assailed the monarch's high estate.
(Ah, let us mourn!—for never morrow
    Shall dawn upon him, desolate!)
And round about his home the glory
    That blushed and bloomed,
Is but a dim-remembered story
    Of the old-time entombed.

And travellers, now, within that valley,
    Through the encrimsoned windows see
Vast forms that move fantastically
    To a discordant melody;
While, like a ghastly rapid river,
    Through the pale door
A hideous throng rush out forever
    And laugh—but smile no more.

The Conqueror Worm

Lo! 'tis a gala night
    Within the lonesome latter years!
An angel throng, bewinged, bedight
    In veils, and drowned in tears,
Sit in a theatre, to see
    A play of hopes and fears,
While the orchestra breathes fitfully
    The music of the spheres.

Mimes, in the form of God on high,
    Mutter and mumble low,
And hither and thither fly—
    Mere puppets they, who come and go
At bidding of vast formless things
    That shift the scenery to and fro,
Flapping from out their Condor wings
    Invisible Wo!

That motley drama—oh, be sure
    It shall not be forgot!
With its Phantom chased for evermore,
    By a crowd that seize it not,
Through a circle that ever returneth in
    To the self-same spot,
And much of Madness, and more of Sin,
    And Horror the soul of the plot.

But see, amid the mimic rout,
    A crawling shape intrude!
A blood-red thing that writhes from out
    The scenic solitude!
It writhes!—it writhes!—with mortal pangs
    The mimes become its food,
And the seraphs sob at vermin fangs
    In human gore imbued.

Out—out are the lights—out all!
    And, over each quivering form,
The curtain, a funeral pall,

Comes down with the rush of a storm,
And the angels, all pallid and wan,
Uprising, unveiling, affirm
That the play is the tragedy, "Man,"
And its hero the Conqueror Worm.

Dream-Land

By a route obscure and lonely,
Haunted by ill angels only,
Where an Eidolon, named Night,
On a black throne reigns upright,
I have reached these lands but newly
From an ultimate dim Thule—
From a wild weird clime that lieth, sublime,
Out of Space—out of Time.

Bottomless vales and boundless floods,
And chasms, and caves, and Titan woods,
With forms that no man can discover
For the dews that drip all over;
Mountains toppling evermore
Into seas without a shore;
Seas that restlessly aspire,
Surging, unto skies of fire;
Lakes that endlessly outspread
Their lone waters—lone and dead,—
Their still waters, still and chilly
With the snows of the lolling lily.

By the lakes that thus outspread
Their lone waters, lone and dead,—
Their sad waters, sad and chilly
With the snows of the lolling lily,—
By the mountains—near the river
Murmuring lowly, murmuring ever,—
By the gray woods,—by the swamp
Where the toad and the newt encamp,—
By the dismal tarns and pools
Where dwell the Ghouls,—

By each spot the most unholy—
In each nook most melancholy,—
There the traveller meets aghast
Sheeted Memories of the Past—
Shrouded forms that start and sigh
As they pass the wanderer by—
White-robed forms of friends long given,
In agony, to the Earth—and Heaven.

For the heart whose woes are legion
'Tis a peaceful, soothing region—
For the spirit that walks in shadow
O! it is an Eldorado!
But the traveller, travelling through it,
May not—dare not openly view it;
Never its mysteries are exposed
To the weak human eye unclosed;
So wills its King, who hath forbid
The uplifting of the fringed lid;
And thus the sad Soul that here passes
Beholds it but through darkened glasses.

By a route obscure and lonely,
Haunted by ill angels only,
Where an Eidolon, named NIGHT,
On a black throne reigns upright,
I have wandered home but newly
From this ultimate dim Thule.

Ulalume

The skies they were ashen and sober;
 The leaves they were crispéd and sere—
 The leaves they were withering and sere:
It was night, in the lonesome October
 Of my most immemorial year;
It was hard by the dim lake of Auber,
 In the misty mid region of Weir:—
It was down by the dank tarn of Auber,
 In the ghoul-haunted woodland of Weir.

Here once, through an alley Titanic,
  Of cypress, I roamed with my Soul—
  Of cypress, with Psyche, my Soul.
These were days when my heart was volcanic
  As the scoriac rivers that roll—
  As the lavas that restlessly roll
Their sulphurous currents down Yaanek,
  In the ultimate climes of the Pole—
That groan as they roll down Mount Yaanek,
  In the realms of the Boreal Pole.

Our talk had been serious and sober,
  But our thoughts they were palsied and sere—
  Our memories were treacherous and sere—
For we knew not the month was October,
  And we marked not the night of the year—
  (Ah, night of all nights in the year!)
We noted not the dim lake of Auber,
  (Though once we had journeyed down here)
We remembered not the dank tarn of Auber,
  Nor the ghoul-haunted woodland of Weir.

And now, as the night was senescent,
  And star-dials pointed to morn—
  As the star-dials hinted of morn—
At the end of our path a liquescent
  And nebulous lustre was born,
Out of which a miraculous crescent
  Arose with a duplicate horn—
Astarte's bediamonded crescent,
  Distinct with its duplicate horn.

And I said—"She is warmer than Dian:
  She rolls through an ether of sighs—
  She revels in a region of sighs.
She has seen that the tears are not dry on
  These cheeks where the worm never dies,
And has come past the stars of the Lion,
  To point us the path to the skies—
  To the Lethean peace of the skies—
Come up, in despite of the Lion,

To shine on us with her bright eyes—
Come up, through the lair of the Lion,
        With love in her luminous eyes."

But Psyche, uplifting her finger,
        Said—"Sadly this star I mistrust—
        Her pallor I strangely mistrust—
Ah, hasten!—ah, let us not linger!
        Ah, fly!—let us fly!—for we must."
In terror she spoke; letting sink her
        Wings till they trailed in the dust—
In agony sobbed; letting sink her
        Plumes till they trailed in the dust—
        Till they sorrowfully trailed in the dust.

I replied—"This is nothing but dreaming.
        Let us on, by this tremulous light!
        Let us bathe in this crystalline light!
Its Sybillic splendor is beaming
        With Hope and in Beauty to-night—
        See!—it flickers up the sky through the night!
Ah, we safely may trust to its gleaming
        And be sure it will lead us aright—
We safely may trust to a gleaming
        That cannot but guide us aright
Since it flickers up to Heaven through the night."

Thus I pacified Psyche and kissed her,
        And tempted her out of her gloom—
        And conquered her scruples and gloom;
And we passed to the end of the vista—
        But were stopped by the door of a tomb—
        By the door of a legended tomb:—
And I said—"What is written, sweet sister,
        On the door of this legended tomb?"
        She replied—"Ulalume—Ulalume!—
        'Tis the vault of thy lost Ulalume!"

Then my heart it grew ashen and sober
        As the leaves that were crispéd and sere—
        As the leaves that were withering and sere—

And I cried—"It was surely October,
    On *this* very night of last year,
    That I journeyed—I journeyed down here!—
    That I brought a dread burden down here—
    On this night, of all nights in the year,
    Ah, what demon has tempted me here?
Well I know, now, this dim lake of Auber—
    This misty mid region of Weir:—
Well I know, now, this dank tarn of Auber—
    This ghoul-haunted woodland of Weir."

Said we then—the two, then—"Ah, can it
    Have been that the woodlandish ghouls—
    The pitiful, the merciful ghouls,
To bar up our way and to ban it
    From the secret that lies in these wolds—
    From the thing that lies hidden in these wolds—
Have drawn up the spectre of a planet
    From the limbs of lunary souls—
This sinfully scintillant planet
    From the Hell of the planetary souls?"

Alfred, Lord Tennyson (1809–1892)

Alfred, Lord Tennyson suffered an unhappy childhood in a troubled family, one whose legacy is seen in the themes of his verse—hope for an idyllic future, yearning for the heroic past, respite from loss, and the consolation of death. Alfred and two brothers were writing poetry in their teens; some of these items were collected in a local small-press edition. At Cambridge a group of gifted students he fell in with encouraged him to devote his life to poetry, and he published his first mature work, *Poems, Chiefly Lyrical,* in 1830. Though reaction was mixed, he continued to hone his craft. Tennyson matured into a master technician and creator of often striking poetic imagery. In 1850 he achieved success with the publication of *In Memoriam,* and the following year he was appointed Poet Laureate of England. "The Kraken" was first published in *Poems, Chiefly Lyrical.*

The Kraken

Below the thunders of the upper deep;
Far, far beneath in the abysmal sea,
His ancient, dreamless, uninvaded sleep
The Kraken sleepeth: faintest sunlights flee
About his shadowy sides: above him swell
Huge sponges of millennial growth and height;
And far away into the sickly light,
From many a wondrous grot and secret cell
Unnumbered and enormous polypi
Winnow with giant arms the slumbering green.
There hath he lain for ages and will lie
Battening upon huge seaworms in his sleep,
Until the latter fire shall heat the deep;
Then once by man and angels to be seen,
In roaring he shall rise and on the surface die.

Oliver Wendell Holmes (1809–1894)

American writer Oliver Wendell Holmes was best known in his life-
time for *The Autocrat of the Breakfast Table* (1858) and its successors, a
series of discursive essays. Holmes, a medical doctor, also wrote a loose
trilogy of "medicated" novels, *Elsie Venner* (1861), *The Guardian Angel*
(1867), and *A Mortal Antipathy* (1885), that have weird elements. He
was also a prolific poet. He was the father of the Supreme Court Jus-
tice Oliver Wendell Holmes, Jr. "The Broomstick Train" was first pub-
lished in the late collection *Over the Teacups* (1891).

The Broomstick Train; or, The Return of the Witches

Look out! Look out, boys! Clear the track!
The witches are here! They've all come back!
They hanged them high,—No use! No use!
What cares a witch for a hangman's noose?
They buried them deep, but they wouldn't lie still,
For cats and witches are hard to kill;

They swore they shouldn't and wouldn't die,—
Books said they did, but they lie! they lie!

A couple of hundred years, or so,
They had knocked about in the world below,
When an Essex Deacon dropped in to call,
And a homesick feeling seized them all;
For he came from a place they knew full well,
And many a tale he had to tell.
They longed to visit the haunts of men,
To see the old dwellings they knew again,
And ride on their broomsticks all around
Their wide domain of unhallowed ground.

In Essex county there's many a roof
Well known to him of the cloven hoof;
The small square windows are full in view
Which the midnight hags went sailing through,
On their well-trained broomsticks mounted high,
Seen like shadows against the sky;
Crossing the track of owls and bats,
Hugging before them their coal-black cats.

Well did they know, those gray old wives,
The sights we see in our daily drives:
Shimmer of lake and shine of sea,
Browne's bare hill with its lonely tree,
(It wasn't then as we see it now,
With one scant scalp-lock to shade its brow;)
Dusky nooks in the Essex woods,
Dark, dim, Dante-like solitudes,
Where the tree-toad watches the sinuous snake
Glide through his forests of fern and brake;
Ipswich River; its old stone bridge;
Far off Andover's Indian Ridge,
And many a scene where history tells
Some shadow of bygone terror dwells,—
Of "Norman's Woe" with its tale of dread,
Of the Screeching Woman of Marblehead,
(The fearful story that turns men pale:
Don't bid me tell it,—my speech would fail.)

*   *   *

Who would not, will not, if he can,
Bathe in the breezes of fair Cape Ann,—
Rest in the bowers her bays enfold,
Loved by the sachems and squaws of old?
Home where the white magnolias bloom,
Sweet with the bayberry's chaste perfume,
Hugged by the woods and kissed by the sea!
Where is the Eden like to thee?
For that "couple of hundred years, or so,"
There had been no peace in the world below;
The witches still grumbling, "It isn't fair;
Come, give us a taste of the upper air!
We've had enough of your sulphur springs,
And the evil odor that round them clings;
We long for a drink that is cool and nice,—
Great buckets of water with Wenham ice;
We've served you well up-stairs, you know;
You're a good old—fellow—come, let us go!"

I don't feel sure of his being good,
But he happened to be in a pleasant mood,—
As fiends with their shins full sometimes are,—
(He'd been drinking with "roughs" at a Boston bar.)
So what does he do but up and shout
To a graybeard turnkey, "Let 'em out!"

To mind his orders was all he knew;
The gates swung open, and out they flew.
"Where are our broomsticks?" the beldams cried.
"Here are your broomsticks," an imp replied.
"They've been in—the place you know—so long
They smell of brimstone uncommon strong;
But they've gained by being left alone,—
Just look, and you'll see how tall they've grown."
"And where is my cat?" a vixen squalled.
"Yes, where are our cats?" the witches bawled,
And began to call them all by name:
As fast as they called the cats, they came:
There was bob-tailed Tommy and long-tailed Tim,
And wall-eyed Jacky and green-eyed Jim,

And splay-foot Benny and slim-legged Beau,
And Skinny and Squally, and Jerry and Joe,
And many another that came at call,—
It would take too long to count them all.
All black,—one could hardly tell which was which,
But every cat knew his own old witch;
And she knew hers as hers knew her,—
Ah, didn't they curl their tails and purr!

No sooner the withered hags were free
Than out they swarmed for a midnight spree;
I couldn't tell all they did in rhymes,
But the Essex people had dreadful times.
The Swampscott fishermen still relate
How a strange sea-monster stole their bait;
How their nets were tangled in loops and knots,
And they found dead crabs in their lobster-pots.
Poor Danvers grieved for her blasted crops,
And Wilmington mourned over mildewed hops.
A blight played havoc with Beverly beans,—
It was all the work of those hateful queans!
A dreadful panic began at "Pride's,"
Where the witches stopped in their midnight rides,
And there rose strange rumors and vague alarms
'Mid the peaceful dwellers at Beverly Farms.

Now when the Boss of the Beldams found
That without his leave they were ramping round,
He called,—they could hear him twenty miles,
From Chelsea beach to the Misery Isles;
The deafest old granny knew his tone
Without the trick of the telephone.
"Come here, you witches! Come here!" says he,—
"At your games of old, without asking me!
I'll give you a little job to do
That will keep you stirring, you godless crew!"

They came, of course, at their master's call,
The witches, the broomsticks, the cats, and all;
He led the hags to a railway train
The horses were trying to drag in vain.

"Now, then," says he, "you've had your fun,
And here are the cars you've got to run.
The driver may just unhitch his team,
We don't want horses, we don't want steam;
You may keep your old black cats to hug,
But the loaded train you've got to lug."

Since then on many a car you'll see
A broomstick plain as plain can be;
On every stick there's a witch astride,—
The string you see to her leg is tied.
She will do a mischief if she can,
But the string is held by a careful man,
And whenever the evil-minded witch
Would cut some caper, he gives a twitch.
As for the hag, you can't see her,
But hark! you can hear her black cat's purr,
And now and then, as a car goes by,
You may catch a gleam from her wicked eye.
Often you've looked on a rushing train,
But just what moved it was not so plain.
It couldn't be those wires above,
For they could neither pull nor shove;
Where was the motor that made it go
You couldn't guess, *but now you know.*

Remember my rhymes when you ride again
On the rattling rail by the broomstick train!

———————————

Robert Browning (1812–1889)

British poet Robert Browning was inspired to pursue poetry in his teens, when he discovered the work of Shelley. Allied to the Romantics in his expansive spirit, the mature Browning was, by contrast, a realist in method—finding the infinite in the finite, eschewing poetic delicacy for vigor. He initially attempted to write verse drama for the stage, but shifted by the early 1840s to a shorter lyric mode. He published *Dramatic Lyrics* in 1842 and *Dramatic Romances and Lyrics* in 1845, each of which contains enduring poems. Browning's style, deemed experimental by the Victorians, owes something to John Donne with its colloquial phrasing and irregular rhythms. Supernatural elements persist throughout his long writing career, from the early work *Paracelsus* (1835) to "Childe Roland to the Dark Tower Came" (in *Men and Women*, 1855) to "Gerard de Lairesse" (in *Parleyings with Certain People of Importance in Their Day*, 1887).

Chillde Roland to the Dark Tower Came

I
My first thought was, he lied in every word,
    That hoary cripple, with malicious eye
    Askance to watch the working of his lie
On mine, and mouth scarce able to afford
Suppression of the glee, that pursed and scored
    Its edge, at one more victim gained thereby.

II
What else should he be set for, with his staff?
    What, save to waylay with his lies, ensnare
    All travellers who might find him posted there,
And ask the road? I guessed what skull-like laugh
Would break, what crutch 'gin write my epitaph
    For pastime in the dusty thoroughfare,

III
If at his counsel I should turn aside
    Into that ominous tract which, all agree,
    Hides the Dark Tower. Yet acquiescingly
I did turn as he pointed: neither pride
Nor hope rekindling at the end descried,
    So much as gladness that some end might be.

IV
For, what with my whole world-wide wandering,
    What with my search drawn out thro' years, my hope
    Dwindled into a ghost not fit to cope
With that obstreperous joy success would bring,—
I hardly tried now to rebuke the spring
    My heart made, finding failure in its scope.

V

As when a sick man very near to death
        Seems dead indeed, and feels begin and end
        The tears and takes the farewell of each friend,
And hears one bid the other go, draw breath
Freelier outside, ("since all is o'er," he saith,
        "And the blow fallen no grieving can amend;")

VI

While some discuss if near the other graves
        Be room enough for this, and when a day
        Suits best for carrying the corpse away,
With care about the banners, scarves and staves:
And still the man hears all, and only craves
        He may not shame such tender love and stay.

VII

Thus, I had so long suffered in this quest,
        Heard failure prophesied so oft, been writ
        So many times among "The Band"—to wit,
The knights who to the Dark Tower's search addressed
Their steps—that just to fail as they, seemed best,
        And all the doubt was now—should I be fit?

VIII

So, quiet as despair, I turned from him,
        That hateful cripple, out of his highway
        Into the path he pointed. All the day
Had been a dreary one at best, and dim
Was settling to its close, yet shot one grim
        Red leer to see the plain catch its estray.

IX

For mark! no sooner was I fairly found
        Pledged to the plain, after a pace or two,
        Than, pausing to throw backward a last view
O'er the safe road, 'twas gone; grey plain all round:
Nothing but plain to the horizon's bound.
        I might go on; nought else remained to do.

X

So, on I went. I think I never saw
    Such starved ignoble nature; nothing throve:
    For flowers—as well expect a cedar grove!
But cockle, spurge, according to their law
Might propagate their kind, with none to awe,
    You'd think; a burr had been a treasure-trove.

XI

No! penury, inertness and grimace,
    In some strange sort, were the land's portion. "See
    Or shut your eyes," said Nature peevishly,
"It nothing skills: I cannot help my case:
"'Tis the Last Judgment's fire must cure this place,
    "Calcine its clods and set my prisoners free."

XII

If there pushed any ragged thistle-stalk
    Above its mates, the head was chopped; the bents
    Were jealous else. What made those holes and rents
In the dock's harsh swarth leaves, bruised as to baulk
All hope of greenness? 'tis a brute must walk
    Pashing their life out, with a brute's intents.

XIII

As for the grass, it grew as scant as hair
    In leprosy; thin dry blades pricked the mud
    Which underneath looked kneaded up with blood.
One stiff blind horse, his every bone a-stare,
Stood stupefied, however he came there:
    Thrust out past service from the devil's stud!

XIV

Alive? he might be dead for aught I know,
    With that red gaunt and colloped neck a-strain,
    And shut eyes underneath the rusty mane;
Seldom went such grotesqueness with such woe;
I never saw a brute I hated so;
    He must be wicked to deserve such pain.

XV

I shut my eyes and turned them on my heart.
      As a man calls for wine before he fights,
      I asked one draught of earlier, happier sights,
Ere fitly I could hope to play my part.
Think first, fight afterwards—the soldier's art:
      One taste of the old time sets all to rights.

XVI

Not it! I fancied Cuthbert's reddening face
      Beneath its garniture of curly gold,
      Dear fellow, till I almost felt him fold
An arm in mine to fix me to the place,
That way he used. Alas, one night's disgrace!
      Out went my heart's new fire and left it cold.

XVII

Giles then, the soul of honour—there he stands
      Frank as ten years ago when knighted first.
      What honest men should dare (he said) he durst.
Good—but the scene shifts—faugh! what hangman-hands
Pin to his breast a parchment? his own bands
      Read it. Poor traitor, spit upon and curst!

XVIII

Better this present than a past like that;
      Back therefore to my darkening path again!
      No sound, no sight as far as eye could strain.
Will the night send a howlet or a bat?
I asked: when something on the dismal flat
      Came to arrest my thoughts and change their train.

XIX

A sudden little river crossed my path
      As unexpected as a serpent comes.
      No sluggish tide congenial to the glooms;
This, as it frothed by, might have been a bath
For the fiend's glowing hoof—to see the wrath
      Of its black eddy bespate with flakes and spumes.

XX

So petty yet so spiteful! All along,
  Low scrubby alders kneeled down over it;
  Drenched willows flung them headlong in a fit
Of mute despair, a suicidal throng:
The river which had done them all the wrong,
  Whate'er that was, rolled by, deterred no whit.

XXI

Which, while I forded,—good saints, how I feared
  To set my foot upon a dead man's cheek,
  Each step, or feel the spear I thrust to seek
For hollows, tangled in his hair or beard!
—It may have been a water-rat I speared,
  But, ugh! it sounded like a baby's shriek.

XXII

Glad was I when I reached the other bank.
  Now for a better country. Vain presage!
  Who were the strugglers, what war did they wage,
Whose savage trample thus could pad the dank
Soil to a plash? Toads in a poisoned tank,
  Or wild cats in a red-hot iron cage—

XXIII

The fight must so have seemed in that fell cirque.
  What penned them there, with all the plain to choose?
  No foot-print leading to that horrid mews,
None out of it. Mad brewage set to work
Their brains, no doubt, like galley-slaves the Turk
  Pits for his pastime, Christians against Jews.

XXIV

And more than that—a furlong on—why, there!
  What bad use was that engine for, that wheel,
  Or brake, not wheel—that harrow fit to reel
Men's bodies out like silk? with all the air
Of Tophet's tool, on earth left unaware,
  Or brought to sharpen its rusty teeth of steel.

XXV

Then came a bit of stubbed ground, once a wood,
  Next a marsh, it would seem, and now mere earth
  Desperate and done with; (so a fool finds mirth,
Makes a thing and then mars it, till his mood
Changes and off he goes!) within a rood—
  Bog, clay and rubble, sand and stark black dearth.

XXVI

Now blotches rankling, coloured gay and grim,
  Now patches where some leanness of the soil's
Broke into moss or substances like boils;
Then came some palsied oak, a cleft in him
Like a distorted mouth that splits its rim
  Gaping at death, and dies while it recoils.

XXVII

And just as far as ever from the end!
  Nought in the distance but the evening, nought
  To point my footstep further! At the thought,
A great black bird, Apollyon's bosom-friend,
Sailed past, nor beat his wide wing dragon-penned
  That brushed my cap—perchance the guide I sought.

XXVIII

For, looking up, aware I somehow grew,
  'Spite of the dusk, the plain had given place
  All round to mountains—with such name to grace
Mere ugly heights and heaps now stolen in view.
How thus they had surprised me,—solve it, you!
  How to get from them was no clearer case.

XXIX

Yet half I seemed to recognize some trick
  Of mischief happened to me, God knows when—
  In a bad dream perhaps. Here ended, then,
Progress this way. When, in the very nick
Of giving up, one time more, came a click
  As when a trap shuts—you're inside the den!

XXX

Burningly it came on me all at once,
  This was the place! those two hills on the right,
  Crouched like two bulls locked horn in horn in fight;
While to the left, a tall scalped mountain . . . Dunce,
Dotard, a-dozing at the very nonce,
  After a life spent training for the sight!

XXXI

What in the midst lay but the Tower itself?
  The round squat turret, blind as the fool's heart,
  Built of brown stone, without a counterpart
In the whole world. The tempest's mocking elf
Points to the shipman thus the unseen shelf
  He strikes on, only when the timbers start.

XXXII

Not see? because of night perhaps?—why, day
  Came back again for that! before it left,
  The dying sunset kindled through a cleft:
The hills, like giants at a hunting, lay,
Chin upon hand, to see the game at bay,—
  "Now stab and end the creature—to the heft!"

XXXIII

Not hear? when noise was everywhere! it tolled
  Increasing like a bell. Names in my ears
  Of all the lost adventurers my peers,—
How such a one was strong, and such was bold,
And such was fortunate, yet each of old
  Lost, lost! one moment knelled the woe of years.

XXXIV

There they stood, ranged along the hill-sides, met
  To view the last of me, a living frame
  For one more picture! in a sheet of flame
I saw them and I knew them all. And yet
Dauntless the slug-horn to my lips I set,
  And blew. *"Childe Roland to the Dark Tower came."*

James Russell Lowell (1819–1891)

American author James Russell Lowell was a major exponent of eighteenth-century literature in the United States. The verse collection *A Year's Life* (1841) was his first book. The year 1848 was a bellwether for the author's popularity, as he published *The Biglow Papers* (satirical verses with an anti-slavery theme), *The Vision of Sir Launfal* (a long poem about the quest for the Grail), *A Fable for Critics* (a verse evaluation of contemporary American authors), and the second series of *Poems*. Henceforth his literary production comprised largely prose essays. Though usually technically competent, much of his verse lacks depth and poetic fire, and his legacy is that of a "man of letters" rather than of a poet. "The Ghost-Seer" was first published in the *Broadway Journal* (8 March 1845).

The Ghost-Seer

Ye who, passing graves by night,
Glance not to the left or right,
Lest a spirit should arise,
Cold and white, to freeze your eyes,
Some weak phantom, which your doubt
Shapes upon the dark without
From the dark within, a guess
At the spirit's deathlessness,
Which ye entertain with fear
In your self-built dungeon here,
Where ye sell your God-given lives
Just for gold to buy you gyves,—
Ye without a shudder meet
In the city's noonday street,
Spirits sadder and more dread
Than from out the clay have fled,
Buried, beyond hope of light,
In the body's haunted night!
See ye not that woman pale?
There are bloodhounds on her trail!
Bloodhounds two, all gaunt and lean,
(For the soul their scent is keen,)
Want and Sin, and Sin is last,

They have followed far and fast;
Want gave tongue, and, at her howl,
Sin awakened with a growl.
Ah, poor girl! she had a right
To a blessing from the light;
Title-deeds to sky and earth
God gave to her at her birth;
But, before they were enjoyed,
Poverty had made them void,
And had drunk the sunshine up
From all nature's ample cup,
Leaving her a first-born's share
In the dregs of darkness there.
Often, on the sidewalk bleak,
Hungry, all alone, and weak,
She has seen, in night and storm,
Rooms o'erflow with firelight warm,
Which, outside the window-glass,
Doubled all the cold, alas!
Till each ray that on her fell
Stabbed her like an icicle,
And she almost loved the wail
Of the bloodhounds on her trail.
Till the floor becomes her bier,
She shall feel their pantings near,
Close upon her very heels,
Spite of all the din of wheels;
Shivering on her pallet poor,
She shall hear them at the door
Whine and scratch to be let in,
Sister bloodhounds, Want and Sin!

Hark! that rustle of a dress,
Stiff with lavish costliness!
Here comes one whose cheek would flush
But to have her garment brush
'Gainst the girl whose fingers thin
Wove the weary broidery in,
Bending backward from her toil,
Lest her tears the silk might soil,
And, in midnights chill and murk,

Stitched her life into the work,
Shaping from her bitter thought
Heart's-ease and forget-me-not,
Satirizing her despair
With the emblems woven there.
Little doth the wearer heed
Of the heart-break in the brede;
A hyena by her side
Skulks, down-looking,—it is Pride.
He digs for her in the earth,
Where lie all her claims of birth,
With his foul paws rooting o'er
Some long-buried ancestor,
Who, perhaps a statue won
By the ill deeds he had done,
By the innocent blood he shed,
By the desolation spread
Over happy villages,
Blotting out the smile of peace.
There walks Judas, he who sold
Yesterday his Lord for gold,
Sold God's presence in his heart
For a proud step in the mart;
He hath dealt in flesh and blood;
At the bank his name is good;
At the bank, and only there,
'Tis a marketable ware.
In his eyes that stealthy gleam
Was not learned of sky or stream,
But it has the cold, hard glint
Of new dollars from the mint.
Open now your spirit's eyes,
Look through that poor clay disguise
Which has thickened, day by day,
Till it keeps all light at bay,
And his soul in pitchy gloom
Gropes about its narrow tomb,
From whose dank and slimy walls
Drop by drop the horror falls.
Look! a serpent lank and cold

Hugs his spirit fold on fold;
From his heart, all day and night,
It doth suck God's blessed light.
Drink it will, and drink it must,
Till the cup holds naught but dust;
All day long he hears it hiss,
Writhing in its fiendish bliss;
All night long he sees its eyes
Flicker with foul ecstasies,
As the spirit ebbs away
Into the absorbing clay.
Who is he that skulks, afraid
Of the trust he has betrayed,
Shuddering if perchance a gleam
Of old nobleness should stream
Through the pent, unwholesome room,
Where his shrunk soul cowers in gloom,
Spirit sad beyond the rest
By more instinct for the best?
'Tis a poet who was sent
For a bad world's punishment,
By compelling it to see
Golden glimpses of To Be,
By compelling it to hear
Songs that prove the angels near;
Who was sent to be the tongue
Of the weak and spirit-wrung,
Whence the fiery-winged Despair
In men's shrinking eyes might flare.
'Tis our hope doth fashion us
To base use or glorious:
He who might have been a lark
Of Truth's morning, from the dark
Raining down melodious hope
Of a freer, broader scope,
Aspirations, prophecies,
Of the spirit's full sunrise,
Chose to be a bird of night,
That, with eyes refusing light,
Hooted from some hollow tree

Of the world's idolatry.
'Tis his punishment to hear
Sweep of eager pinions near,
And his own vain wings to feel
Drooping downward to his heel,
All their grace and import lost,
Burdening his weary ghost:
Ever walking by his side
He must see his angel guide,
Who at intervals doth turn
Looks on him so sadly stern,
With such ever-new surprise
Of hushed anguish in her eyes,
That it seems the light of day
From around him shrinks away,
Or drops blunted from the wall
Built around him by his fall.
Then the mountains, whose white peaks
Catch the morning's earliest streaks,
He must see, where prophets sit,
Turning east their faces lit,
Whence, with footsteps beautiful,
To the earth, yet dim and dull,
They the gladsome tidings bring
Of the sunlight's hastening:
Never can these hills of bliss
Be o'erclimbed by feet like his!

But enough! Oh, do not dare
From the next the veil to tear,
Woven of station, trade, or dress,
More obscene than nakedness,
Wherewith plausible culture drapes
Fallen Nature's myriad shapes!
Let us rather love to mark
How the unextinguished spark
Still gleams through the thin disguise
Of our customs, pomps, and lies,
And, not seldom blown to flame,
Vindicates its ancient claim.

Charles Baudelaire (1821–1867)

Charles Pierre Baudelaire attended military school and later law school, but he decided he would rather be a writer and spent his time with artists and bohemians. He developed an addiction to opium and contracted syphilis before he turned twenty-one; these events would shape his literary output even as they destroyed his health. He wrote poetry sporadically, but published art criticism in periodicals that gained him a reputation as an advocate of Romanticism. He found wider notice in 1856 with his translations of Poe's verse. In 1857 Baudelaire published *Les Fleurs du mal*, which contained material so explicit that he was found guilty of offenses against public morals, fined, and forced to remove six poems from the second edition of 1861. Later work included further art and literary criticism, *Les Paradis artificiels: Opium et haschisch* (1860), and *Le Spleen de Paris* (*Petits Poèmes en prose*) (1869). In 1863 Baudelaire moved to Brussels, but suffered a stroke three years later that paralyzed him and left him unable to speak. He was returned to his family home, where he died at age forty-six. His literary influence is difficult to overstate, as Decadent, Symbolist, and above all Modernist. Both poems printed below are from *Les Fleurs du mal*. Clark Ashton Smith's translation of "Le Revenant" ("The Phantom") first appeared in *Weird Tales* (May 1929). His translation of "L'Irrémédiable" ("The Irremediable") first appeared in the *Auburn Journal* (23 July 1925).

The Phantom

Like an ill angel tawny-eyed,
I will return, and stilly glide
With shadows of the lunar dusk
Into thy chamber aired with musk,

And I will give thee, ere I go,
The kisses of a moon of snow,
And long caresses, chill, unsleeping,
Of serpents on the marbles creeping.

When lifts again the bloodless dawn,
From out thy bed I shall be gone—
Where all, till eve, is void and drear:

Let others reign by love and ruth
Over thy life and all thy youth,
But I am fain to rule by fear.

The Irremediable

I.
An Entity, an Eidolon,
Fallen from out some azure clime
Into a Styx of lead and slime
Nor star nor sun has looked upon;

A wandering angel indiscreet,
Lost in the love of things difform,
Who down abysmal dreams of harm
Falls beating as great swimmers beat,

And fights in mortal anguish stark
Some eddy of a demon sea
That sings and shouts deliriously
And dances in the whirling dark;

A hapless man, bewitched, bewrayed,
Whose futile gropings fain would find
In reptile-swarming darkness blind
The lost light and the key mislaid;

A lost soul without lamp descending,
To whom the gulf-arisen smell
Betrays a dank, profounder hell
And railless fall of stairs unending

Where slimy monsters ward the way,
Whose eyes of phosphor, luminous, large,
Make darker still the nighted marge,
Burning in bulks obscure for aye;

A vessel at the frozen pole
As in a trap of crystal caught;
And searching how her keel was brought
Thereto by fatal strait and shoal:—

Clear emblems, perfect similes
Of an irremediable doom,
That prove how well the Devil's loom
Can weave our sombre destinies!

II.
Self-mirrored, in close colloquy,
The heart its image sees in sooth:
The dark and lucid well of Truth
Where a star trembles lividly,

Flambeau of grace from sullen hells,
Pharos ironic and infernal,
Sole glory, solacement eternal—
A Conscience still in Evil dwells.

[tr. Clark Ashton Smith]

William Allingham (1824–1889)

Irish poet William Allingham became a friend of Tennyson, Carlyle, Dante Gabriel Rossetti, and other noted writers, and his recollections of them are found in his diary, published in 1907. He also published several volumes of poems, including *Poems* (1850) and *Laurence Bloomfield in Ireland* (1864), and collections and anthologies of poems for children. "A Dream" first appeared in *Songs, Ballads and Stories* (1877).

A Dream

I heard the dogs howl in the moonlight night;
I went to the window to see the sight;
All the Dead that ever I knew
Going one by one and two by two.

On they pass'd, and on they pass'd;
Townsfellows all, from first to last;
Born in the moonlight of the lane,
Quench'd in the heavy shadow again.

Schoolmates, marching as when we play'd
At soldiers once—but now more staid;
Those were the strangest sight to me
Who were drown'd, I knew, in the awful sea.

Straight and handsome folk; bent and weak too;
Some that I loved, and gasp'd to speak to;
Some but a day in their churchyard bed;
Some that I had not known were dead.

A long, long crowd—where each seem'd lonely,
Yet of them all there was one, one only,
Raised a head or look'd my way:
She linger'd a moment,—she might not stay.

How long since I saw that fair pale face!
Ah! Mother dear! might I only place
My head on thy breast, a moment to rest,
While thy hand on my tearful cheek were prest!

On, on, a moving bridge they made
Across the moon-stream, from shade to shade,
Young and old, women and men;
Many long-forgot, but remember'd then.

And first there came a bitter laughter;
A sound of tears the moment after;
And then a music so lofty and gay,
That every morning, day by day,
I strive to recall it if I may.

George MacDonald (1824–1905)

Scottish writer George MacDonald is now best known for the allegorical fantasies *Phantastes* (1858) and *Lilith* (1895), along with such stories for children as *At the Back of the North Wind* (1871) and *The Princess and the Goblin* (1872). He also wrote a substantial amount of poetry. "The Homeless Ghost" first appeared in *Poems* (1857).

The Homeless Ghost

Still flowed the music, flowed the wine.
  The youth in silence went;
Through naked streets, in cold moonshine,
  His homeward way he bent,
Where, on the city's seaward line,
  His lattice seaward leant.

He knew not why he left the throng,
  But that he could not rest;
That something pained him in the song,
  And mocked him in the jest;
And a cold moon-glitter lay along
  One lovely lady's breast.

He sat him down with solemn book
  His sadness to beguile;
A skull from off its bracket-nook
  Threw him a lipless smile;
But its awful, laughter-mocking look
  Was a passing moonbeam's wile.

An hour he sat, and read in vain,
  Nought but mirrors were his eyes;
For to and fro through his helpless brain
  Went the dance's mysteries;
Till a gust of wind against the pane,
  Mixed with a sea-bird's cries,
And the sudden spatter of drifting rain
  Bade him mark the altered skies.

The moon was gone, intombed in cloud;
  The wind began to rave;
The ocean heaved within its shroud,
  For the dark had built its grave;
But like ghosts brake forth, and cried aloud,
  The white crests of the wave.

Big rain. The wind howled out, aware
  Of the tread of the watery west;
The windows shivered, back waved his hair,

The fireside seemed the best;
But lo! a lady sat in his chair,
    With the moonlight across her breast.

The moonbeam passed. The lady sat on.
    Her beauty was sad and white.
All but her hair with whiteness shone,
    And her hair was black as night;
And her eyes, where darkness was never gone,
    Although they were full of light.

But her hair was wet, and wept like weeds
    On her pearly shoulders bare;
And the clear pale drops ran down like beads,
    Down her arms, to her fingers fair;
And her limbs shine through, like thin-filmed seeds,
    Her dank white robe's despair.

She moved not, but looked in his wondering face,
    Till his blushes began to rise;
But she gazed, like one on the veiling lace,
    To something within his eyes;
A gaze that had not to do with place,
    But thought and spirit tries.

Then the voice came forth, all sweet and clear,
    Though jarred by inward pain;
She spoke like one that speaks in fear
    Of the judgment she will gain,
When the soul is full as a mountain-mere,
    And the speech but a flowing vein.

"Thine eyes are like mine, and thou art bold;
    Nay, heap not the dying fire;
It warms not me, I am too cold,
    Cold as the churchyard spire;
If thou cover me up with fold on fold,
    Thou kill'st not the coldness dire."

Her voice and her beauty, like molten gold,
    Thrilled through him in burning rain.
He was on fire, and she was cold,

Cold as the waveless main;
But his heart-well filled with woe, till it rolled
    A torrent that calmed him again.

"Save, me, Oh, save me!" she cried; and flung
    Her splendour before his feet;—
"I am weary of wandering storms among,
    And I hate the mouldy sheet;
I can dare the dark, wind-vexed and wrung,
    Not the dark where the dead things meet.

"Ah! though a ghost, I'm a lady still—"
    The youth recoiled aghast.
With a passion of sorrow her great eyes fill;
    Not a word her white lips passed.
He caught her hand; 'twas a cold to kill,
    But he held it warm and fast.

"What can I do to save thee, dear?"
    At the word she sprang upright.
To her ice-lips she drew his burning ear,
    And whispered—he shivered—she whispered light.
She withdrew; she gazed with an asking fear;
    He stood with a face ghost-white.

"I wait—ah, would I might wait!" she said;
    "But the moon sinks in the tide;
Thou seest it not; I see it fade,
    Like one that may not bide.
Alas! I go out in the moonless shade;
    Ah, kind! let me stay and hide."

He shivered, he shook, he felt like clay;
    And the fear went through his blood;
His face was an awful ashy grey,
    And his veins were channels of mud.
The lady stood in a white dismay,
    Like a half-blown frozen bud.

"Ah, speak! am I so frightful then?
    I live; though they call it death;
I am only cold—say *dear* again"—

But scarce could he heave a breath;
The air felt dank, like a frozen fen,
    And he a half-conscious wraith.

"Ah, save me!" once more, with a hopeless cry,
    That entered his heart, and lay;
But sunshine and warmth and rosiness vie
    With coldness and moonlight and grey.
He spoke not. She moved not; yet to his eye,
    She stood three paces away.

She spoke no more. Grief on her face
    Beauty had almost slain.
With a feverous vision's unseen pace
    She had flitted away again;
And stood, with a last dumb prayer for grace,
    By the window that clanged with rain.

He stood; he stared. She had vanished quite.
    The loud wind sank to a sigh;
Grey faces without paled the face of night,
    As they swept the window by;
And each, as it passed, pressed a cheek of fright
    To the glass, with a staring eye.

And over, afar from over the deep,
    Came a long and cadenced wail;
It rose, and it sank, and it rose on the steep
    Of the billows that build the gale.
It ceased; but on in his bosom creep
    Low echoes that tell the tale.

He opened his lattice, and saw afar,
    Over the western sea,
Across the spears of a sparkling star,
    A moony vapour flee;
And he thought, with a pang that he could not bar,
    The lady it might be.

He turned and looked into the room;
    And lo! it was cheerless and bare;
Empty and drear as a hopeless tomb,—

And the lady was not there;
Yet the fire and the lamp drove out the gloom,
    As he had driven the fair.

And up in the manhood of his breast
    Sprang a storm of passion and shame;
It tore the pride of his fancied best
    In a thousand shreds of blame;
It threw to the ground his ancient crest,
    And puffed at his ancient name.

He had turned a lady, and lightly clad,
    Out in the stormy cold.
Was she a ghost?—Divinely sad
    Are the guests of Hades old.
A wandering ghost? Oh! terror bad,
    That refused an earthly fold!

And sorrow for her his shame's regret
    Into humility wept;
He knelt and he kissed the footprints wet,
    And the track by her thin robe swept;
He sat in her chair, all ice-cold yet,
    And moaned until he slept.

He woke at dawn. The flaming sun
    Laughed at the bye-gone dark.
"I am glad," he said, "that the night is done,
    And the dream slain by the lark."
And the eye was all, until the gun
    That boomed at the sun-set—hark!

And then, with a sudden invading blast,
    He knew that it was no dream,
And all the night belief held fast,
    Till thinned by the morning beam.
Thus radiant mornings and pale nights passed
    On the backward-flowing stream.

He loved a lady with heaving breath,
    Red lips, and a smile alway;
And her sighs an odour inhabiteth,

All of the rose-hued may;
But the warm bright lady was false as death,
    And the ghost is true as day.

And the spirit-face, with its woe divine,
    Came back in the hour of sighs;
As to men who have lost their aim, and pine,
    Old faces of childhood rise:
He wept for her pleading voice, and the shine
    Of her solitary eyes.

And now he believed in the ghost all night,
    And believed in the day as well;
And he vowed, with a sorrowing tearful might,
    All she asked, whate'er befel,
If she came to his room, in her garment white,
    Once more at the midnight knell.

She came not. He sought her in churchyards old
    That lay along the sea;
And in many a church, when the midnight tolled,
    And the moon shone wondrously;
And down to the crypts he crept, grown bold;
    But he waited in vain: ah me!

And he pined and sighed for love so sore,
    That he looked as he were lost;
And he prayed her pardon more and more,
    As one who had sinned the most;
Till, fading at length, away he wore,
    And he was himself a ghost.

But if he found the lady then,
    The lady sadly lost,
Or she had found 'mongst living men
    A love that was a host,
I know not, till I drop my pen,
    And am myself a ghost.

George Meredith (1828–1909)

British novelist and poet George Meredith gained celebrity with the novels *The Shaving of Shagpat* (1856) and *The Ordeal of Richard Feverel* (1859), although among his earliest book publications were the poetry volumes *Poems* (1851) and *Modern Love* (1862). He went on to publish such novels as *Rhoda Fleming* (1865), *The Egoist* (1879), and *Diana of the Crossways* (1885), although he also continued to publish poetry, in such volumes as *Poems and Lyrics of the Joy of Earth* (1883) and *Ballads and Poems of Tragic Life* (1887). As a publisher's reader for the firm of Chapman & Hall he helped to build the reputations of several leading British writers. Late in life, finally attaining financial success with his writing, he received the Order of Merit from King Edward VII. "Phantasy" was first published in *Once a Week* (23 November 1861) and collected in *Modern Love*.

Phantasy

Within a Temple of the Toes,
    Where twirled the passionate Wili,
I saw full many a market rose,
    And sighed for my village lily.

With cynical Adrian then I took flight
    To that old dead city whose carol
Bursts out like a reveller's loud in the night,
    As he sits astride his barrel.

We two were bound the Alps to scale,
    Up the rock-reflecting river;
Old times blew thro' me like a gale,
    And kept my thoughts in a quiver.

Hawking ruin, wood-slope, and vine
    Reeled silver-laced under my vision,
And into me passed, with the green-eyed wine
    Knocking hard at my head for admission.

I held the village lily cheap,
    And the dream around her idle:

Lo, quietly as I lay to sleep,
    The bells led me off to a bridal.

My bride wore the hood of a Béguine,
    And mine was the foot to falter;
Three cowled monks, rat-eyed, were seen;
    The Cross was of bones o'er the altar.

The Cross was of bones; the priest that read,
    A spectacled necromancer:
But at the fourth word, the bride I led
    Changed to an Opera dancer.

A young ballet-beauty, who perked in her place,
    A darling of pink and spangles;
One fair foot level with her face,
    And the hearts of men at her ankles.

She whirled, she twirled, the mock-priest grinned,
    And quickly his mask unriddled;
'Twas Adrian! loud his old laughter dinned;
    Then he seized a fiddle, and fiddled.

He fiddled, he glowed with the bottomless fire,
    Like Sathanas in feature:
All through me he fiddled a wolfish desire
    To dance with that bright creature.

And gathering courage I said to my soul,
    Throttle the thing that hinders!
When the three cowled monks, from black as coal,
    Waxed hot as furnace-cinders.

They caught her up, twirling: they leapt between-whiles:
    The fiddler flickered with laughter:
Profanely they flew down the awful aisles,
    Where I went sliding after.

Down the awful aisles, by the fretted walls,
    Beneath the Gothic arches:—
King Skull in the black confessionals
    Sat rub-a-dub-dubbing his marches.

Then the silent cold stone warriors frowned,
    The pictured saints strode forward:
A whirlwind swept them from holy ground;
    A tempest puffed them nor'ward.

They shot through the great cathedral door;
    Like mallards they traversed ocean:
And gazing below, on its boiling floor,
    I marked a horrid commotion.

Down a forest's long alleys they spun like tops:
    It seemed that for ages and ages,
Thro' the Book of Life bereft of stops,
    They waltzed continuous pages.

And ages after, scarce awake,
    And my blood with the fever fretting,
I stood alone by a forest-lake,
    Whose shadows the moon were netting.

Lilies, golden and white, by the curls
    Of their broad flat leaves hung swaying.
A wreath of languid twining girls
    Streamed upward, long locks disarraying.

Their cheeks had the satin frost-glow of the moon;
    Their eyes the fire of Sirius.
They circled, and droned a monotonous tune,
    Abandoned to love delirious.

Like lengths of convolvulus torn from the hedge,
    And trailing the highway over,
The dreamy-eyed mistresses circled the sedge,
    And called for a lover, a lover!

I sank, I rose through seas of eyes,
    In odorous swathes delicious:
They fanned me with impetuous sighs,
    They bit me with kisses vicious.

My ears were spelled, my neck was coiled,
    And I with their fury was glowing,

When the marbly waters bubbled and boiled
 At a watery noise of crowing.

They dragged me low and low to the lake:
 Their kisses more stormily showered;
On the emerald brink, in the white moon's wake,
 An earthly damsel cowered.

Fresh heart-sobs shook her knitted hands
 Beneath a tiny suckling,
As one by one of the doleful bands
 Dived like a fairy duckling.

And now my turn had come—O me!
 What wisdom was mine that second!
I dropped on the adorer's knee;
 To that sweet figure I beckoned.

Save me! save me! for now I know
 The powers that Nature gave me,
And the value of honest love I know:—
 My village lily! save me!

Come 'twixt me and the sisterhood,
 While the passion-born phantoms are fleeing!
Oh, he that is true to flesh and blood
 Is true to his own being!

And he that is false to flesh and blood
 Is false to the star within him:
And the mad and hungry sisterhood
 All under the tides shall win him!

My village lily! save me! save!
 For strength is with the holy:—
Already I shuddered to feel the wave,
 As I kept sinking slowly:—

I felt the cold wave and the under-tug
 Of the Brides, when—starting and shrinking—
Lo, Adrian tilts the water-jug!
 And Bruges with morn is blinking.

Merrily sparkles sunny prime
    On gabled peak and arbour:
Merrily rattles belfry-chime
    The song of Sevilla's Barber.

Thomas Bailey Aldrich (1836–1907)

American poet and novelist Thomas Bailey Aldrich covered the Civil War as a correspondent and subsequently became the editor of the *Atlantic Monthly* (1881–90). He is celebrated for such stories as "Marjorie Daw" and the novel *The Story of a Bad Boy* (1870). He published numerous collections of poetry, including *The Bells* (1855), *Cloth of Gold* (1874), and *Judith and Holofernes* (1896). "Eidolons" first appeared in Aldrich's early volume *A Nest of Sonnets* (1856) under the title "Ghosts." "The Lorelei" was first published in *Flower and Thorn: Later Poems* (1876). "Apparitions" was collected in *Poems* (1885).

Eidolons

Those forms we fancy shadows, those strange lights
That flash on lone morasses, the quick wind
That smites us by the roadside are the Night's
Innumerable children. Unconfined
By shroud or coffin, disembodied souls,
Still on probation, steal into the air
From ancient battlefields and churchyard knolls
At the day's ending. Pestilence and despair
Fly with the startled bats at set of sun;
And wheresoever murders have been done,
In crowded palaces or lonely woods,
Where'er a soul has sold itself and lost
Its high inheritance, there, hovering, broods
Some mute, invisible, accursèd ghost.

The Lorelei

Yonder we see it from the steamer's deck,
The haunted Mountain of the Lorelei—
The hanging crags sharp-cut against a sky
Clear as a sapphire without flaw or fleck.
'Twas here the Siren lay in wait to wreck
The fisher-lad. At dusk, as he rowed by,
Perchance he heard her tender amorous cry,
And, seeing the wondrous whiteness of her neck,
Perchance would halt, and lean towards the shore;
Then she by that soft magic which she had
Would lure him, and in gossamers of her hair,
Gold upon gold, would wrap him o'er and o'er,
Wrap him, and sing to him, and drive him mad,
Then drag him down to no man knoweth where.

Apparitions

At noon of night, and at the night's pale end,
　　Such things have chanced to me
As one, by day, would scarcely tell a friend
　　For fear of mockery.

Shadows, you say, mirages of the brain!
　　I know not, faith, not I.
Is it more strange the dead should walk again
　　Than that the quick should die?

Algernon Charles Swinburne (1837–1909)

British poet and critic Algernon Charles Swinburne's verse is character-
ized by technical virtuosity and inventiveness. His flamboyant empha-
sis on sound over sense—cited by critics both as an artistic strength
and as a weakness—broke from Victorian literary fashion and antici-
pated elements of modern poetics. His widely noted verse drama *Ata-
lanta in Calydon* (1865) was followed by two series of *Poems and
Ballads* (1866, 1878). Swinburne's highly strung temperament was

undermined by alcoholism, causing periodic fits of intense nervous excitement and ultimately a complete breakdown in 1879. He recovered completely and during the remaining three decades of his life published upwards of twenty volumes of poetry, prose, and drama. "The Witch-Mother" appeared in *Poems and Ballads: Third Series* (1889).

The Witch-Mother

"O Where Will ye gang to and where will ye sleep,
    Against the night begins?"
"My bed is made wi' cauld sorrows,
    My sheets are lined wi' sins.

"And a sair grief sitting at my foot,
    And a sair grief at my head;
And dule to lay me my laigh pillows,
    And teen till I be dead.

"And the rain is sair upon my face,
    And sair upon my hair;
And the wind upon my weary mouth,
    That never may man kiss mair.

"And the snow upon my heavy lips,
    That never shall drink nor eat;
And shame to cledding, and woe to wedding,
    And pain to drink and meat.

"But woe be to my bairns' father,
    And ever ill fare he:
He has tane a braw bride hame to him,
    Cast out my bairns and me."

"And what shall they have to their marriage meat
    This day they twain are wed?"
"Meat of strong crying, salt of sad sighing,
    And God restore the dead."

"And what shall they have to their wedding wine
    This day they twain are wed?"
"Wine of weeping, and draughts of sleeping,
    And God raise up the dead."

She's tane her to the wild woodside,
  Between the flood and fell:
She's sought a rede against her need
  Of the fiend that bides in hell.

She's tane her to the wan burnside,
  She's wrought wi' sang and spell:
She's plighted her soul for doom and dole
  To the fiend that bides in hell.

She's set her young son to her breast,
  Her auld son to her knee:
Says, "Weel for you the night, bairnies,
  And weel the morn for me."

She looked fu' lang in their een, sighing,
  And sair and sair grat she:
She has slain her young son at her breast,
  Her auld son at her knee.

She's sodden their flesh wi' saft water,
  She's mixed their blood with wine:
She's tane her to the braw bride-house,
  Where a' were boun' to dine.

She poured the red wine in his cup,
  And his een grew fain to greet:
She set the baked meats at his hand,
  And bade him drink and eat.

Says, "Eat your fill of your flesh, my lord,
  And drink your fill of your wine;
For a' thing's yours and only yours
  That has been yours and mine."

Says, "Drink your fill of your wine, my lord,
  And eat your fill of your bread:
I would they were quick in my body again,
  Or I that bare them dead."

He struck her head frae her fair body,
  And dead for grief he fell:
And there were twae mair sangs in heaven,

And twae mair sauls in hell.

Thomas Hardy (1840–1928)

British novelist, dramatist, and poet Thomas Hardy published his first novel, *Desperate Remedies* (1871), anonymously. Such later works as *Far from the Madding Crowd* (1874), *The Return of the Native* (1878), *The Mayor of Casterbridge* (1886), and *Tess of the d'Urbervilles* (1891) established him as the leading British novelist of his age. Many of his novels and tales are set in an imaginary region of England, called Wessex, that reflects the topography and social climate of his native Dorset. Hostile reaction to the novel *Jude the Obscure* (1895), chiefly because of its frank treatment of sexual themes, caused Hardy to abandon the novel and take to poetry and drama. In his later years he produced such works as the verse drama *The Dynasts* (1904–08) and *Satires of Circumstance* (1914). Much of his work is infused with a religious skepticism that reflects Hardy's lifelong struggle to reconcile the idea of a benevolent God with the realities of human suffering. "The Dead Man Walking" was first published in *Time's Laughingstock and Other Verses* (1909).

The Dead Man Walking

They hail me as one living,
　　But don't they know
That I have died of late years,
　　Untombed although?

I am but a shape that stands here,
　　A pulseless mould,
A pale past picture, screening
　　Ashes gone cold.

Not at a minute's warning,
　　Not in a loud hour,
For me ceased Time's enchantments
　　In hall and bower.

There was no tragic transit,

No catch of breath,
When silent seasons inched me
        On to this death. . . .

—A Troubadour-youth I rambled
        With Life for lyre,
The beats of being raging
        In me like fire.

But when I practised eyeing
        The goal of men,
It iced me, and I perished
        A little then.

When passed my friend, my kinsfolk,
        Through the Last Door,
And left me standing bleakly,
        I died yet more;

And when my Love's heart kindled
        In hate of me,
Wherefore I knew not, died I
        One more degree.

And if when I died fully
        I cannot say,
And changed into the corpse-thing
        I am to-day;

Yet is it that, though whiling
        The time somehow
In walking, talking, smiling,
        I live not now.

_____

Ambrose Bierce (1842–1914?)

American journalist and short story writer Ambrose Bierce established
his celebrity as a fiery and satirical journalist for such papers as the *San
Francisco News Letter* (1867–72), the *Argonaut* (1877–79), the *Wasp*
(1881–86), and especially the *San Francisco Examiner* (1887–1906).

His chilling tales of supernatural and psychological horror appeared in *Tales of Soldiers and Civilians* (1891) and *Can Such Things Be?* (1893). His poetry, usually scattered in his newspaper columns, was gathered in *Black Beetles in Amber* (1892) and *Shapes of Clay* (1903). Donald Sidney-Fryer gathered Bierce's weird verse in *A Vision of Doom* (1980). "A Vision of Doom" was first published in *Shapes of Clay*.

A Vision of Doom

I stood upon a hill. The setting sun
Was crimson with a curse and a portent,
And scarce his angry ray lit up the land
That lay below, whose lurid gloom appeared
Freaked with a moving mist, which, reeking up
From dim tarns hateful with some horrid ban,
Took shapes forbidden and without a name.
Gigantic night-birds, rising from the reeds
With cries discordant, startled all the air,
And bodiless voices babbled in the gloom—
The ghosts of blasphemies long ages stilled,
And shrieks of women, and men's curses. All
These visible shapes, and sounds no mortal ear
Had ever heard, some spiritual sense
Interpreted, though brokenly; for I
Was haunted by a consciousness of crime,
Some giant guilt, but whose I knew not. All
These things malign, by sight and sound revealed,
Were sin-begotten; that I knew—no more—
And that but dimly, as in dreadful dreams
The sleepy senses babble to the brain
Imperfect witness. As I stood, a voice,
But whence it came I knew not, cried aloud
Some words to me in a forgotten tongue,
Yet straight I knew me for a ghost forlorn,
Returned from the illimited inane.
Again, but in a language that I knew,
As in reply to something which in me
Had shaped itself a thought, but found no words,
It spake from the dread mystery about:

"Immortal shadow of a mortal soul
That perished with eternity, attend.
What thou beholdest is as void as thou:
The shadow of a poet's dream—himself
As thou, his soul as thine, long dead,
But not like thine outlasted by its shade.
His dreams alone survive eternity
As pictures in the unsubstantial void.
Excepting thee and me (and we because
The poet wove us in his thought) remains
Of nature and the universe no part
Nor vestige but the poet's dreams. This dread,
Unspeakable land about thy feet, with all
Its desolation and its terrors—lo!
'Tis but a phantom world. So long ago
That God and all the angels since have died
That poet lived—yourself long dead—his mind
Filled with the light of a prophetic fire,
And standing by the Western sea, above
The youngest, fairest city in the world,
Named in another tongue than his for one
Ensainted, saw its populous domain
Plague-smitten with a nameless shame. For there
Red-handed murder rioted; and there
The people gathered gold, nor cared to loose
The assassin's fingers from the victim's throat,
But said, each in his vile pursuit engrossed:
'Am I my brother's keeper? Let the Law
Look to the matter.' But the Law did not.
And there, O pitiful! the babe was slain
Within its mother's breast and the same grave
Held babe and mother; and the people smiled,
Still gathering gold, and said: 'The Law, the Law.'
Then the great poet, touched upon the lips
With a live coal from Truth's high altar, raised
His arms to heaven and sang a song of doom—
Sang of the time to be, when God should lean
Indignant from the Throne and lift His hand,
And that foul city be no more!—a tale,
A dream, a desolation and a curse!

No vestige of its glory should survive
In fact or memory: its people dead,
Its site forgotten, and its very name
Disputed."

"Was the prophecy fulfilled?"

The sullen disc of the declining sun
Was crimson with a curse and a portent,
And scarce his angry ray lit up the land
Freaked with a moving mist, which, reeking up
From dim tarns hateful with a horrid ban,
Took shapes forbidden and without a name.
And bodiless voices babbled in the gloom.
But not to me came any voice again;
And, covering my face with thin, dead hands,
I wept, and woke, and cried aloud to God!

Julian Hawthorne (1846–1934)

American writer Julian Hawthorne, son of Nathaniel Hawthorne, was a prolific novelist, journalist, and editor. He wrote numerous novels, including *Idolatry: A Romance* (1874) and *Dust* (1884). He also wrote a controversial book about his parents, *Nathaniel Hawthorne and His Wife* (1884). In 1913 he was convicted of mail fraud involving the promotion of mining stock and spent a year in jail. In his later years he wrote a number of tales of horror and fantasy. "Were-Wolf" first appeared in the *Chap-Book* (May 1, 1895).

Were-Wolf

Runs the wind along the waste,
Run the clouds across the moon,
Ghastly shadows run in haste
From snowy dune to dune—
Blue shadows o'er the ghastly white
Spectral gleaming in the night.
But ghastlier, more spectral still,

What fearful thing speeds hither,
Running, running, running
Swifter than cloud or wind?
What omen of nameless ill,
Whence coming, speeding whither,
Running, running, running,
Leaves all save fear behind?

Leaning, leaning in the race,
Breath keen-drawn through nostrils tense,
Fell eyes in ruthless face,
What goblin of malevolence
Runs through the frozen night
In superhuman flight?
See it run, run, run,
Outstripping the shadows that fly!
Hear the fiend's heart beat, beat,
Beat, beat, beat in its breast!
Running, running, running on
Under the frozen sky,
Fleet, so fearfully fleet,
Pausing never to rest.
Clutched—what it clutched so tight
In its lean, cold hands as it speeds?
Something soft, something white,
Something human, that bleeds?
Is it an infant's curly head,
And innocent limbs, gnawed and red?
Fleeter and yet more fleet
It leans, leans and runs;
Dabbled with blood are its awful lips,
Grinning in horrible glee.
The wolves that follow with scurrying feet,
Sniffing that goblin scent, at once
Scatter in terror, while it slips
Away to the shore of the frozen sea.

Away! is it man? is it woman,
On such dread meat to feed?
Away! is it beast? is it human?
Or is it a fiend indeed?

Fiend from human loins begotten,
Hell-inspired, God-forgotten!
Now the midnight hour draws on:
Human form no fiend may keep
Or ever that mystic hour is told.
Lower, lower, lower it bends.
Midnight is come—is come and gone!
Down on all fours see it plunge and leap!
A human yell in wolf's howl ends! . . .
What gaunt, grey thing gallops on o'er the wold?

W. E. Henley (1849–1903)

British poet, critic, and editor William Ernest Henley spend lengthy pe-
riods of time confined to hospital in his twenties because of a foot am-
putation and other complications of tubercular disease; there he began
writing and submitting to magazines the poetry that established his lit-
erary reputation. These poems, set largely in impressionistic free verse,
were collected in *A Book of Verses* (1888). The rest of his best-known
work is contained in *London Voluntaries* (1893) and *In Hospital* (1903).
While usually realistic in tone, his work sometimes highlights the sordid
with a weird sort of glamor, to unsettling effect. Restored to active life,
Henley established himself as an outstanding magazine editor who
promoted some of the finest writing talent of the day including Kipling,
Hardy, Shaw, and Wells. The following poem, the fourth poem of
"London Voluntaries," appeared in *London Voluntaries.*

[Untitled]

Largo e mesto

Out of the poisonous East,
Over a continent of blight,
Like a maleficent Influence released
From the most squalid cellarage of hell,
The Wind-Fiend, the abominable—
The Hangman Wind that tortures temper and light—
Comes slouching, sullen and obscene,
Hard on the skirts of the embittered night;

And in a cloud unclean
Of excremental humours, roused to strife
By the operation of some ruinous change,
Wherever his evil mandate run and range,
Into a dire intensity of life,
A craftsman at his bench, he settles down
To the grim job of throttling London Town.

So, by a jealous lightlessness beset
That might have oppressed the dragons of old time
Crunching and groping in the abysmal slime,
A cave of cut-throat thoughts and villainous dreams,
Hag-rid and crying with cold and dirt and wet,
The afflicted City, prone from mark to mark
In shameful occultation, seems
A nightmare labyrinthine, dim and drifting,
With wavering gulfs and antic heights, and shifting,
Rent in the stuff of a material dark,
Wherein the lamplight, scattered and sick and pale,
Shows like the leper's living blotch of bale:
Uncoiling monstrous into street on street
Paven with perils, teeming with mischance,
Where man and beast go blindfold and in dread,
Working with oaths and threats and faltering feet
Somewhither in the hideousness ahead;
Working through wicked airs and deadly dews
That make the laden robber grin askance
At the good places in his black romance,
And the poor, loitering harlot rather choose
Go pinched and pined to bed
Than lurk and shiver and curse her wretched way
From arch to arch, scouting some threepenny prey.

Forgot his dawns and far-flushed afterglows,
His green garlands and windy eyots forgot,
The old Father-River flows,
His watchfires cores of menace in the gloom,
As he came oozing from the Pit, and bore,
Sunk in his filthily transfigured sides,
Shoals of dishonoured dead to tumble and rot
In the squalor of the universal shore:

His voices sounding through the gruesome air
As from the Ferry where the Boat of Doom
With her blaspheming cargo reels and rides:
The while his children, the brave ships,
No more adventurous and fair,
Nor tripping it light of heel as home-bound brides,
But infamously enchanted,
Huddle together in the foul eclipse,
Or feel their course by inches desperately,
As through a tangle of alleys murder-haunted,
From sinister reach to reach out—out—to sea.

And Death the while—
Death with his well-worn, lean, professional smile,
Death in his threadbare working trim—
Comes to your bedside, unannounced and bland,
And with expert, inevitable hand
Feels at your windpipe, fingers you in the lung,
Or flicks the clot well into the labouring heart:
Thus signifying unto old and young,
However hard of mouth or wild of whim,
'Tis time—'tis time by his ancient watch—to part
From books and women and talk and drink and art.
And you go humbly after him
To a mean suburban lodging: on the way
To what or where
Not Death, who is old and very wise, can say:
And you—how should you care
So long as, unreclaimed of hell,
The Wind-Fiend, the insufferable,
Thus vicious and thus patient, sits him down
To the black job of burking London Town?

Guy de Maupassant (1850–1893)

French short story writer and novelist Guy de Maupassant was born near Dieppe and educated in various local schools. He served in the Franco-Prussian War (1870–71), which later served as the setting for many of his literary works. While working as a civil servant in Paris, he began writing under the tutelage of Gustave Flaubert and Emile Zola, both of whom he knew. He wrote hundreds of short stories, many of them tales of horror and the supernatural, and several distinctively fusing psychological and supernatural horror. The most celebrated of them is "The Horla" (1886; "Le Horla"). Many of these tales were written toward the end of his life, when syphilis caused him to become afflicted with paranoia and a fear of death. Maupassant also wrote a number of realistic novels. The poem "Terreur," usually translated as "Horror," was included in his collection *Des Vers* (1880).

Horror

That evening, in my study, I had read
The writings of an author long since dead.
    'Twas midnight, when my soul was seized with fear—
    A fear of what? I know not; none was near,
Friend to console, or foe to do me harm;
And yet I shuddered, breathless with alarm,
    As if a portent bade me understand
    Some nameless act of horror was at hand.
    I thought that some one stood behind my chair,
Smiling a cruel smile, a grisly leer,
Whose moveless lines would never disappear;
    Yet not an uttered accent moved the air.
    I was in torture lest he touch my hair,
And, bending over me, that cursed face,
A long lean hand upon my shoulder place;
    For were that hand to stroke me I should die.
Ah, he was drawing nearer to my seat,
Closer and closer on those soundless feet;
    And were it for my soul's salvation, I
Would not have ventured in that moment dread
To make one movement, or to turn my head.
And just as birds, when furious tempests blow,
Are buffeted and beaten to and fro,
Hither and thither turned my startled thought,
As if some refuge from despair I sought.
Sweat drenched my members, as if death were near,
Yet all was silence in that chamber drear,
Save my own chattering teeth that shook for fear.

But suddenly, I heard a creaking sound,
As if some viewless forms went hurrying by;
With terror dazed, I uttered a wild cry.
Ah, never yet had such a fearful note
Found utterance in any human throat;
Then fell I stiff and senseless to the ground.

[tr. anon. (1903)]

Edwin Markham (1852–1940)

American poet Edwin Markham gained enormous celebrity with the publication of "The Man with the Hoe" (1899), a protest against the exploitation of the poor. It was collected in *The Man with the Hoe and Other Poems* (1899). Other poetry collections include *Lincoln and Other Poems* (1901) and *Gates of Paradise and Other Poems* (1920). "Wail of the Wandering Dead" and "The Wharf of Dreams" were first collected in *The Man with the Hoe and Other Poems*.

Wail of the Wandering Dead

Death, too, is a chimera and betrays,
    And yet they promised we should enter rest;
Death is as empty as the cup of days,
    And bitter milk is in her wintry breast.

There is no worth in any world to come,
    Nor any in the world we left behind;
And what remains of all our masterdom?—
    Only a cry out of the crumbling mind.

We played all comers at the old Gray Inn,
    But played the King of Players to our cost.
We played Him fair and had no chance to win:
    The dice of God were loaded and we lost.

We wander, wander, and the nights come down
    With starless darkness and the rush of rains;
We drift as phantoms by the songless town,

We drift as litter on the windy lanes.

Hope is the fading vision of the heart,
  A mocking spirit throwing up wild hands.
She led us on with music at the start,
  To leave us at dead fountains in the sands.

Now all our days are but a cry for sleep,
  For we are weary of the petty strife.
Is there not somewhere in the endless deep
  A place where we can lose the feel of life?

Where we can be as senseless as the dust
  The night wind blows about a dried-up well?
Where there is no more labor, no more lust,
  Nor any flesh to feel the Tooth of Hell?

Our feet are ever sliding, and we seem
  As old and weary as the pyramids.
Come, God of Ages, and dispel the dream,
  Fold the worn hands and close the sinking lids.

There is no new road for the dead to take:
  Wild hearts are we among the worlds astray—
Wild hearts are we that cannot wholly break,
  But linger on though life has gone away.

We are the sons of Misery and Eld:
  Come, tender Death, with all your hushing wings,
And let our broken spirits be dispelled—
  Let dead men sink into the dusk of things.

The Wharf of Dreams

Strange wares are handled on the wharves of sleep:
  Shadows of shadows pass, and many a light
  Flashes a signal fire across the night;
Barges depart whose voiceless steersmen keep
Their way without a star upon the deep;
  And from lost ships, homing with ghostly crews,
  Come cries of incommunicable news,
While cargoes pile the piers, a moon-white heap—

Budgets of dream-dust, merchandise of song,
Wreckage of hope and packs of ancient wrong,
    Nepenthes gathered from a secret strand,
Fardels of heartache, burdens of old sins,
Luggage sent down from dim ancestral inns,
    And bales of fantasy from No-Man's Land.

Emile Verhaeren (1855–1916)

Emile Verhaeren was born in Belgium, where he briefly practiced law before pursuing a literary career. His first collection of poems, *Les Flamandes,* was published in 1883. Over a career spanning three decades he subsequently published two dozen volumes of poems (written in French) in addition to several plays and essay collections. Known as an exponent of Symbolist poetry, he sought to evoke rather than to describe, and used images as signifiers of the ineffable. Writing and traveling prolifically, he experienced a nervous breakdown and retreated to England to convalesce; the poetry volumes *Les Soirs* (1887), *Les Débâcles* (1888), and *Les Flambeaux noirs* (1890) begin to reflect a darker and more reflective Verhaeren. Returning to Belgium, he composed several volumes at the peak of his imaginative powers: *Les Campagnes Hallucinées* (1893), *Les Villages illusoires* (1895), and *Les Villes tentaculaires* (1895). "The Miller" ("Le Meunier") was collected in *Les Villages illusoires.*

The Miller

The old keeper of the black mill
was being buried, in winter—evening
of biting wind and piercing chill—
in a ground of cinder and hemlock.

Sunset glinted with uncertain gleam
off the shovel of the sexton.
A dog wandered near the pit
and barked at the flare of light.

At each spadeful the shovel

flickered like a twisted mirror,
shone, gouged, and buried
itself in the severed earth.
The sun sank in suspect shadows.
Silhouetted, the grave-digger,
like a gigantic mantis,
seemed grappling with fear.
The spade trembled in his hands;
the ground opened in spite of him,
and nothing seemed to fill the hole that,
like the night, yawned before him.

In the town down there,
No one had offered a shroud for the dead.

In the town down there,
No one had said a prayer for the dead.

In the town down there,
No one but the corpse sounded a death knell.

In the town down there,
No one wanted to nail the coffin shut.

And the houses and cottages
along the road facing the cemetery,
so as to witness nothing—
all had closed their shutters.

The grave-digger felt himself alone
with this dead man who had no shroud,
for whom all the villagers felt hate
and fear in their very blood.

For upon this hill, gloomy with evening,
the old miller of the black windmill
had long lived in agreement
with the cosmos and the infinite;
with the crazed flight of storms streaming
from billowing tresses of the north wind.
For long his heart had listened
to what the dark and golden mouths

of the stars reveal
to those attentive to the eternal.
He, austere as brambles and gray as heather,
had forged an identity with that mystery
by which mere things make souls aware,
and speak to them, and counsel them.
That great current flowing in every animate thing
had pervaded his mind with such power that,
in his most solitary and profound self,
this rustic knew the initiation and procession of the world.

This eternal did not sense
how long it was that he had been
secluded up here, far from the village,
observing the flight of birds in their quest,
and the sigils of fire amidst the clouds,

Awed by the silence of which
he had noiselessly
woven his existence;
awed still further
by the golden eyes
of his windmill, abruptly ablaze in darkness.

And none would have taken note
of the miller's agony and demise,
were it not for those four wings
which he flourished to the unknown
like eternal supplications;
were it not that one morning
they were perfectly fixed,
black and immobile
as a cross that marks one's fate.

The grave-digger saw the swelling shadows
massing like crowds;
and the village and its shuttered windows
melted into the distance and disappeared;

The pervasive unease
became peopled with cries of solitude
in black and brown veils;

the wind gusted as if sentient;
the wavering of hostile horizons
became rigid with febrile trembling;
until the moment when—wild-eyed,
swinging his shovel madly,
the multifold arms of the night
threatening behind him—
like a thief the sexton fled.
                                    So,
Then came silence, absolute, universal.
In the rended earth the hole appeared gigantic;
nothing moved any more;

And alone, the insatiable plains
absorbed into their immensity
of northern shadow
the dead man
whose life had been rendered limitless and,
by their mystery, exalted to the infinite.

                              [tr. Steven J. Mariconda]

A. E. Housman (1859–1936)

British poet and scholar Alfred Edward Housman studied classics at St. John's College, Oxford, and, as Kennedy Professor of Latin at Trinity College, Cambridge, went on to become one of the most distinguished classical scholars of his time. He edited important editions of the Roman poets Juvenal, Lucan, and Manilius, and wrote numerous papers on classical subjects. As a poet he ultimately gained celebrity for the 63-poem cycle *A Shropshire Lad* (1896), although he self-published the first edition. Focusing grimly but with exquisite lyricism on death and pessimism, the individual poems of the cycle were frequently set to music. Housman collected his later poems in the volume *Last Poems* (1922). His sister Clemence Housman wrote the classic horror tale *The Were-Wolf* (1896), and his brother Laurence Housman also dabbled in the weird. "Hell Gate" was gathered in *Last Poems*.

Hell Gate

      Onward led the road again
Through the sad uncoloured plain
Under twilight brooding dim,
And along the utmost rim
Wall and rampart risen to sight
Cast a shadow not of night,
And beyond them seemed to glow
Bonfires lighted long ago.
And my dark conductor broke
Silence at my side and spoke,
Saying, "You conjecture well:
Yonder is the gate of hell."

      Ill as yet the eye could see
The eternal masonry,
But beneath it on the dark
To and fro there stirred a spark.
And again the sombre guide
Knew my question, and replied:
"At hell gate the damned in turn
Pace for sentinel and burn."

      Dully at the leaden sky
Staring, and with idle eye
Measuring the listless plain,
I began to think again.
Many things I thought of then,
Battle, and the loves of men,
Cities entered, oceans crossed,
Knowledge gained and virtue lost,
Cureless folly done and said,
And the lovely way that led
To the slimepit and the mire
And the everlasting fire.
And against a smoulder dun
And a dawn without a sun
Did the nearing bastion loom,
And across the gate of gloom
Still one saw the sentry go,

Trim and burning, to and fro,
One for women to admire
In his finery of fire.
Something, as I watched him pace,
Minded me of time and place,
Soldiers of another corps
And a sentry known before.

      Ever darker hell on high
Reared its strength upon the sky,
And our footfall on the track
Fetched the daunting echo back.
But the soldier pacing still
The insuperable sill,
Nursing his tormented pride,
Turned his head to neither side,
Sunk into himself apart
And the hell-fire of his heart.
But against our entering in
From the drawbridge Death and Sin
Rose to render key and sword
To their father and their lord.
And the portress foul to see
Lifted up her eyes on me
Smiling, and I made reply:
"Met again, my lass," said I.
Then the sentry turned his head,
Looked, and knew me, and was Ned.

      Once he looked, and halted straight,
Set his back against the gate,
Caught his musket to his chin,
While the hive of hell within
Sent abroad a seething hum
As of towns whose king is come
Leading conquest home from far
And the captives of his war,
And the car of triumph waits,
And they open wide the gates.
But across the entry barred
Straddled the revolted guard,

Weaponed and accoutred well
From the arsenals of hell;
And beside him, sick and white,
Sin to left and Death to right
Turned a countenance of fear
On the flaming mutineer.
Over us the darkness bowed,
And the anger in the cloud
Clenched the lightning for the stroke;
But the traitor musket spoke.

    And the hollowness of hell
Sounded as its master fell,
And the mourning echo rolled
Ruin through his kingdom old.
Tyranny and terror flown
Left a pair of friends alone,
And beneath the nether sky
All that stirred was he and I.

    Silent, nothing found to say,
We began the backward way;
And the ebbing lustre died
From the soldier at my side,
As in all his spruce attire
Failed the everlasting fire.
Midmost of the homeward track
Once we listened and looked back,
But the city, dusk and mute,
Slept, and there was no pursuit.

Katharine Tynan (1861–1931)

Irish poet and novelist Katharine Tynan was a close associate of
W. B. Yeats and, later, a correspondent of the Irish poet Francis
Ledwidge. Among her many volumes of poetry are *Louise de la Val-
lière and Other Poems* (1885), *Irish Love-Songs* (1892), *Irish Poems*
(1913), and *Twilight Songs* (1927). Her novels include *The House of
the Foxes* (1915) and *A Mad Marriage* (1922). "The Witch" first ap-
peared in *Ballads and Lyrics* (1891).

The Witch

Margaret Grady—I fear she will burn—
Charmed the butter off my churn;
'Tis I would know it the wide world over,
Yellow as saffron, scented with clover.

At Omagh market the witch displayed it:
Ill she had gathered, ill she had made it.
Hid in my cloak's hood, one glance I threw it,
Passed on smiling; my troth! I knew it!

Sheila, the kindest cow in the parish,
Mild and silken, and good to cherish,
Shame her own gold butter should leave her
To enrich the milk of a low-bred heifer!

I said not Yea or Nay to the mocker,
But called the fairy-man over from Augher;
Like a russet he is that's withered,
Bent in two with his wisdom gathered.

He touched the butter, he peered and pondered,
And crooned strange rhymes while I watched and wondered:
Then he drew me out through the gloaming
O'er the fields where the mist was coming.

He bewitched me so that I know not
Where they may grow, where they may grow not;
Those witch-hazels he plucked and plaited,
Crooning on while the twigs he mated.

There's the wreath on the churn-dash yonder.
All the neighbours view it with wonder;
And 'spite of Father Tom I avow it
The yield is doubled since that came to it.

I bless the fairy-man though he be evil;
Yet fairy-spells come not from the Devil;
And Margaret Grady—I fear she will burn—
I do forgive her, with hate and scorn.

Madison Cawein (1865–1914)

Madison Cawein was in his lifetime known as the "Keats of Kentucky." His poetry is traditional in form and reflects a deep appreciation of nature and a devotion to mythology and classical European literature. His outlook was doubtless colored by his parents: his father was an herbalist who prepared homeopathic remedies, his mother a spiritualist. Over the period bookended by *Blooms of the Berry* (1887) and *The Cup of Comus* (1915), Cawein published more than thirty volumes and about 2700 poems. After the turn of the century his health and finances declined, and his work suffered. In 1908 a five-volume edition of *The Poems of Madison Cawein* appeared; a single-volume selection, *Poems,* followed three years later with a foreword by William Dean Howells, who had written a favorable notice of the author's first collection. The four poems printed below are all from *The Vale of Tempe* (1911).

The Forest of Shadows

Deep in the hush of a mighty wood
    I came to a place of dread and dream,
And forms of shadows, whose shapes elude
    The searching swords of the Sun's dim gleam,
Builders of silence and solitude.
And there where a glimmering water crept
    From rock to rock with a slumberous sound,
    Tired to tears, on the mossy ground,
Under a tree I lay and slept.

Was it the heart of an olden oak?
    Was it the soul of a flower that died?
Or was it the wildrose there that spoke,
    The wilding lily that palely sighed?—
For all on a sudden it seemed I awoke:
And the leaves and the flowers were all intent
    On a visible something of light and bloom—
    A presence, felt as a wild perfume
Or beautiful music, that came and went.

And all the grief, I had known, was gone;
　　And all the anguish of heart and soul;
And the burden of care that had made me wan
　　Lifted and left me strong and whole
As once in the flush of my youth's dead dawn.
And, lo! it was night. And the oval moon,
　　A silvery silence, paced the wood:
　　And there in its light like snow she stood,
As starry still as a star aswoon.

At first I thought that I looked into
　　A shadowy water of violet,
Where the faint reflection of one I knew,
　　Long dead, gazed up from its mirror wet,
Till she smiled in my face as the living do;
Till I felt her touch, and heard her say,
　　In a voice as still as a rose unfolds,—
　　"You have come at last; and now nothing holds;
Give me your hand; let us wander away.

"Let us wander away through the Shadow Wood,
　　Through the Shadow Wood to the Shadow Land,
Where the trees have speech and the blossoms brood
　　Like visible music; and hand in hand
The winds and the waters go rainbow-hued:
Where ever the voice of beauty sighs;
　　And ever the dance of dreams goes on;
　　Where nothing grows old; and the dead and gone,
And the loved and lost, smile into your eyes.

"Let us wander away! let us wander away!—
　　Do you hear them calling, 'Come here and live'?
Do you hear what the trees and the flowers say,
　　Wonderful, wild, and imperative,
Hushed as the lines of the dawn of day?
They say, 'Your life, that was rose and rue
　　In a world of shadows where all things die,
　　Where beauty is dust and love, a lie,
Is finished.—Come here! we are waiting for you!'"

And she took my hand: and the trees around
　　Seemed whispering something I dared not hear:

And the taciturn flowers, that strewed the ground,
      Seemed thinking something I felt with fear,
A beautiful something that made no sound.
And she led me on through the forest old,
      Where the moon and the midnight stood on guard,—
      Sentinel spirits that shimmered the sward,
Silver and sable and glimmering gold.

And then in an instant I knew. I knew
      What the trees had whispered, the winds had said;
What the flowers had thought in their hearts of dew,
      And the stars had syllabled overhead,
And she bent above me and smiled, "'Tis true!
Heart of my heart, you have heard aright.—
      Look in my eyes and draw me near!
      Look in my eyes and have no fear!—
Heart of my heart, you died to-night!"

The Wood Water

An evil, stealthy water, dark as hate,
      Sunk from the light of day,
'Thwart which is hung a ruined water-gate,
      Creeps on its stagnant way.

Moss and the spawny duckweed, dim as air,
      And green as copperas,
Choke its dull current; and, like hideous hair,
      Tangles of twisted grass.

Above it sinister trees,—as crouched and gaunt
      As huddled Terror,—lean;
Guarding some secret in that nightmare haunt,
      Some horror they have seen.

Something the sunset points at from afar,
      Spearing the sullen wood
And hag-gray water with a single bar
      Of flame as red as blood.

Something the stars, conspiring with the moon,
    Shall look on, and remain
Frozen with fear; staring as in a swoon,
    Striving to flee in vain.

Something the wisp that, wandering in the night,
    Above the ghastly stream,
Haply shall find; and, filled with frantic fright,
    Light with its ghostly gleam.

Something that lies there, under weed and ooze,
    With wide and awful eyes
And matted hair, and limbs the waters bruise,
    That strives, yet can not rise.

The Night-Wind

I
I have heard the wind on a winter's night,
    When the snow-cold moon looked icily through
My window's flickering firelight,
    Where the frost his witchery drew:
I have heard the wind on a winter's night,
Wandering ways that were frozen white,
    Wail in my chimney-flue:
And its voice was the voice,—so it seemed to me,—
    The voice of the world's vast misery.

II
I have heard the wind on a night of spring,
    When the leaves unclasped their girdles of gold,
And the bird on the bough sang slumbering,
    In the lilac's fragrant fold:
I have heard the wind on a night of spring,
Shaking the musk from its dewy wing,
    Sigh in my garden old:
And it seemed that it said, as it sighed above,
"I am the voice of the Earth's great love."

III

I have heard the wind on a night of fall,
        When a devil's-dance was the rain's downpour,
And the wild woods reeled to its demon call,
        And the carpet fluttered the floor:
I have heard the wind on a night of fall,
Heaping the leaves by the garden wall,
        Weep at my close-shut door:
And its voice, so it seemed, as it sorrowed there,
Was the old, old voice of the world's despair.

IV

I have heard the wind on a summer night,
        When the myriad stars stormed heaven with fire,
And the moon-moth glimmered in phantom flight,
        And the crickets creaked in choir:
I have heard the wind on a summer night,
Rocking the red rose and the white,
        Murmur in bloom and brier:
And its voice was the voice,—so it seemed to me,—
Of Earth's primordial mystery.

Hallowmas

All hushed of glee,
The last chill bee
Clings wearily
To the dying aster.
The leaves drop faster:
And all around, red as disaster,
The forest crimsons with tree on tree.

A butterfly,
The last to die,
Wings heavily by,
Weighed down with torpor.
The air grows sharper;
And the wind in the trees, like some sad harper,
Sits and sorrows with sigh on sigh.

The far crows call;
The acorns fall;
And over all
The Autumn raises
Dun mists and hazes,
Through which her soul, it seemeth, gazes
On ghosts and dreams in carnival.

The end is near;
The dying Year
Leans low to hear
Her own heart breaking,
And Beauty taking
Her flight, and all my dreams forsaking
My soul, bowed down 'mid the sad and sere.

W. B. Yeats (1865–1939)

William Butler Yeats was the leader of the Irish literary renaissance and ranks among poetry's greatest artists by virtue of the technical excellence and imaginative depth he maintained over a four-decade writing career. Passionate about Irish history, art, and nationalism, he also delved deeply into mysticism, folklore, and metaphysics. A playwright as well as a poet, Yeats co-founded and wrote for the national Abbey Theatre. His primary poetry collections include *The Wanderings of Oisin* (1889), *The Celtic Twilight* (1893), *The Wind among the Reeds* (1899), *The Wild Swans at Coole* (1917), and *The Tower* (1928). Yeats was elected to the Irish Free Senate in 1922 and awarded the Nobel Prize for literature in 1923. The ornate language and mythic themes of Yeats's early work gave way in maturity to a more vigorous style and a focus on contemporary issues; in his final phase he treated the esoteric themes developed in his eccentric philosophical treatise *A Vision* (1925), using a paradoxically spare and powerful verse idiom. "The Phantom Ship" was first published in the *Providence Sunday Journal* (May 27, 1888).

The Phantom Ship

Flames the shuttle of the lightning across the driving sleet,
Ay, and shakes in sea-green waverings along the fishers' street;
Gone the stars and gone the white moon, gone and puffed away and
    dead.
Never storm arose so swiftly; scarce the children were in bed,
Scarce the old and wizen houses had their doors and windows shut.
Ah! it dwelt within the twilight as the worm within the nut.
"Waken, waken, sleepy fishers; no hour is this for sleep,"
Cries a voice at roaring midnight beside the moonless deep.
Half dizzy with the lightning there runs a gathering band—
"Watcher, wherefore have ye called us?" Eyes go after his lean hand,
And the fisher men and women from the dripping harbour wall
See the darkness slow disgorging a vessel blind with squall.
"Bring the ropes now! Stand ye by now! See, she rounds the har-
    bour clear.
God! they're mad to fly such canvas!" Ah! what bell-notes do they
    hear?
Say what ringer rings at midnight; for, in the belfry high,
Slow the chapel bell is tolling as though the dead passed by.
Round she comes in stays before them; cease the winds, and on
    their poles
Cease the sails their flapping uproar, and the hull no longer rolls.
Now a scream from all those fishers, for there on deck there be
All the drowned that ever were drowned from that village by the
    sea;
And the ghastly ghost-flames glimmer all along the taffrail rails
On the drowned men's hands and faces, on the spars and on the
    sails.
Hush'd the fishers, till a mother calls by name her drownèd son;
Then each wife and maid and mother calls by name some drownèd
    one.
Stands each grey and silent phantom on the same regardless spot—
Joys and fears in their grey faces that the live earth knoweth not;
Down the vapours fall and hide them from the children of a day,
And the winds come down and blow them with the vapours far
    away.

Hang the mist-threads for a little while like cobwebs in the air;
Then the stars grow out of heaven with their countenances fair.

"Pray for the souls in purgatory," the pale priest trembling cries.

Prayed those forgotten fishers, till in the eastern skies
Came olive fires of morning and on the darkness fed,
By the slow heaving ocean—mumbling mother of the dead.

Dora Sigerson Shorter (1866–1918)

Irish poet Dora Sigerson Shorter was a leading figure in the Irish Renaissance of the late 19th and early 20th centuries. She was married to the British journalist Clement K. Shorter. Among her several volumes of poetry are *My Lady's Slipper and Other Verses* (1899), *Madge Linsey and Other Poems* (1913), and *Tricolour: Poems of the Irish Revolution* (1922). "The Skeleton in the Cupboard" first appeared in *The Fairy Changeling and Other Poems* (1898). "The Fetch" first appeared in *Ballads and Poems* (1899). Both were included in *Collected Poems of Dora Sigerson Shorter* (1907).

The Skeleton in the Cupboard

Just this one day in all the year
Let all be one, let all be dear;
Wife, husband, child in fond embrace,
And thrust the phantom from its place.
No bitter words, no frowning brow,
Disturb the Christmas festal, now
The skeleton's behind the door.

Nor let the child, with looks askance,
Find out its sad inheritance
From souls that held no happiness
Of home, where love is seldom guest;
But in his coming years retain
This one sweet night that had no pain;
The skeleton's behind the door.

In vain you raise the wassail bowl,
And pledge your passion, soul to soul.
You hear the sweet bells ring in rhyme,
You wreathe the room for Christmas-time
In vain. The solemn silence falls,
The death-watch ticks within the walls;
The skeleton taps on the door.

Then let him back into his place,
Let us sit out the old disgrace;
Nor seek the phantom now to lay
That haunted us through every day;
For plainer is the ghost; useless
Is this pretence of happiness;
The skeleton taps on the door.

The Fetch

"What makes you so late at the trysting?
What caused you so long to be?
For a weary time I have waited
From the hour you promised me."

"I would I were here by your side, love,
Full many an hour ago,
For a thing I passed on the roadway
All mournful and so slow."

"And what have you passed on the roadside
That kept you so long and late?"
"It is weary the time behind me
Since I left my father's gate.

"As I hastened on in the gloaming
By the road to you to-night,
There I saw the corpse of a young maid
All clad in a shroud of white."

"And was she some comrade cherished,
Or was she a sister dead,

That you left thus your own beloved
Till the trysting-hour had fled?"

"Oh! I would that I could discover,
But never did see her face,
And I knew I must turn and follow
Till I came to her resting place."

"And did it go up by the town path,
Did it go down by the lake?
I know there are but the two churchyards
Where a corpse its rest may take."

"They did not go up by the town path,
Nor stopped by the lake their feet,
They buried the corpse all silently
Where the four cross-roads do meet."

"And was it so strange a sight, then,
That you should go like a child,
Thus to leave me wait all forgotten—
By a passing sight beguiled?"

"'Twas my name that I heard them whisper,
Each mourner that passed by me;
And I had to follow their footsteps,
Though their faces I could not see."

"And right well I should like to know, now,
Who might be this fair young maid,
So come with me, my own true love,
If you be not afraid."

He did not go down by the lakeside,
He did not go by the town,
But carried her to the four cross-roads,
And he there did set her down.

"Now, I see no track of a foot here,
I see no mark of a spade,
And I know right well in this white road
That never a grave was made."

And he took her hand in his right hand
And led her to town away,
And there he questioned the good old priest,
Did he bury a maid that day.

And he took her hand in his right hand,
Down to the church by the lake,
And there he questioned the pale young priest
If a maiden her life did take.

But neither had heard of a new grave
In all the parish around,
And no one could tell of a young maid
Thus put in unholy ground.

So he loosed her hand from his hand,
And turned on his heel away,
And, "I know now you are false," he said,
"From the lie you told to-day."

And she said, "Alas! what evil thing
Did to-night my senses take?"
She knelt her down by the water-side
And wept as her heart would break.

And she said, "Oh, what fairy sight then
Was it thus my grief to see?
I will sleep well 'neath the still water,
Since my love has turned from me."

And her love he went to the north land,
And far to the south went he,
And her distant voice he still could hear
Call weeping so bitterly.

And he could not rest in the daytime,
He could not sleep in the night,
So he hastened back to the old road,
With the trysting place in sight.

What first he heard was his own love's name,
And keening both loud and long,

What first he saw was his love's dear face,
At the head of a mourning throng.

And all white she was as the dead are,
And never a move made she,
But passed him by in her lone black pall,
Still sleeping so peacefully.

And all cold she was as the dead are,
And never a word she spake,
When they said, "Unholy is her grave
For she her life did take."

And silent she was as the dead are,
And never a cry she made,
When there came, more sad than the keening,
The ring of a digging spade.

No rest she had in the old town church,
No grave by the lake so sweet,
They buried her in unholy ground,
Where the four cross roads do meet.

Æ (George William Russell) (1867–1935)

George William Russell (who wrote under the pseudonym Æ) was
trained as a painter, but he made his mark as a political activist,
journalist, editor, public speaker, and poet. His first book of verse,
Homeward: Songs by the Way (1894), established him—with Yeats,
Joyce, and others—as a leading figure in the Irish Literary Revival.
Russell was editor of the *Irish Homestead,* a journal of the coopera-
tive farming movement, and wrote extensively on politics and eco-
nomics. He claimed to be clairvoyant, and his deep involvement
with mysticism and theosophy is reflected in the essays in *The Can-
dle of Vision* (1918) and several other volumes, as well as in his po-
etry. Editions of his *Collected Poems* were issued in 1913 and 1926.
"A Vision of Beauty" was published in the revised edition of *Home-
ward: Songs by the Way* (1895).

A Vision of Beauty

Where we sat at dawn together, while the star-rich heavens shifted,
We were weaving dreams in silence, suddenly the veil was lifted.
By a hand of fire awakened, in a moment caught and led
Upward to the heaven of heavens—through the star-mists overhead
Flare and flaunt the monstrous highlands; on the sapphire coast of
    night
Fall the ghostly froth and fringes of the ocean of the light.
Many coloured shine the vapours: to the moon-eye far away
'Tis the fairy ring of twilight, mid the spheres of night and day,
Girdling with a rainbow cincture round the planet where we go,
We and it together fleeting, poised upon the pearly glow;
We and it and all together flashing through the starry spaces
In a tempest dream of beauty lighting up the face of faces.
Half our eyes behold the glory; half within the spirit's glow
Echoes of the noiseless revels and the will of Beauty go.
By a hand of fire uplifted—to her star-strewn palace brought,
To the mystic heart of beauty and the secret of her thought:
Here of yore the ancient Mother in the fire mists sank to rest,
And she built her dreams about her, rayed from out her burning
    breast:
Here the wild will woke within her lighting up her flying dreams,
Round and round the planets whirling break in woods and flowers
    and streams,
And the winds are shaken from them as the leaves from off the rose,
And the feet of earth go dancing in the way that beauty goes,
And the souls of earth are kindled by the incense of her breath
As her light alternate lures them through the gates of birth and
    death.
O'er the fields of space together following her flying traces,
In a radiant tumult thronging, suns and stars and myriad races
Mount the spirit spires of beauty, reaching onward to the day
When the Shepherd of the Ages draws his misty hordes away
Through the glimmering deeps to silence, and within the awful fold
Life and joy and love forever vanish as a tale is told,
Lost within the Mother's being. So the vision flamed and fled,
And before the glory fallen every other dream lay dead.

V. The Twentieth Century

George Sterling (1869–1926)

American poet George Sterling was born in Long Island but moved to California in the 1890s. Under the tutelage of Ambrose Bierce, he published several books of poetry, including *The Testimony of the Suns* (1903), *A Wine of Wizardry* (1909), *Sails and Mirage* (1921), and *Selected Poems* (1923). He himself was the early mentor of Clark Ashton Smith. His weird verses have now been gathered in *The Thirst of Satan: Poems of Fantasy and Terror* (2003). "A Dream of Fear" and "A Wine of Wizardry" were published in *A Wine of Wizardry;* "The Thirst of Satan" appeared in *Beyond the Breakers and Other Poems* (1914).

A Dream of Fear

Unseen the ghostly hand that led,
  I walked where all was darkness, save
  What light the moon, half-wasted, gave
Above a city of the dead.

So lone it was, so grey, I deemed
  That death itself was scarce so old;
  The moonlight fell forlorn and cold
On tombs where Time lay dead, it seemed.

Within its gates I heard the sound
  Of winds in cypress-caverns caught
  Of huddling trees that moaned, and sought
To whisper what their roots had found.

Within its gates my soul was led,
  Down nettle-choked and haunted way—
  An atom of the Dark's dismay,
In deaf immensities of dread.

In broken crypts where ghouls had slept
  I saw how muttering devils sate

(Knowing the final grasp of Fate)
And told grim auguries, and wept.

The night was mad with nameless fear.
    The Powers of Darkness feared the gloom.
    From sentried sky to anxious tomb
Ran messages I bent to hear.

Mine ears were sealed, nor heard I save
    The secret known to Endor's witch—
    Whispered to lemur and to lich
From lips made wiser by the grave.

O'er tarns where spectral vapors flowed
    Antares shook with bloody light,
    And guarded on its haughty flight
The offended fire of Alphard glowed.

The menace of infinity
    Constrained the cavern of the skies.
    I felt the gaze of solemn eyes
In hostile gulfs intent to see;

Gage of whose imminent designs,
    Satanic Armageddon broke,
    Where monstrous vans in blackness spoke
The flight of Evil on the Signs—

Abysmal occultation cast
    By kingdoms of the sunken noon,
    And shadow-shafts that smote the moon
At altars of the cloven Vast!

To worlds that faltered on their way
    Python's intolerable hiss
    Told from the jaws of his abyss
Malign amazement and dismay.

By god or demon undestroyed,
    In malediction sate the stars,
    Concentered from Titanic wars
To cry the judgments of the Void.

Assigned, implacable, supreme,
      The heralds of the Curse came down:
      I felt the eternal bastions' frown;
I saw colossal cerements gleam.

Convoking trumpets shook the gloom.
      Their incommunicable word
      Announced o'er Time's foundations, stirred,
All vasts and covenants of doom.

I saw the light of dreadful fanes,
      I heard enormous valves resound,
      For aeons sealed in crypts profound,
And clangor of ascending chains.

A Wine of Wizardry

> *"When mountains were stained as with wine*
> *By the dawning of Time, and as wine*
> *Were the seas."* AMBROSE BIERCE.

Without, the battlements of sunset shine,
'Mid domes the sea-winds rear and overwhelm.
Into a crystal cup the dusky wine
I pour, and, musing at so rich a shrine,
I watch the star that haunts its ruddy gloom.
Now Fancy, empress of a purpled realm,
Awakes with brow caressed by poppy-bloom,
And wings in sudden dalliance her flight
To strands where opals of the shattered light
Gleam in the wind-strewn foam, and maidens flee
A little past the striving billows' reach,
Or seek the russet mosses of the sea,
And wrinkled shells that lure along the beach,
And please the heart of Fancy; yet she turns,
Tho' trembling, to a grotto rosy-sparred,
Where wattled monsters redly gape, that guard
A cowled magician peering on the damned
Thro' vials wherein a splendid poison burns,
Sifting Satanic gules athwart his brow.
So Fancy will not gaze with him, and now

She wanders to an iceberg oriflammed
With rayed, auroral guidons of the North—
Wherein hath winter hidden ardent gems
And treasuries of frozen anadems,
Alight with timid sapphires of the snow.
But she would dream of warmer gems, and so
Ere long her eyes in fastnesses look forth
O'er blue profounds mysterious whence glow
The coals of Tartarus on the moonless air,
As Titans plan to storm Olympus' throne,
'Mid pulse of dungeoned forges down the stunned,
Undominated firmament, and glare
Of Cyclopean furnaces unsunned.

Then hastens she in refuge to a lone,
Immortal garden of the eastern hours,
Where Dawn upon a pansy's breast hath laid
A single tear, and whence the wind hath flown
And left a silence. Far on shadowy tow'rs
Droop blazoned banners, and the woodland shade,
With leafy flames and dyes autumnal hung,
Makes beautiful the twilight of the year.
For this the fays will dance, for elfin cheer,
Within a dell where some mad girl hath flung
A bracelet that the painted lizards fear—
Red pyres of muffled light! Yet Fancy spurns
The revel, and to eastern hazard turns,
And glaring beacons of the Soldan's shores,
When in a Syrian treasure-house she pours,
From caskets rich and amethystine urns,
Dull fires of dusty jewels that have bound
The brows of naked Ashtaroth around.
Or hushed, at fall of some disastrous night,
When sunset, like a crimson throat to hell,
Is cavernous, she marks the seaward flight
Of homing dragons dark upon the West;
Till, drawn by tales the winds of ocean tell,
And mute amid the splendors of her quest,
To some red city of the Djinns she flees
And, lost in palaces of silence, sees
Within a porphyry crypt the murderous light

Of garnet-crusted lamps whereunder sit
Perturbéd men that tremble at a sound,
And ponder words on ghastly vellum writ,
In vipers' blood, to whispers from the night—
Infernal rubrics, sung to Satan's might,
Or chaunted to the Dragon in his gyre.
But she would blot from memory the sight,
And seeks a stainéd twilight of the South,
Where crafty gnomes with scarlet eyes conspire
To quench Aldebaran's affronting fire,
Low sparkling just beyond their cavern's mouth,
Above a wicked queen's unhallowed tomb.
There lichens brown, incredulous of fame,
Whisper to veinéd flowers her body's shame,
'Mid stillness of all pageantries of bloom.
Within, lurk orbs that graven monsters clasp;
Red-embered rubies smolder in the gloom,
Betrayed by lamps that nurse a sullen flame,
And livid roots writhe in the marble's grasp,
As moaning airs invoke the conquered rust
Of lordly helms made equal in the dust.
Without, where baleful cypresses make rich
The bleeding sun's phantasmagoric gules,
Are fungus-tapers of the twilight witch
(Seen by the bat above unfathomed pools)
And tiger-lilies known to silent ghouls,
Whose king hath digged a somber carcanet
And necklaces with fevered opals set.
But Fancy, well affrighted at his gaze,
Flies to a violet headland of the West,
About whose base the sun-lashed billows blaze,
Ending in precious foam their fatal quest,
As far below the deep-hued ocean molds,
With waters' toil and polished pebbles' fret,
The tiny twilight in the jacinth set,
With wintry orb the moonstone-crystal holds,
Snapt coral twigs and winy agates wet,
Translucencies of jasper, and the folds
Of banded onyx, and vermilion breast
Of cinnabar. Anear on orange sands,

With prows of bronze the sea-stained galleys rest,
And swarthy mariners from alien strands
Stare at the red horizon, for their eyes
Behold a beacon burn on evening skies,
As fed with sanguine oils at touch of night.
Forth from that pharos-flame a radiance flies,
To spill in vinous gleams on ruddy decks;
And overside, when leap the startled waves
And crimson bubbles rise from battle-wrecks,
Unresting hydras wrought of bloody light
Dip to the ocean's phosphorescent caves.

So Fancy's carvel seeks an isle afar,
Led by the Scorpion's rubescent star,
Until in templed zones she smiles to see
Black incense glow, and scarlet-bellied snakes
Sway to the tawny flutes of sorcery.
There priestesses in purple robes hold each
A sultry garnet to the sea-linkt sun,
Or, just before the colored morning shakes
A splendor on the ruby-sanded beach,
Cry unto Betelgeuse a mystic word.
But Fancy, amorous of evening, takes
Her flight to groves whence lustrous rivers run,
Thro' hyacinth, a minster wall to gird,
Where, in the hushed cathedral's jeweled gloom,
Ere Faith return, and azure censers fume,
She kneels, in solemn quietude, to mark
The suppliant day from gorgeous oriels float
And altar-lamps immure the deathless spark;
Till, all her dreams made rich with fervent hues,
She goes to watch, beside a lurid moat,
The kingdoms of the afterglow suffuse
A sentinel mountain stationed toward the night—
Whose broken tombs betray their ghastly trust,
Till bloodshot gems stare up like eyes of lust.
And now she knows, at agate portals bright,
How Circe and her poisons have a home,
Carved in one ruby that a Titan lost,
Where icy philters brim with scarlet foam,
'Mid hiss of oils in burnished caldrons tost,

While thickly from her prey his life-tide drips,
In turbid dyes that tinge her torture-dome;
As craftily she gleans her deadly dews,
With gyving spells not Pluto's queen can use,
Or listens to her victim's moan, and sips
Her darkest wine, and smiles with wicked lips.
Nor comes a god with any power to break
The red alembics whence her gleaming broths
Obscenely fume, as asp or adder froths,
To lethal mists whose writhing vapors make
Dim augury, till shapes of men that were
Point, weeping, at tremendous dooms to be,
When pillared pomps and thrones supreme shall stir,
Unstable as the foam-dreams of the sea.

But Fancy still is fugitive, and turns
To caverns where a demon altar burns,
And Satan, yawning on his brazen seat,
Fondles a screaming thing his fiends have flayed,
Ere Lilith come his indolence to greet,
Who leads from hell his whitest queens, arrayed
In chains so heated at their master's fire
That one new-damned had thought their bright attire
Indeed were coral, till the dazzling dance
So terribly that brilliance shall enhance.
But Fancy is unsatisfied, and soon
She seeks the silence of a vaster night,
Where powers of wizardry, with faltering sight
(Whenas the hours creep farthest from the noon)
Seek by the glow-worm's lantern cold and dull
A crimson spider hidden in a skull,
Or search for mottled vines with berries white,
Where waters mutter to the gibbous moon.
There, clothed in cerements of malignant light,
A sick enchantress scans the dark to curse,
Beside a caldron vext with harlots' blood,
The stars of that red Sign which spells her doom.

Then Fancy cleaves the palmy skies adverse
To sunset barriers. By the Ganges' flood
She sees, in her dim temple, Siva loom

And, visioned with the monstrous ruby, glare
On distant twilight where the burning-ghaut
Is lit with glowering pyres that seem the eyes
Of her abhorrent dragon-worms that bear
The pestilence, by Death in darkness wrought.
So Fancy's wings forsake the Asian skies,
And now her heart is curious of halls
In which dead Merlin's prowling ape hath spilt
A vial squat whose scarlet venom crawls
To ciphers bright and terrible, that tell
The sins of demons and the encharneled guilt
That breathes a phantom at whose cry the owl,
Malignly mute above the midnight well,
Is dolorous, and Hecate lifts her cowl
To mutter swift a minatory rune;
And, ere the tomb-thrown echoings have ceased,
The blue-eyed vampire, sated at her feast,
Smiles bloodily against the leprous moon.

But evening now is come, and Fancy folds
Her splendid plumes, nor any longer holds
Adventurous quest o'er stainéd lands and seas—
Fled to a star above the sunset lees,
O'er onyx waters stilled by gorgeous oils
That toward the twilight reach emblazoned coils.
And I, albeit Merlin-sage hath said,
"A vyper lurketh in ye wine-cuppe redde,"
Gaze pensively upon the way she went,
Drink at her font, and smile as one content.

The Thirst of Satan

In dream I saw the starry disarray
        (That battle-dust of matter's endless war)
        Astir with some huge passing, and afar
Beheld the troubled constellations sway
In winds of insurrection and dismay,
        Till, from that magnitude whose ages are
        But moments in the cycle of the star,
There swept a Shadow on our ghost of day—

A Shape that clutched the deviating earth
    And checked its headlong flight and held it fast,
        Draining the bitter oceans one by one.
Then, to the laughter of infernal mirth,
    The ruined chalice droned athwart the Vast,
        Hurled in the face of the offended sun.

Edwin Arlington Robinson (1869–1935)

American poet Edwin Arlington Robinson is best remembered for his brief dramatic poems about the people of rural New England. Robinson's early life was marked by personal and professional setbacks, and he endured years of poverty before his work began to attract notice. His poetry is correspondingly terse in its vocabulary and rhythm, and bleak in its examination of the tragic complexities of life. *The Torrent and the Night Before* (1896), privately printed at his own expense, was followed by *The Children of the Night* (1897), *The Town Down the River* (1910), and *The Man against the Sky* (1916). The last-named attracted some measure of critical acclaim. Robinson went on to write long narrative poems such as *Merlin* (1917), *Lancelot* (1920), *Tristram* (1927), *The Man Who Died Twice* (1924), and *Amaranth* (1934). "The Dead Village" was first collected in *The Children of the Night*, "The Dark House" in *The Man against the Sky*.

The Dead Village

Here there is death. But even here, they say,
Here where the dull sun shines this afternoon
As desolate as ever the dead moon
Did glimmer on dead Sardis, men were gay;
And there were little children here to play,
With small soft hands that once did keep in tune
The strings that stretch from heaven, till too soon
The change came, and the music passed away.

Now there is nothing but the ghosts of things,—
No life, no love, no children, and no men;
And over the forgotten place there clings

The strange and unrememberable light
That is in dreams. The music failed, and then
God frowned, and shut the village from His sight.

The Dark House

Where a faint light shines alone,
Dwells a Demon I have known.
Most of you had better say
"The Dark House," and go your way.
Do not wonder if I stay.

For I know the Demon's eyes,
And their lure that never dies.
Banish all your fond alarms,
For I know the foiling charms
Of her eyes and of her arms,

And I know that in one room
Burns a lamp as in a tomb;
And I see the shadow glide,
Back and forth, of one denied
Power to find himself outside.

There he is who is my friend,
Damned, he fancies, to the end—
Vanquished, ever since a door
Closed, he thought, for evermore
On the life that was before.

And the friend who knows him best
Sees him as he sees the rest
Who are striving to be wise
While a Demon's arms and eyes
Hold them as a web would flies.

All the words of all the world,
Aimed together and then hurled,
Would be stiller in his ears
Than a closing of still shears
On a thread made out of years.

But there lives another sound,
More compelling, more profound;
There's a music, so it seems,
That assuages and redeems,
More than reason, more than dreams.

There's a music yet unheard
By the creature of the word,
Though it matters little more
Than a wave-wash on a shore—
Till a Demon shuts a door.

So, if he be very still
With his Demon, and one will,
Murmurs of it may be blown
To my friend who is alone
In a room that I have known.

After that from everywhere
Singing life will find him there;
Then the door will open wide,
And my friend, again outside,
Will be living, having died.

———————————

Christopher Brennan (1870–1932)

The Australian Christopher Brennan decided to become a poet after encountering the poetry of Stéphane Mallarmé while on a traveling scholarship in Germany. His first volume of poetry was *XXI Poems* (1897). His major poetic work was *Poems: 1913* (1914), a volume that was meant to be read as a unity. His other volumes include *A Chant of Doom and Other Verses* (1918) and the posthumous *The Burden of Tyre* (1953). Brennan's work was immensely influential on subsequent generations of Australian poets, including A. D. Hope, Judith Wright, and Vincent Buckley. The following untitled poem appeared in *Poems: 1913*.

[Untitled]

The forest has its horrors, as the sea:
and ye that enter from the staling lea
into the early freshness kept around
the waiting trunks that watch its rarer bound,
after the glistening song that, sprinkled, leaves
an innocence upon the glancing leaves;
O ye that dream to find the morning yet
secret and chaste, beside her mirror set,
some glimmering source o'ershadow'd, where the light
is coolness felt, whom filter'd glints invite
thro' the slow-shifting green transparency;
O ye that hearken towards pale mystery
a rustle of hidden pinions, and obey
the beckoning of each little leaf asway:
return, return, or e'er to warn you back
the shadow bend along your rearward track
longer and longer from the brooding west;
return, and evening shall bosom your rest
in the warm gloom that wraps the blazing hearth:
there hear from wither'd lips long wean'd of mirth
the tale that lulls old watches;—How they rode,
brave-glittering once, where the brave morning glow'd
along the forest-edges, and were lost
for ever, where the crossing trunks are most;
and, far beyond the dim arcades of song,
where moon-mist weaves a dancing elfin throng,
and far beyond the luring glades that brood
around a maiden thought of Quietude,
the savage realm begins, of lonely dread,
black branches from the fetid marish bred
that lurks to trap the loyal careless foot,
and gaping trunks protrude a snaky root
o'er slinking paths that centre, where beneath
a sudden rock on the short blasted heath,
bare-set, a cavern lurks and holds within
its womb, obscene with some corroding sin,

coil'd on itself and stirring, a squat shade;
before the entrance rusts a broken blade.

The forest hides its horrors, as the sea.

Paul Laurence Dunbar (1872–1906)

African-American poet Paul Laurence Dunbar became a pioneer in the use of African-American dialect in poetry. Among his poetry volumes are *Oak and Ivy* (1893), *Lyrics of Lowly Life* (1896), *Lyrics of the Hearthside* (1899), *Lyrics of Love and Laughter* (1903), and *Lyrics of Sunshine and Shadow* (1905). He also wrote several novels, including *The Uncalled* (1898) and *The Sport of the Gods* (1902). "The Haunted Oak" first appeared in the *Century Magazine* (December 1900).

The Haunted Oak

Pray why are you so bare, so bare,
    Oh, bough of the old oak-tree;
And why, when I go through the shade you throw,
    Runs a shudder over me?

My leaves were green as the best, I trow,
    And sap ran free in my veins,
But I saw in the moonlight dim and weird
    A guiltless victim's pains.

I bent me down to hear his sigh;
    I shook with his gurgling moan,
And I trembled sore when they rode away,
    And left him here alone.

They'd charged him with the old, old crime,
    And set him fast in jail:
Oh, why does the dog howl all night long,
    And why does the night wind wail?

He prayed his prayer and he swore his oath,
    And he raised his hand to the sky;

But the beat of hoofs smote on his ear,
    And the steady tread drew nigh.

Who is it rides by night, by night,
    Over the moonlit road?
And what is the spur that keeps the pace,
    What is the galling goad?

And now they beat at the prison door,
    "Ho, keeper, do not stay!
We are friends of him whom you hold within,
    And we fain would take him away

"From those who ride fast on our heels
    With mind to do him wrong;
They have no care for his innocence,
    And the rope they bear is long."

They have fooled the jailer with lying words,
    They have fooled the man with lies;
The bolts unbar, the locks are drawn,
    And the great door open flies.

Now they have taken him from the jail,
    And hard and fast they ride,
And the leader laughs low down in his throat,
    As they halt my trunk beside.

Oh, the judge, he wore a mask of black,
    And the doctor one of white,
And the minister, with his oldest son,
    Was curiously bedight.

Oh, foolish man, why weep you now?
    'Tis but a little space,
And the time will come when these shall dread
    The mem'ry of your face.

I feel the rope against my bark,
    And the weight of him in my grain,
I feel in the throe of his final woe
    The touch of my own last pain.

And never more shall leaves come forth
    On a bough that bears the ban;
I am burned with dread, I am dried and dead,
    From the curse of a guiltless man.

And ever the judge rides by, rides by,
    And goes to hunt the deer,
And ever another rides his soul
    In the guise of a mortal fear.

And ever the man he rides me hard,
    And never a night stays he;
For I feel his curse as a haunted bough,
    On the trunk of a haunted tree.

———————————

Walter de la Mare (1873–1956)

British author Walter de la Mare was a prolific novelist, short story writer, and poet. Much of his work is laced with the weird, including the novel *The Return* (1910) and the story collections *The Riddle and Other Stories* (1923), *The Connoisseur and Other Stories* (1926), and *On the Edge* (1930), which included such celebrated tales as "Seaton's Aunt," "The Tree," "All Hallows," and "Mr. Kempe." Much of his work for children, including *Ding Dong Bell* (1924) and *Broomsticks and Other Tales* (1925), incorporates elements of fantasy and terror. De la Mare also wrote a lengthy introduction to his son Colin de la Mare's anthology *They Walk Again* (1931). His poetry also contains liberal doses of weirdness. "Fear" first appeared in *Poems* (1906). "The Listeners" was collected in *The Listeners and Other Poems* (1912). "Drugged" was collected in *The Veil and Other Poems* (1922).

Fear

I know where lurk
The eyes of Fear;
I, I alone,
Where shadowy-clear,

Watching for me,
Lurks Fear.

'Tis ever still
And dark, despite
All singing and
All candlelight,
'Tis ever cold,
And night.

He touches me;
Says quietly,
"Stir not, nor whisper,
I am nigh;
Walk noiseless on,
I am by!"

He drives me
As a dog a sheep;
Like a cold stone
I cannot weep.
He lifts me,
Hot from sleep,

In marble hands
To where on high
The jewelled horror
Of his eye
Dares me to struggle
Or cry.

No breast wherein
To chase away
That watchful shape!
Vain, vain to say,
"Haunt not with night
The day!"

The Listeners

"Is there anybody there?" said the Traveller,
    Knocking on the moonlit door;
And his horse in the silence champed the grasses
    Of the forest's ferny floor:
And a bird flew up out of the turret,
    Above the Traveller's head:
And he smote upon the door again a second time;
    "Is there anybody there?" he said.
But no one descended to the Traveller;
    No head from the leaf-fringed sill
Leaned over and looked into his grey eyes,
    Where he stood perplexed and still.
But only a host of phantom listeners
    That dwelt in the lone house then
Stood listening in the quiet of the moonlight
    To that voice from the world of men:
Stood thronging the faint moonbeams on the dark stair,
    That goes down to the empty hall,
Hearkening in an air stirred and shaken
    By the lonely Traveller's call.
And he felt in his heart their strangeness,
    Their stillness answering his cry,
While his horse moved, cropping the dark turf,
    'Neath the starred and leafy sky;
For he suddenly smote on the door, even
    Louder, and lifted his head:—
"Tell them I came, and no one answered,
    That I kept my word," he said.
Never the least stir made the listeners,
    Though every word he spake
Fell echoing through the shadowiness of the still house
    From the one man left awake:
Ay, they heard his foot upon the stirrup,
    And the sound of iron on stone,
And how the silence surged softly backward,
    When the plunging hoofs were gone.

Drugged

Inert in his chair,
In a candle's guttering glow;
His bottle empty,
His fire sunk low;
With drug-sealed lids shut fast,
Unsated mouth ajar,
This darkened phantasm walks
Where nightmares are:

In a frenzy of life and light,
Crisscross—a menacing throng—
They gibe, they squeal at the stranger,
Jostling along,
Their faces cadaverous grey:
While on high from an attic stare
Horrors, in beauty apparelled,
Down the dark air.

A stream gurgles over its stones,
The chambers within are a-fire.
Stumble his shadowy feet
Through shine, through mire;
And the flames leap higher.
In vain yelps the wainscot mouse;
In vain beats the hour;
Vacant, his body must drowse
Until daybreak flower—

Staining these walls with its rose,
And the draughts of the morning shall stir
Cold on cold brow, cold hands.
And the wanderer
Back to flesh house must return.
Lone soul—in horror to see,
Than dream more meagre and awful,
Reality.

Robert W. Service (1874–1958)

Canadian poet and novelist Robert W. Service was born in Scotland but came to Canada when he was twenty. He became celebrated for his ballad poetry, collected in *Songs of a Sourdough* (1907; later titled *The Spell of the Yukon and Other Verses*), *Rhymes of a Rolling Stone* (1912), *Bar-Room Ballads* (1940), and many other volumes. He also wrote several novels, including *The Master of the Microbe* (1926) and *The House of Fear* (1927). "The Cremation of Sam McGee" first appeared in *The Spell of the Yukon and Other Verses*.

The Cremation of Sam McGee

> *There are strange things done in the midnight sun*
> > *By the men who moil for gold;*
> *The Arctic trails have their secret tales*
> > *That would make your blood run cold;*
> *The Northern Lights have seen queer sights,*
> > *But the queerest they ever did see*
> *Was that night on the marge of Lake Lebarge*
> > *I cremated Sam McGee.*

Now Sam McGee was from Tennessee, where the cotton blooms and blows.
Why he left his home in the South to roam 'round the Pole, God only knows.
He was always cold, but the land of gold seemed to hold him like a spell;
Though he'd often say in his homely way that "he'd sooner live in hell."

On a Christmas Day we were mushing our way over the Dawson trail.
Talk of your cold! through the parka's fold it stabbed like a driven nail.
If our eyes we'd close, then the lashes froze till sometimes we couldn't see;
It wasn't much fun, but the only one to whimper was Sam McGee.

And that very night, as we lay packed tight in our robes beneath the snow,

And the dogs were fed, and the stars o'erhead were dancing heel and
    toe,
He turned to me, and "Cap," says he, "I'll cash in this trip, I guess;
And if I do, I'm asking that you won't refuse my last request."

Well, he seemed so low that I couldn't say no; then he says with a
    sort of moan:
"It's the cursèd cold, and it's got right hold till I'm chilled clean
    through to the bone.
Yet 'taint being dead—it's my awful dread of the icy grave that
    pains;
So I want you to swear that, foul or fair, you'll cremate my last re-
    mains."

A pal's last need is a thing to heed, so I swore I would not fail;
And we started on at the streak of dawn; but God! he looked ghastly
    pale.
He crouched on the sleigh, and he raved all day of his home in Ten-
    nessee;
And before nightfall a corpse was all that was left of Sam McGee.

There wasn't a breath in that land of death, and I hurried, horror-
    driven,
With a corpse half hid that I couldn't get rid, because of a promise
    given;
It was lashed to the sleigh, and it seemed to say: "You may tax your
    brawn and brains,
But you promised true, and it's up to you to cremate those last re-
    mains."

Now a promise made is a debt unpaid, and the trail has its own stem
    code.
In the days to come, though my lips were dumb, in my heart how I
    cursed that load.
In the long, long night, by the lone firelight, while the huskies,
    round in a ring,
Howled out their woes to the homeless snows—O God! how I
    loathed the thing.

And every day that quiet clay seemed to heavy and heavier grow;
And on I went, though the dogs were spent and the grub was get-
    ting low;

The trail was bad, and I felt half mad, but I swore I would not give in;
And I'd often sing to the hateful thing, and it hearkened with a grin.

Till I came to the marge of Lake Lebarge, and a derelict there lay;
It was jammed in the ice, but I saw in a trice it was called the "Alice May."
And I looked at it, and I thought a bit, and I looked at my frozen chum;
Then "Here," said I, with a sudden cry, "is my cre-ma-tor-eum."

Some planks I tore from the cabin floor, and I lit the boiler fire;
Some coal I found that was lying around, and I heaped the fuel higher;
The flames just soared, and the furnace roared—such a blaze you seldom see;
And I burrowed a hole in the glowing coal, and I stuffed in Sam McGee.

Then I made a hike, for I didn't like to hear him sizzle so;
And the heavens scowled, and the huskies howled, and the wind began to blow.
It was icy cold, but the hot sweat rolled down my cheeks, and I don't know why;
And the greasy smoke in an inky cloak went streaking down the sky.

I do not know how long in the snow I wrestled with grisly fear;
But the stars came out and they danced about ere again I ventured near;
I was sick with dread, but I bravely said: "I'll just take a peep inside.
I guess he's cooked, and it's time I looked;" . . . then the door I opened wide.

And there sat Sam, looking cool and calm, in the heart of the furnace roar;
And he wore a smile you could see a mile, and he said: "Please close that door.
It's fine in here, but I greatly fear you'll let in the cold and storm—
Since I left Plumtree, down in Tennessee, it's the first time I've been warm."

There are strange things done in the midnight sun
   By the men who moil for gold;

The Arctic trails have their secret tales
That would make your blood run cold;
The Northern Lights have seen queer sights,
But the queerest they ever did see
Was that night on the marge of Lake Lebarge
I cremated Sam McGee.

Robert Frost (1874–1963)

Robert Frost, bard of New England, was born in San Francisco. His father's death in 1885 prompted the family to resettle in Massachusetts. Frost married in 1895 and attended Harvard as a special student, but soon took up farming to make a living. In 1912 he moved his family to England to concentrate on writing, there publishing *A Boy's Will* (1913) and *North of Boston* (1915) to great accolades. Frost returned to the United States a major success, garnering fame and many academic residencies. Over a long and prolific career he won the Pulitzer Prize for poetry four times. Frost's personal life, by contrast, was often dark: his marriage was problematic, and his children died young and suffered from mental illness. Frost's verse is so technically accomplished as to appear virtually artless; similarly, a deep undercurrent of pessimism and existential despair tinges what is widely perceived as a Norman Rockwell-like wholesomeness of subject. "Ghost House" and "The Demiurge's Laugh" were both first collected in *A Boy's Will*.

Ghost House

I dwell in a lonely house I know
That vanished many a summer ago,
    And left no trace but the cellar walls,
    And a cellar in which the daylight falls
And the purple-stemmed wild raspberries grow.

O'er ruined fences the grapevines shield
The woods come back to the mowing field;
    The orchard tree has grown one copse
    Of new wood and old where the woodpecker chops;
The footpath down to the well is healed.

I dwell with a strangely aching heart
In that vanished abode there far apart
  On that disused and forgotten road
  That has no dust-bath now for the toad.
Night comes; the black bats tumble and dart;

The whippoorwill is coming to shout
And hush and cluck and flutter about:
  I hear him begin far enough away
  Full many a time to say his say
Before he arrives to say it out.

It is under the small, dim, summer star.
I know not who these mute folk are
  Who share the unlit place with me—
  Those stones out under the low-limbed tree
Doubtless bear names that the mosses mar.

They are tireless folk, but slow and sad—
Though two, close-keeping, are lass and lad—
  With none among them that ever sings,
  And yet, in view of how many things,
As sweet companions as might be had.

The Demiurge's Laugh

It was far in the sameness of the wood;
  I was running with joy on the Demon's trail,
Though I knew what I hunted was no true god.
  It was just as the light was beginning to fail
That I suddenly heard—all I needed to hear:
It has lasted me many and many a year.

The sound was behind me instead of before,
  A sleepy sound, but mocking half,
As of one who utterly couldn't care.
  The Demon arose from his wallow to laugh,
Brushing the dirt from his eye as he went;
And well I knew what the Demon meant.

I shall not forget how his laugh rang out.
    I felt as a fool to have been so caught,
And checked my steps to make pretense
    It was something among the leaves I sought
(Though doubtful whether he stayed to see).
Thereafter I sat me against a tree.

William Hope Hodgson (1877–1918)

British writer William Hope Hodgson published four noteworthy
novels of the supernatural, *The Boats of the "Glen Carrig"* (1907),
The House on the Borderland (1908), *The Ghost Pirates* (1909), and
The Night Land (1912). He also wrote many tales of horror and the
supernatural, gathered in *Carnacki the Ghost-Finder* (1913), *Men of
the Deep Waters* (1914), and other volumes. Most of his poetry was
published posthumously, following his death in a battle in World
War I. "Storm" first appeared in *The Calling of the Sea* (1920).

Storm

At sea; the night,
    Borne on a thunder-cloud,
Rushed vastly o'er the sky, and hid from sight
    The sun, as in a shroud.

And loathsome gloom
    Rolled o'er the fretful sea;
Rolled o'er, a curtain dark that hid the doom
    That waited there for me.

The tempest's howl
    I heard far o'er the deeps
Ring hollowly, a strange unearthly growl,
    Among the watery steeps.

Anon the wide
    Of that grim over-cast
Was cleft in twain and rent from side to side
    With lightnings from the vast.

And muttered roars,
    Of blasts that hoarsely bray,
Came from the void where the eternal shores
    Uprear their disarray.

The twanging shrouds
    Sang in that wintry breath.
The sea tossed up her belly to the clouds,
    And roared, insane, for death.

The ship drove high
    Upon a spumy swell;
Drove high, deep surging, 'neath that lonesome sky
    And diving—into silence fell.

Park Barnitz (1878–1901)

American poet David Park Barnitz is best known for his 1901 volume *The Book of Jade,* a classic of decadent poetry. Barnitz was born in West Virginia, but soon moved to Iowa when his Lutheran minister father was reassigned there. He attended college early, where his propensity for literature led him to study Sanskrit. In 1897 he entered Harvard to pursue Asian studies, including Hindu and Buddhist thought, receiving an M.A. There he composed *The Book of Jade,* the first half largely dealing with love, the second half with death. The book's theme is the utter negation of both the real and the ideal. Dense with imagery of decay and merciless in its use of irony, it reflects the influence of Eastern philosophy, Mallarmé, Poe, and especially Baudelaire, to whose memory it is dedicated. After graduation Barnitz returned home; his book was published anonymously, and not long after he died suddenly at the age of twenty-three, apparently the victim of congenital heart disease. "Mad Sonnet" and "Mankind" both appeared in *The Book of Jade.*

Mad Sonnet

Lo, in the night I cry out, in the night,
God! and my voice shall howl into the sky!
I am weary of seeing shapeless things that fly,
And flap into my face in their vile flight;

I am weary of dead things that crowd into my sight,
I am weary of hearing horrible corpses that cry,
God! I am weary of that lidless Eye
That comes and stares at me, O God of light!

All, all the world is become a dead blur,
God! God! and I, stricken with hideous blight,
Crouch in the black corners, and I dare not stir.

I am aweary of my evil plight.
If thou art not a dead corpse in thy sky,
Send thou down Death into my loathed sty!

Mankind

They do not know that they are wholly dead,
Nor that their bodies are to the worms given o'er;
They pass beneath the sky forevermore;
With their dead flesh the earth is cumbered.

Each day they drink of wine and eat of bread,
And do the things that they have done before;
And yet their hearts are rotten to the core,
And from their eyes the light of life is fled.

Surely the sun is weary of their breath,
They have no ears, and they are dumb and blind;
Long time their bodies hunger for the grave.

How long, O God, shall these dead corpses rave?
When shall the earth be clean of humankind?
When shall the sky cease to behold this death?

Edward Thomas (1878–1917)

British writer Edward Thomas wrote numerous travel volumes and the novel *The Happy-Go-Lucky Morgans* (1913). British poet Ralph Hodgson introduced Thomas to Robert Frost, who encouraged him to write poetry. Thomas's *Poems* (1917) appeared the same year that he died at the Battle of Arras in France. "Out in the Dark" was first published in *Last Poems* (1918).

Out in the Dark

Out in the dark over the snow
The fallow fawns invisible go
With the fallow doe;
And the winds blow
Fast as the stars are slow.

Stealthily the dark haunts round
And, when the lamp goes, without sound
At a swifter bound
Than the swiftest hound,
Arrives, and all else is drowned;

And star and I and wind and deer,
Are in the dark together,—near,
Yet far,—and fear
Drums on my ear
In that sage company drear.

How weak and little is the light,
All the universe of sight,
Love and delight,
Before the might,
If you love it not, of night.

––––––––––––––

Herman George Scheffauer (1878–1927)

American poet and translator Herman George Scheffauer became a pupil of Ambrose Bierce in San Francisco and published several volumes of poetry, including *Of Both Worlds* (1903) and *Looms of Life* (1908). He later emigrated to Germany, the land of his ancestors, and wrote a number of screeds against Woodrow Wilson and other American political figures. He also became one of the earliest English translators of the work of Thomas Mann. "Phantasmagoria" and "Lilith of Eld" were collected in *Of Both Worlds;* "The Shadow o'er the City," commemorating the San Francisco earthquake and fire of 1906, was collected in *Looms of Life.*

Phantasmagoria

Lost on this shadowland's phantasmal shore,
    By the bleak moor I stand, whose utmost bound
    Glooms to the realms of kings huge sorrows crowned
With iron crowns and Woe that dies no more,
No more while Memory lives. Clouds roll, winds roar
    Wild through the spectral heavens where spirits drowned
    With pain, float on the gray air-deeps;—no sound
Save sighing o'er those scenes well-loved of yore.
Unhappy, wandering shapes! with torment dire
    In this cloud-purgatory pent, in view
    Of coolest skies and waters meek and blue
As Jesus' eye, you feel once more the fire
Of old Earth passionate ere you expire
    In mists, where weakly this sad sun shines through.

Lilith of Eld

They tasted the sweet despair
    That flowed from her mortal kiss,
And they hung by one silken hair
    Above a black abyss!

For many had gone to wreck
    On the gleam of her coral lips,
By her shining finger's beck
    That boded no eclipse.

Then her smile had buried them
    As the waves the broken bark,

For what could bide or stem
  That magic dread and dark?

Deep down from her starry eyes
  The path led straight to hell,
And never the soul could rise
  That to their bottom fell.

She trod on the hearts of men,
  As they were pavement stones;
She danced, a light o' the fen,
  Across their charnel bones.

And the thoughts! the thoughts that rushed
  Like eagles from her eye—
And the smile—the smile that crushed
  The slaves it lured to die.

But a curse fell out of the night;
  It singled forth her head;
She vanished out of our sight
  And the world cried: She is dead!

She lived! she loved! she mourned!
  For a love she ne'er could own;
Her heart was racked and scorned
  With the vengeance she had sown.

And he, to whom this tale
  She told, lives doomed to write
The terror, tears and bale
  Of her—through night and night.

The Shadow o'er the City

(San Francisco)

Vast hung the moon o'er ruins black and prone,
  And where the torn, flame-stricken summits blight
  The heavens, there crouched all vigilant in light,
Two marble lions by a palace lone
Whose portals hungry weeds had overgrown,

Whose mangled walls gave ingress to the Night
And all her stars. There Silence sat upright,
Ash-crowned, and wrought a menace round her throne.

Low in the vales each litten thoroughfare
    Trembled, as Life, with roses tossing red,
        Danced in her glittering garments through the town;
But high across the still, moon-fettered air,
    Full on the living streets I saw the dead
        Look darkly and inexorably down.

Lord Dunsany (1878–1957)

Anglo-Irish novelist and dramatist Lord Dunsany (Edward John Moreton Drax Plunkett) became a pioneering writer of fantasy with such volumes as *The Gods of Pegāna* (1905), *A Dreamer's Tales* (1910), and *The Book of Wonder* (1912). He also wrote many fantasy novels, including *The King of Elfland's Daughter* (1924), *The Blessing of Pan* (1927), and *The Curse of the Wise Woman* (1933), and many plays. Late in life he published several volumes of poetry, including *Mirage Water* (1938), *War Poems* (1941), and *Wandering Songs* (1943). "Songs from an Evil Wood" (*Saturday Review* [London], February 24, 1917) and "The Watchers" (*Saturday Evening Post*, May 4, 1929) are taken from *Fifty Poems* (1929).

Songs from an Evil Wood

I
There is no wrath in the stars,
    They do not rage in the sky;
I look from the evil wood
    And find myself wondering why.

Why do they not scream out
    And grapple star against star,
Seeking for blood in the wood,
    As all things round me are?

They do not glare like the sky
        Or flash like the deeps of the wood;
But they shine softly on
        In their sacred solitude.

To their high happy haunts
        Silence from us has flown,
She whom we loved of old
        And know it now she is gone.

When will she come again
        Though for one second only?
She whom we loved is gone
        And the whole world is lonely.

II
Somewhere lost in the haze
        The sun goes down in the cold,
And birds in this evil wood
        Chirrup home as of old;

Chirrup, stir and are still,
        On the high twigs frozen and thin.
There is no more noise of them now,
        And the long night sets in.

Of all the wonderful things
        That I have seen in the wood
I marvel most at the birds,
        At their chirp and their quietude.

For a giant smites with his club
        All day the tops of the hill,
Sometimes he rests at night,
        Oftener he beats them still.

And a dwarf with a grim black mane
        Raps with repeated rage
All night in the valley below
        On the wooden walls of his cage.

And the elder giants come
        Sometimes, tramping from far,

Through the weird and flickering light
    Made by an earthly star.

And the giant with his club,
    And the dwarf with rage in his breath,
And the elder giants from far,
    They are all the children of Death.

They are all abroad to-night
    And are breaking the hills with their brood,
And the birds are all asleep,
    Even in Plugstreet Wood.

The Watchers

The world of old in its orbit moving
    Chanced to pass (if there's chance at all)
Near to the path of two Spirits' roving,
    Who stood and looked at the large green ball.

Morning flashed upon tusk and pinion,
    Tooth and talon, of tribes at war.
"Who, we wonder, will win dominion?
    Which will rule in the little star?"

Little scope there appeared for wonder:
    The mammoth strode from the forest's dusk.
Who but he, with his hooves of thunder?
    Who but he, with his lightning tusk?

Yet there seemed in his monstrous striding,
    Heaving weight and enormous ears,
Something gross. So, before deciding,
    "Come again in a million years."

Through the vault where the stars are sprinkled
    Ages passed from the world away.
All of that time Orion twinkled:
    Nothing changed in the Milky Way.

Again they stood where the world was rolling,
    Again they watched, and saw, this time, Man,

Heard the roar of his engines coaling,
　　Scanned his cities to guess his plan,

Peered through clouds that his smoke turned sour,
　　Even spied on his hopes and fears.
"Yes," they said, "he has surely power.
　　But, come again in a million years."

Wilfrid Wilson Gibson (1878–1962)

British poet Wilfrid Wilson Gibson was born in Northumberland but moved to London in 1912. His first published book of poetry was *Mountain Lovers* (1902). He served in the British Army during World War I, but did not go overseas; nevertheless, he wrote many stirring poems about the war. His poems were collected in such volumes as *Poems (1904–1917)* (1917), *Collected Poems: 1905–1925* (1926), and *The Island Stag* (1947). He also wrote several plays. "The Whisperers" and "The Lodging House" appeared in *Borderlands and Thoroughfares* (1914).

The Whisperers

As beneath the moon I walked,
Dog-at-heel my shadow stalked,
Keeping ghostly company:
And as we went gallantly
Down the fell-road, dusty-white,
Round us in the windy night
Bracken, rushes, bent and heather
Whispered ceaselessly together:
"Would he ever journey more,
Ever stride so carelessly,
If he knew what lies before,
And could see what we can see?"

As I listened, cold with dread,
Every hair upon my head
Strained to hear them talk of me,

Whispering, whispering ceaselessly:
"Folly's fool the man must be,
Surely, since, though where he goes
He knows not, his shadow knows:
And his secret shadow never
Utters warning words, or ever
Seeks to save him from his fate,
Reckless, blindfold, and unknown,
Till death tells him all, too late,
And his shadow walks alone."

The Lodging House

When up the fretful, creaking stair,
From floor to floor
I creep
On tiptoe, lest I wake from their first beauty-sleep
The unknown lodgers lying, layer on layer,
In the packed house from roof to basement
Behind each landing's unseen door;
The well-known steps are strangely steep,
And the old stairway seems to soar,
For my amazement
Hung in air,
Flight on flight
Through pitchy night,
Evermore and evermore.
And when at last I stand outside
My garret-door I hardly dare
To open it,
Lest, when I fling it wide,
With candle lit
And reading in my only chair,
I find myself already there . . .

And so must crawl back down the sheer black pit
Of hell's own stair,
Past lodgers sleeping layer on layer,
To seek a home I know not where.

John Masefield (1878–1967)

As a British youth John Masefield apprenticed aboard a naval train-
ing "school ship" and was later best known as an author of plain-
spoken poems of the sea and rural England. A prolific and long-lived
writer, his first book, *Salt-Water Ballads* (1902), remains one of his
best loved. This volume was followed by poetic dramas such as *The
Campden Wonder* (1907), novels such as *Captain Margaret* (1908),
and long narrative poems such as *The Everlasting Mercy* (1911),
which shocked many with frank depiction of country life. Masefield
also wrote children's novels and autobiography. An edition of his
Collected Poems was issued in 1923. He served as Poet Laureate of
the United Kingdom from 1930 until his death. "The Haunted" was
first collected in *King Cole and Other Poems* (1923).

The Haunted

Here, in this darkened room of this old house,
    I sit beside the fire. I hear again,
Within, the scutter where the mice carouse,
    Without, the gutter dropping with the rain.
Opposite, are black shelves of wormy books,
    To left, glazed cases, dusty with the same,
Behind, a wall, with rusty guns on hooks,
    To right, the fire, that chokes one panting flame.
Over the mantel, black as funeral cloth,
    A portrait hangs, a man, whose flesh the worm
Has mawed this hundred years, whose clothes the moth
    A century since, has channelled to a term.
I cannot see his face: I only know
He stares at me, that man of long ago.

I light the candles in the long brass sticks,
    I see him now, a pale-eyed, simpering man,
Framed in carved wood, wherein the death-watch ticks,
    A most dead face: yet when the work began
That face, the pale puce coat, the simpering smile,
    The hands that hold a book, the eyes that gaze,
Moved to the touch of mind a little while.
    The painter sat in judgment on his ways:

The painter turned him to and from the light,
     Talked about art, or bade him lift his head,
Judged the lips' paleness and the temples' white,
     And now his work abides; the man is dead.
But is he dead? This dusty study drear
Creaks in its panels that the man is here.

Here, beyond doubt, he lived, in that old day.
     "He was a Doctor here," the student thought.
Here, when the puce was new, that now is grey,
     That simpering man his daily practice wrought.
Here he let blood, prescribed the pill and drop,
     The leech, the diet; here his verdict given
Brought agonies of hoping to a stop,
     Here his condemned confessioners were shriven.
What is that book he holds, the key, too dim
     To read, to know; some little book he wrote,
Forgotten now, but still the key to him.
     He sacrificed his vision for his coat.
I see the man; a simpering mask that hid
A seeing mind that simpering men forbid.

Those are his books no doubt, untoucht, undusted,
     Unread, since last he left them on the shelves,
Octavo sermons that the fox has rusted,
     Sides splitting off from brown decaying twelves.
This was his room, this darkness of old death,
     This coffin-room with lights like embrasures,
The place is poisonous with him; like a breath
     On glass, he stains the spirit; he endures.
Here is his name within the sermon book,
     And verse, "When hungry Worms my Body eat";
He leans across my shoulder as I look,
     He who is God or pasture to the wheat.
He who is Dead is still upon the soul
A check, an inhibition, a control.

I draw the bolts. I am alone within.
     The moonlight through the coloured glass comes faint,
Mottling the passage wall like human skin,
     Pale with the breathings left of withered paint.

But others walk the empty house with me,
   There is no loneliness within these walls
No more than there is stillness in the sea
   Or silence in the eternal waterfalls.
There in the room, to right, they sit at feast;
   The dropping grey-beard with the cold blue eye,
The lad, his son, that should have been a priest,
   And he, the rake, who made his mother die.
And he, the gambling man, who staked the throw,
They look me through, they follow when I go.

They follow with still footing down the hall,
   I know their souls, those fellow-tenants mine,
Their shadows dim those colours on the wall,
   They point my every gesture with a sign.
That grey-beard cast his aged servant forth
   After his forty years of service done,
The gambler supped up riches as the north
   Sups with his death the glories of the sun.
The lad betrayed his trust; the rake was he
   Who broke two women's hearts to ease his own:
They nudge each other as they look at me,
   Shadows, all four, and yet as hard as stone.
And there, he comes, that simpering man, who sold
His mind for coat of puce and penny gold.

O ruinous house, within whose corridors
   None but the wicked and the mad go free.
(On the dark stairs they wait, behind the doors
   They crouch, they watch, or creep to follow me.)
Deep in old blood your ominous bricks are red,
   Firm in old bones your walls' foundations stand,
With dead men's passions built upon the dead,
   With broken hearts for lime and oaths for sand.
Terrible house, whose horror I have built,
   Sin after sin, unseen, as sand that slips
Telling the time, till now the heapèd guilt
   Cries, and the planets circle to eclipse.
You only are the Daunter, you alone
Clutch, till I feel your ivy on the bone.

John G. Neihardt (1881–1973)

American poet John Gneiseneau Neihardt was born in Illinois but moved with his family to Nebraska when he was ten; he subsequently became one of the most famous writers of that state. He drew upon the local culture, including the Native American reservations near his home, for much of his poetry. His first volume was *The Divine Enchantment* (1900), but he gained celebrity with a multi-volume poetic cycle, "A Cycle of the West," beginning with *The Song of Hugo Glass* (1915) and concluding with *The Song of Jed Smith* (1941). His many years of discussions with the Oglala holy man Black Elk led to the best-selling treatise *Black Elk Speaks* (1932). "The Voice of Nemesis" was included in *The Quest* (1916).

The Voice of Nemesis

You knew me of old and feared me,
Dreading my face revealed;
Temples and altars you reared me,
Wooed me with shuddering names;
Masking your fear in meekness,
You pæaned the doom I wield,
Wrought me a robe of your weakness,
A crown of your woven shames.

Image of all earth's error,
Big as the bulk of its guilt,
Lo, I darkled with terror,
A demon of spite and grudge;
You made me a vessel of fury
Brimmed with the blood you spilt;
With devils of hell for jury,
You throned me a pitiless judge.

For ever the wage of sorrow
Paid for the lawless deed;
Never the gray to-morrow
Paused for a pious price;
Never by prayer and psalter
Perished the guilty seed;

Vain was the wall at the altar,
The smoke of the sacrifice.

I come like a crash of thunder;
I come as a slow-toothed dread;
With fire and sword to plunder
Or only with lust and sloth.
By star or sun I creep or run,
And lo, my will was sped
By the might of the Mede, the hate of the Hun,
The bleak northwind of the Goth!

Yet, older than malice and cunning,
The love and the hate of your creed,
I smile in the blossom sunning,
I am hurricane lightning-shod!
Revealed in a myriad dresses,
I am master or slave at need.
You grope for my face with your guesses,
And kneel to your guess for a god.

I am one in the fall of the pebble,
The call of the sea to the stream,
The wrath of the starving rebel,
The plunge of the vernal thaw;
The yearning of things to be level,
The stir of the deed in the dream;
I am these—I am angel and devil—
I am Law!

Siegfried Sassoon (1886–1967)

British poet Siegfried Sassoon published some poetry prior to World
War I, but it was his service in that war and the poetry that he wrote
during and after the conflict that made his reputation, with such vol-
umes as *Counter-Attack* (1918) and *Suicide in the Trenches* (1918).
After the war he gained celebrity for *Memoirs of a Fox-Hunting Man*
(1928), the first of three volumes of fictionalized autobiography that
have come to be called the Sherston Trilogy. His *Collected Poems*

1908–1956 appeared in 1961. "Haunted" and "Goblin Revel" both appeared in *The Old Huntsman and Other Poems* (1917).

Haunted

Evening was in the wood, louring with storm.
A time of drought had sucked the weedy pool
And baked the channels; birds had done with song.
Thirst was a dream of fountains in the moon,
Or willow-music blown across the water
Leisurely sliding on by weir and mill.

Uneasy was the man who wandered, brooding,
His face a little whiter than the dusk.
A drone of sultry wings flicker'd in his head.
The end of sunset burning thro' the boughs
Died in a smear of red; exhausted hours
Cumber'd, and ugly sorrows hemmed him in.

He thought: "Somewhere there's thunder," as he strove
To shake off dread; he dared not look behind him,
But stood, the sweat of horror on his face.

He blunder'd down a path, trampling on thistles,
In sudden race to leave the ghostly trees.
And: "Soon I'll be in open fields," he thought,
And half remembered starlight on the meadows,
Scent of mown grass and voices of tired men,
Fading along the field-paths; home and sleep
And cool-swept upland spaces, whispering leaves,
And far off the long churring night-jar's note.

But something in the wood, trying to daunt him,
Led him confused in circles through the thicket.
He was forgetting his old wretched folly,
And freedom was his need; his throat was choking.
Barbed brambles gripped and clawed him round his legs,
And he floundered over snags and hidden stumps.
Mumbling: "I will get out! I must get out!"
Butting and thrusting up the baffling gloom,

Pausing to listen in a space 'twixt thorns,
He peers around with peering, frantic eyes.

An evil creature in the twilight looping,
Flapped blindly in his face. Beating it off,
He screeched in terror, and straightway something clambered
Heavily from an oak, and dropped, bent double,
To shamble at him zigzag, squat and bestial.

Headlong he charges down the wood, and falls
With roaring brain—agony—the snap't spark—
And blots of green and purple in his eyes.
Then the slow fingers groping on his neck,
And at his heart the strangling clasp of death.

Goblin Revel

In gold and grey, with fleering looks of sin,
I watch them come; by two, by three, by four,
Advancing slow, with loutings they begin
Their woven measure, widening from the door;
While music-men behind are straddling in
With flutes to brisk their feet across the floor,—
And jangled dulcimers, and fiddles thin
That taunt the twirling antic through once more.

They pause, and hushed to whispers, steal away.
With cunning glances; silent go their shoon
On creakless stairs; but far away the dogs
Bark at some lonely farm: and haply they
Have clambered back into the dusky moon
That sinks beyond the marshes loud with frogs.

Vincent Starrett (1886–1974)

American critic and bookman Charles Vincent Starrett, born in To-
ronto, was a longtime journalist in Chicago, working for several
Chicago newspapers as book critic. He published important scholar-
ship on Arthur Machen and Ambrose Bierce. Among his critical

volumes are *Buried Caesars* (1923) and *The Private Life of Sherlock Holmes* (1933). *Books Alive* (1940), *Bookman's Holiday* (1942), and other volumes collect some of his newspaper reviews. His poetry is scattered over various volumes and anthologies. "Villon Strolls at Midnight" is taken from *Estrays* (1920), a volume that included poetry by Starrett, George Seymour, Thomas Kennedy, and Basil Thompson.

Villon Strolls at Midnight

"There is an eerie music, Tabary,
    In the malevolence of the wind tonight:
    Think you the spirits of the damned make flight
O' midnights? Gad, a wench I used to see
Heard all the ghosts of history ride past
    Her window on a shrieking gale like this . . .
    Look! Where the moonlight and the shadows kiss!
Saw you aught move? . . . Poor jade, she died unmassed.
See, where the gibbet rises, gaunt and slim!
    (Curse me! The wind hath thrust my entrails through.)
    It beareth fruit tonight—Not me, nor you! . . .
Hark to the clatter of the bones of him.
    They rattle like—Ah, do you catch your breath?—
    Like castanets clapped in the hands of Death!"

Georg Heym (1887–1912)

Georg Heym was born in Lower Silesia (now Poland) and studied law in Berlin. There he formed Der Neue Club of Berlin with other young, disaffected authors in opposition to what they perceived to be the apathy and decadence of the Wilhelmine era. Held together by a rather vague emotive philosophy—a Neues Pathos—they went on to stage a Neopathetisches Cabaret where the members held public readings. The group later came to be classified as literary Expressionists in their attempt to penetrate reality's appearance and render its essence in a condensed, intensified—and usually distorted—manner. Heym's first published books were the drama *Der Athener Ausfahrt* (1907; The Athens Departure) and the treatise *Versuch einer neuen Religion* 1909; An Attempt at a New Religion); the poetry volumes *Der Gott der Stadt* (1910; The God of the City) and *Der ewige Tag* (1911; The Eternal Day) followed. Heym's work is filled with grotesque, apocalyptic imagery, evoking powerful demonic forces that threaten incipient destruction. The author died tragically attempting to save a friend from drowning during an ice skating outing. *Umbra Vitae* (1912), *Marathon* (1914), and *Der Dieb: Ein Novellenbuch* (1913; The Thief: A Book of Stories) were issued posthumously. "The Demons of the Cities" ("Die Damonen der Stadte") was first collected in *Der ewige Tag*.

The Demons of the Cities

They stride amidst the night of the city,
the very darkness flinching from their step;
black clouds of smoke and soot swirl
like jack-tar's beards about their jaws.

Their vast shadows mottle the sea of houses,
spattering the lamplight along the avenue,
and slide like heavy fog along the pavement,
groping tentatively, slowly, building by building.

Feet planted now in a square of the plaza,
knees resting now upon a building's turret,
their bodies fill the heavens where dark rain streams,
pan pipes chorusing through the tumult of clouds.

Shuffling their feet in refrain with the ritornello
above the ocean of roofs in a dismal dirge—
a mighty death song, now muffled, now shrill,
ululating wildly and swelling into the night.

They parallel the river, black and wide,
like a reptile with back mottled yellow
by the street lamps, sluggishly slithering,
as darkness smothers like a veil the stars.

Leaning heavily on the pier of a bridge
they grope with their hands into the swarm
of pedestrians, like fauns who on the edge

of a swamp forage with an arm in the ooze.

One stands up. The white moon is obscured
as if by a black mask. The pitch of night
descends like a leaden curtain from dark sky
and hastens the houses' retreat, as if into a pit.

The city's clavicle cracks, and there bursts
the seam of a roof, awash in lambent flame.
At once the demons straddle the building
and shriek like feral cats to the firmament.

In a room crowded suddenly with palpable dark
screams a young mother-to-be struggling in labor.
Her vital body bolts erect from the mattress
and she is encircled by the colossal devils.

She clutches herself, trembling on a rack of pain,
and the room spins about her with their howls.
Now comes forth the fruit: her womb gapes red
and bleeding, rended from around the infant.

The devils crane their necks forth like giraffes.
The newborn has no head. The mother offers
it up with extended arms. Splaying at her spine,
webbed fingers of fear topple her backwards.

And now the demons are grown immense, soaring,
their crowns of horn ripping the reddening sky.
Earthquakes are thundering through the city,
the clattering of hooves arising to the fire aloft.

[tr. Steven J. Mariconda]

Rupert Brooke (1887–1915)

British poet Rupert Brooke attended Rugby and King's College, Cambridge, where he became a member of the Cambridge Apostles, a group of writers and philosophers. He was later associated with the Bloomsbury group and was acquainted with such writers as Virginia Woolf and Lytton Strachey. He began writing poetry as early as 1905. As a result of an emotional crisis in 1913, he traveled to the United States and Canada, returning by way of the South Seas. His poetry of this period reflects his wide-ranging travels. In 1914 he joined the Royal Navy and saw action in Antwerp and elsewhere; but in early 1915 he developed sepsis from a mosquito bite and died on April 23, 1915. His poems were gathered posthumously as *The Collected Poems of Rupert Brooke* (1915). "Dead Men's Love" was apparently written in the period 1908–11.

Dead Men's Love

There was a damned successful Poet;
    There was a Woman like the Sun.
And they were dead. They did not know it.
    They did not know their time was done.
        They did not know his hymns
        Were silence; and her limbs,
        That had served Love so well,
        Dust, and a filthy smell.

And so one day, as ever of old,
    Hands out, they hurried, knee to knee;
On fire to cling and kiss and hold
    And, in the other's eyes, to see
        Each his own tiny face,
        And in that long embrace
        Feel lip and breast grow warm
        To breast and lip and arm.

So knee to knee they sped again,
    And laugh to laugh they ran, I'm told,
Across the streets of Hell . . .
            And then
    They suddenly felt the wind blow cold,
        And knew, so closely pressed,
        Chill air on lip and breast,
        And, with a sick surprise,
        The emptiness of eyes.

Samuel Loveman (1887–1976)

American poet and bookman Samuel Loveman worked as a rare book specialist in bookstores in Cleveland and New York City for much of his life. His long poem *The Hermaphrodite* appeared in 1926. His shorter poetry was scattered in many amateur journals and little magazines; some of it was collected in *The Hermaphrodite and Other Poems* (1936). A more extensive collection of his verse, along with short stories and other work, is found in *Out of the Immortal Night: Selected Works of Samuel Loveman* (2004). "Ship of Dreams" first appeared in the *Kansas Zephyr* (February 1906).

Ship of Dreams

Over the silent mere it drifts,
Far through the purple dusk and night,
Into the depths and foaming rifts,
Leaving a wake of pallid light.

Fantastic shadows come and go,
Vanishing in the amber sea;
Wraiths shimmer from the shallop's bow,
And beck and point and whisper to me.

Over the western rim it dips,
Parting a glint, a gleam of gold:
Breeze-born a song from deathless lips
And all the world is bitter cold.

Conrad Aiken (1889–1973)

American writer Conrad Aiken was raised by his great-great-aunt after his father killed his mother and himself when Conrad was eleven. He was a fellow student of T. S. Eliot at Harvard and studied under George Santayana. His earliest book publications were such poetry volumes as *Earth Triumphant* (1911) and *The Jig of Forslin* (1916). His literary corpus includes novels, short stories, and criticism. He is the author of two celebrated horror tales, "Mr. Arcularis" (1931) and

"Silent Snow, Secret Snow" (1932), both included in *Among the Lost People* (1934); the former was turned into a play of the same title (1957). "La Belle Morte" was included in *The Jig of Forslin*.

La Belle Morte

I.

As one who dreams, in a light sleep, may hear
Sounds through his dream,—bells, or passing steps
On the floor above him, or in the street below,—
Rhythmic, precise and clear:
Or voices muttering in an adjacent room,
Lifting a moment, to die again;—
Yet all the while he will pursue his dream,
Guessing a sinister purport in well-known sounds,
And still in his own deep silent world remain:
So now I guess the world from which I came,
In flares of light, ghosts of remembered sound,
Which haunt me here . . . A voice, a street, a bell . . .
Whence do I come, and why? And what's my name?

And you, who cut an orange upon a plate,
With a small silver knife, and lean, and smile,—
You whose mouth is a sly carnivorous flower,
Whose flesh is softer and cooler than rainy wind,—
I gaze upon you, and muse strange aberrations,
I hear unearthly music, ghostly flutes;
I dance in a black eclipse, and through my veins
Is a cold froth of sea; and you are forgotten . . .

And you, who when your act is over peer
Witchlike between the curtains, above the footlights,
Holding the curtains with jewelled hands, to smile
A slow and mordant smile from cavernous eyes—
What hideous things amuse you secretly?
What have you drunk to make your lips so red?
And when the moon creeps up, and stars dance coldly,
And crickets cry in the dew, and dead leaves fall,
Do you spread bat-wings from a starlit wall? . . .

   *   *   *

Music dissolves and dies,—and sings again,
Changing its mood; the lights wink out in darkness,
A shrill wind crosses us, we are blown and stagger.
Our footsteps ring intense. The lights return.
And we have silently changed . . . To what, to whom?

II.

Midnight it was, or just before;
And as I dipt for the hundredth time
The small white quill to add a rhyme
To the cold page, in candlelight,
Whereon my treatise slowly grew,—
Someone harshly knocked at the door;
And marvelling I became aware
That with that knock the entire night
Went mad; a sudden tempest blew;
And shrieking goblins rode the air.

Alarmed, not knowing why, I rose
And dropt my quill across the page.
What demon now, what archimage,
So roiled the dark? And my blood froze
When through the keyhole, with the wind,
A freezing whisper, strangely thinned,
Called my name out, called it twice . . .
My heart lay still, lay black as ice.
The candle trembled in my hands;
Between my fingers the dim light went;
Shadows hurried and shrank and blent,
Huddled, grotesque, in sarabands,
Amazed my eyes, till dumb I stood,
And seemed to see upon that air
Goblins with serpents in their hair,
Mouths contorted for soundless cries,
And hands like claws, and wounded throats,
And winking embers instead of eyes.
The blood went backward to my heart.
Thrice in the night a horn was blown.
And then it seemed that I had known,

For ages, even before my birth,
When I was out with wind and fire,
And had not bargained yet with earth,
That this same night the horn would blow
To call me forth. And I would go.
And so, as haunted dead might do,
I drew the bolt and dropped the chain,
And stood in dream, and only knew
The door had opened and closed again:
Until between my eyelids came
A woman's face, a sheath of flame,
The wink of opals in dusky hair,
A golden throat, a smile like fire,
And eyes that seemed to burn the air
So luminous were they with desire.
She laid one hand upon my arm
And straight a blaze was in my veins,
It pierced me so I feared a charm,
And shrank; whereat, pale, hurriedly,
She whispered "Quickly! Come with me!
All shall be clear! But now make haste—
Four hours till dawn, no time to waste!"—
The amazing whiteness of her skin
Had snared my eyes, and now her voice
Seethed in my ears, and a ghost of sin
Died, and above it I heard rejoice
Loud violins, in chords ascending,
And laughter of virgins; I blew the light,
And followed her, heedless of the ending,
Into the carnival of that night.

Make haste, beloved! the night passes,
The day breaks, the cock crows,
Mist slinks away in the sunlight,
And the thin blood drips from the rose.

Black stallions rushed us through the air,
Their hooves upon the wind struck fire;
Rivers, and hills, and a moonlit spire
Glided beneath us, and then a flare
Of gusty torches beckoned us down

To a palace-gate in a darkened town.
She took my hand and led me in
Through walls of basalt and walls of jade,
And I wondered, to hear a violin
Sweetly within that marble played.
I heard it sing, a wandering tone,
Imprisoned forever in that deep stone.

And then upon a couch we lay,
And heard invisible spirits play
A ghostly music; the candles muttered,
Rose-leaves trembled upon the floor,
Lay still, or rose on the air and fluttered;
And while the moon went dwindling down
Poisoning with black web the skies,
She narrowed her eyelids, and fixed her eyes,
Fiercely upon me; and searched me so
With speeding fire in every shred
That I, consumed with a witching glow,
Knew scarcely if I were alive or dead:
But lay upon her breast, and kissed
The deep red mouth, and drank the breath,
And heard it gasping, how it hissed
To mimic the ecstasy of death.
Above us in a censer burning
Was dust of lotos-flowers, and there
Ghosts of smoke were ever turning,
And gliding along the sleepy air,
And reaching hands, and showing faces,
Or coiling slowly like blue snakes,
To charm us moveless in our places . . .
But then she softly raised her head
And smiled through brooding eyes, and said
"O lover, I have seen you twice.
You changed my veins to veins of ice.
The first time, it was Easter Eve,—
By the church door you stood alone;
You listened to the priests intone
In pallid voices, mournfully;
The second time you passed by me

In the dusk, but did not see . . ."
Her whisper hissed through every vein
And flowered coldly in my brain . . .
I slept, how long I do not know;
But in my sleep saw huge lights flare,
And felt a rushing of wild air,
And heard great walls rock to and fro . . .
Make haste, beloved! The cock crows,
And the cold blood drips from the rose . . .

. . . And then I woke in my own room,
And saw the first pale creep of sun
Drip through the dewy shutters, and run
Across the floor, and in that gloom
Marvelled to find that I had slept
Still fully dressed, and that I kept
One bruised white rose-leaf in my hand—
From whom?—and could not understand.

For seven days my quill I dipt
To wreathe slow filigrees of script:
For seven nights when midnight came,
I swooned, I swept away on flame,
Rushed on the stallions of the air,
Heard goblins laugh, saw torches flare,
And all night long, while music mourned
Hidden under the trembled floor,
I heard her low strange voice implore
As one who speaks from under the earth,
Imploring music, imploring mirth,
Before the allotted time was done
And cock crew up the sullen sun.
Day by day my face grew pale,
Hollowed and purple were my eyes,
I blinked beneath too brilliant sides:
And sometimes my weak hand would fail,
Blotting the page whereon I wrought . . .
This woman is a witch! I thought . . .
And I resolved that night to find
If this were real, or in my mind.

Viol and flute and violin
Remote through labyrinths complained.
Her hand was foam upon my skin.
And then I closed my eyes and feigned
A sudden sleep; whereat her eyes
Peered, and darkened, and opened wide,
Her white brow flushed, and by my side
Laughing, with little ecstatic cries,
She kissed my mouth, she stroked my hair,
And fed upon me with fevered stare.
"One little drop!" she murmured then—
"One little bubble from this red vein,
And safe I await the sun again—"
I heard my heart hiss loud and slow;
A gust of wind through the curtains came;
It flapped the upright candle-flame.
Her famishing eyes began to glow,
She bared my arm; with a golden pin,
Leaned, and tenderly pricked the skin.
And as the small red bubble rose,
Her eyes grew bright with an evil light,
She fawned upon me; and my heart froze
Seeing her teeth so sharp and white . . .

Vampire! I cried. The flame puffed out.
Two blazing eyes withdrew from me.
The music tore discordantly.
The darkness swarmed with a goblin rout.
Great horns shattered, and walls were falling,
Green eyes glowed, voices were calling;
And suddenly then the night grew still,
The air blew suddenly damp and chill,
Stars above me paled in the sky,
Far off I heard one mournful cry—
Or under the earth—and then I found
I lay alone on the leafy ground.
And when stars died, and the cock crowed,
The first pale pour of sunlight showed
That it was on a grave I lay,
A new-made grave of tumbled clay.

That night I took a priest with me;
And sharp at the midnight, secretly,
By lantern-light, with spade and pick,
Striking on stones with loamy click,
We laid a golden coffin bare,
And sprinkled the holy water there.
And straight we heard a sorrowful cry;
Something upon the dark went by;
The trees thrashed in a sudden gust;
Pebbles rattled in windy dust,
Far off, wildly, pealed a bell,
A voice sobbed, and silence fell.
And I grew sad, to think that I
Should make that marvellous spirit die . . .

Make haste, beloved! The night passes,
The day creeps, the cock crows,
Mist slinks away in the pale sun
And the opened grave must close.

III.

Vampires, they say, blow an unearthly beauty,
Their bodies are all suffused with a soft witch-fire,
Their flesh like opal . . . their hair like the float of night.
Why do we muse upon them, what secret's in them?
Is it because, at last, we love the darkness,
Love all things in it, tired of too much light?
Here on the lamplit pavement, in the city,
Where the high stars are lost in the city's glow,
The eyes of harlots go always to and fro—
They rise from a dark world we know nothing of,
Their faces are white, with a strange love—
And are they vampires, or do I only dream? . . .
Lamps on the long bare asphalt coldly gleam.

And hearing the ragtime from a cabaret,
And catching a glimpse, through turning doors,
Of a spangled dancer swaying with drunken eyes,

Applauded and stared at by pimps and whores—
What decadent dreams before us rise? . . .

The pulse of the music thickens, it grows macabre,
The horns are a stertorous breath,
Someone is dying, someone is raging at death . . .
Around a coffin they dance, they pelt dead roses,
They stand the coffin on end, a loud spring clangs,
And suddenly like a door the coffin uncloses:
And a skeleton leers upon us in evening dress,—
There in the coffin he stands,
With his hat in his white-gloved hands,
And bows, and smiles, and puffs at a cigarette.
Harlots blow kisses to him, and fall, forgotten,
The great clock strikes; soft petals drift to the floor;
One by one the dancers float through the door,
Hair is dust, flesh is rotten,
The coffin goes down into darkness, and we forget . . .

Who told us this? Was it a music we heard,
A picture we saw, a dream we dreamed? . . .
I am pale, I am strangely tired.
A warm dream lay upon me, its red eyes gleamed,
It sucked my breath . . . It sighed . . . It afflicted me . . .
But was that dream desired, or undesired?

We must seek other tunes, another fragrance:
This slows the blood in our hearts, and cloys our veins.
Open the windows. Show us the stars. We drowse.

H. P. Lovecraft (1890–1937)

Howard Phillips Lovecraft, though known as an eminent American writer of the weird tale, considered himself primarily a poet for the first part of his literary career. At this time he was intensely devoted to English verse of the manner of Dryden and Pope. He found a broader audience for his work upon joining two amateur press associations in his early twenties. He soon realized that prose was a more suitable medium of expression for his cosmic imagination, but continued to write poems sporadically for the rest of his life. His best verse falls squarely into two categories—satirical and fantastic. The latter achieves its pinnacle in *Fungi from Yuggoth* (written 1929–30). This poetic sequence on the themes of alienation, expectancy, and continuity embodies the bizarre imagery found in his fiction in the form of thirty-six finely turned sonnets. "Despair" was first published in *Pine Cones* (June 1919). "To a Dreamer" first appeared in the *Coyote* (January 1921). "The Wood" first appeared in the *Tryout* (January 1929). Of the *Fungi from Yuggoth* sonnets, "The Book" first appeared in the *Fantasy Fan* (October 1934), "Zaman's Hill" in *Driftwind* (October 1934), "The Courtyard" in *Weird Tales* (September 1930), "The Howler" in *Driftwind* (November 1932), "A Memory" in *Fungi from Yuggoth* (1943), "Night-Gaunts" in the *Providence Journal* (26 March 1930), "Nyarlathotep" in *Weird Tales* (January 1931), "The Familiars" in *Driftwind* (July 1930), and "Continuity" in *Pioneer* (Summer 1932).

Despair

O'er the midnight moorlands crying,
Thro' the cypress forests sighing,
In the night-wind madly flying,
    Hellish forms with streaming hair;
In the barren branches creaking,
By the stagnant swamp-pools speaking,
Past the shore-cliffs ever shrieking;
    Damn'd daemons of despair.

Once, I think I half remember,
Ere the grey skies of November
Quench'd my youth's aspiring ember,
    Liv'd there such a thing as bliss;
Skies that now are dark were beaming,
Gold and azure, splendid seeming
Till I learn'd it all was dreaming—
    Deadly drowsiness of Dis.

But the stream of Time, swift flowing,
Brings the torment of half-knowing—

Dimly rushing, blindly going
      Past the never-trodden lea;
And the voyager, repining,
Sees the grisly death-fires shining,
Hears the wicked petrel's whining
      As he helpless drifts to sea.

Evil wings in ether beating;
Vultures at the spirit eating;
Things unseen forever fleeting
      Black against the leering sky.
Ghastly shades of bygone gladness,
Clawing fiends of future sadness,
Mingle in a cloud of madness
      Ever on the soul to lie.

Thus the living, lone and sobbing,
In the throes of anguish throbbing,
With the loathsome Furies robbing
      Night and noon of peace and rest.
But beyond the groans and grating
Of abhorrent Life, is waiting
Sweet Oblivion, culminating
      All the years of fruitless quest.

To a Dreamer

I scan thy features, calm and white
Beneath the single taper's light;
Thy dark-fring'd lids, behind whose screen
Are eyes that view not earth's demesne.

And as I look, I fain would know
The paths whereon thy dream-steps go;
The spectral realms that thou canst see
With eyes veil'd from the world and me.

For I have likewise gaz'd in sleep
On things my mem'ry scarce can keep,
And from half-knowing long to spy
Again the scenes before thine eye.

I, too, have known the peaks of Thok;
The vales of Pnath, where dream-shapes flock;
The vaults of Zin—and well I trow
Why thou demand'st that taper's glow.

But what is this that subtly slips
Over thy face and bearded lips?
What fear distracts thy mind and heart,
That drops must from thy forehead start?

Old visions wake—thine op'ning eyes
Gleam black with clouds of other skies,
And as from some demoniac sight
I flee into the haunted night.

The Wood

They cut it down, and where the pitch-black aisles
     Of forest night had hid eternal things,
They scal'd the sky with tow'rs and marble piles
     To make a city for their revellings.

White and amazing to the lands around
     That wondrous wealth of domes and turrets rose;
Crystal and ivory, sublimely crown'd
     With pinnacles that bore unmelting snows.

And through its halls the pipe and sistrum rang,
     While wine and riot brought their scarlet stains;
Never a voice of elder marvels sang,
     Nor any eye call'd up the hills and plains.

Thus down the years, till on one purple night
     A drunken minstrel in his careless verse
Spoke the vile words that should not see the light,
     And stirr'd the shadows of an ancient curse.

Forests may fall, but not the dusk they shield;
     So on the spot where that proud city stood,
The shuddering dawn no single stone reveal'd,
     But fled the blackness of a primal wood.

From Fungi from Yuggoth

I. The Book

The place was dark and dusty and half-lost
In tangles of old alleys near the quays,
Reeking of strange things brought in from the seas,
And with queer curls of fog that west winds tossed.
Small lozenge panes, obscured by smoke and frost,
Just shewed the books, in piles like twisted trees,
Rotting from floor to roof—congeries
Of crumbling elder lore at little cost.

I entered, charmed, and from a cobwebbed heap
Took up the nearest tome and thumbed it through,
Trembling at curious words that seemed to keep
Some secret, monstrous if one only knew.
Then, looking for some seller old in craft,
I could find nothing but a voice that laughed.

VII. Zaman's Hill

The great hill hung close over the old town,
A precipice against the main street's end;
Green, tall, and wooded, looking darkly down
Upon the steeple at the highway bend.
Two hundred years the whispers had been heard
About what happened on the man-shunned slope—
Tales of an oddly mangled deer or bird,
Or of lost boys whose kin had ceased to hope.

One day the mail-man found no village there,
Nor were its folk or houses seen again;
People came out from Aylesbury to stare—
Yet they all told the mail-man it was plain
That he was mad for saying he had spied
The great hill's gluttonous eyes, and jaws stretched wide.

IX. The Courtyard

It was the city I had known before;
The ancient, leprous town where mongrel throngs
Chant to strange gods, and beat unhallowed gongs
In crypts beneath foul alleys near the shore.
The rotting, fish-eyed houses leered at me
From where they leaned, drunk and half-animate,
As edging through the filth I passed the gate
To the black courtyard where the man would be.

The dark walls closed me in, and loud I cursed
That ever I had come to such a den,
When suddenly a score of windows burst
Into wild light, and swarmed with dancing men:
Mad, soundless revels of the dragging dead—
And not a corpse had either hands or head!

XII. The Howler

They told me not to take the Briggs' Hill path
That used to be the highroad through to Zoar,
For Goody Watkins, hanged in seventeen-four,
Had left a certain monstrous aftermath.
Yet when I disobeyed, and had in view
The vine-hung cottage by the great rock slope,
I could not think of elms or hempen rope,
But wondered why the house still seemed so new.

Stopping a while to watch the fading day,
I heard faint howls, as from a room upstairs,
When through the ivied panes one sunset ray
Struck in, and caught the howler unawares.
I glimpsed—and ran in frenzy from the place,
And from a four-pawed thing with human face.

XVII. A Memory

There were great steppes, and rocky table-lands
Stretching half-limitless in starlit night,
With alien campfires shedding feeble light
On beasts with tinkling bells, in shaggy bands.

Far to the south the plain sloped low and wide
To a dark zigzag line of wall that lay
Like a huge python of some primal day
Which endless time had chilled and petrified.

I shivered oddly in the cold, thin air,
And wondered where I was and how I came,
When a cloaked form against a campfire's glare
Rose and approached, and called me by my name.
Staring at that dead face beneath the hood,
I ceased to hope—because I understood.

XX. Night-Gaunts

Out of what crypt they crawl, I cannot tell,
But every night I see the rubbery things,
Black, horned, and slender, with membraneous wings,
And tails that bear the bifid barb of hell.
They come in legions on the north wind's swell,
With obscene clutch that titillates and stings,
Snatching me off on monstrous voyagings
To grey worlds hidden deep in nightmare's well.

Over the jagged peaks of Thok they sweep,
Heedless of all the cries I try to make,
And down the nether pits to that foul lake
Where the puffed shoggoths splash in doubtful sleep.
But oh! If only they would make some sound,
Or wear a face where faces should be found!

XXI. Nyarlathotep

And at the last from inner Egypt came
The strange dark One to whom the fellahs bowed;
Silent and lean and cryptically proud,
And wrapped in fabrics red as sunset flame.
Throngs pressed around, frantic for his commands,
But leaving, could not tell what they had heard;
While through the nations spread the awestruck word
That wild beasts followed him and licked his hands.

Soon from the sea a noxious birth began;
Forgotten lands with weedy spires of gold;
The ground was cleft, and mad auroras rolled
Down on the quaking citadels of man.
Then, crushing what he chanced to mould in play,
The idiot Chaos blew Earth's dust away.

XXVI. The Familiars

John Whateley lived about a mile from town,
Up where the hills begin to huddle thick;
We never thought his wits were very quick,
Seeing the way he let his farm run down.
He used to waste his time on some queer books
He'd found around the attic of his place,
Till funny lines got creased into his face,
And folks all said they didn't like his looks.

When he began those night-howls we declared
He'd better be locked up away from harm,
So three men from the Aylesbury town farm
Went for him—but came back alone and scared.
They'd found him talking to two crouching things
That at their step flew off on great black wings.

XXXVI. Continuity

There is in certain ancient things a trace
Of some dim essence—more than form or weight;
A tenuous aether, indeterminate,
Yet linked with all the laws of time and space.
A faint, veiled sign of continuities
That outward eyes can never quite descry;
Of locked dimensions harbouring years gone by,
And out of reach except for hidden keys.

It moves me most when slanting sunbeams glow
On old farm buildings set against a hill,
And paint with life the shapes which linger still
From centuries less a dream than this we know.
In that strange light I feel I am not far
From the fixt mass whose sides the ages are.

Harold Vinal (1891–1965)

Harold Vinal was born in Maine, whose environs are often the subject of his poems. His primary vocation was editor and publisher, most notably of the quarterly poetry magazine *Voices*. His poems began appearing in regional journals around 1920 and were published in hardcover in the Yale Younger Poets Series volume *White April* (1922), a collection of traditionally styled nature lyrics. Subsequent poetry collections include *Voyager* (1923), *Island Born* (1925), *Nor Youth Nor Age* (1925), *A Stranger in Heaven* (1927), *Hurricane: A Maine Coast Chronicle* (1936), and *The Compass Eye* (1944), and were complemented by the nonfiction volume *Attic for the Nightingale* (1944). His *Selected Poems* appeared in 1948. The following two poems appeared in *White April*.

Apparition

She was mirage and dream and little more,
Moving, it seemed, to dirges played on strings
Of frozen basses in the empty wings
Of theaters behind tragic bolt and door.
She was, at best, a phantom in the mind,
Astonished if one looked at her or spoke—
A statue in a niche, a figure shrined
Between the dark and light—not air, but smoke.

And so she came and went, and though men turned
To gaze at her and marvel, she was one
Too virtuous to be at all concerned.
She crossed the stage of Life, and there was none
Who spoke of her as woman or could boast
Of her as being more than just a ghost.

Ghostly Reaper

Now while the wind is up I hear
A dark scythe swung in air,
A door creaks by the crooked elm—
Who is reaping there?

```
*    *    *
```

Who goes to cut the field tonight
Beside the lily pond?
Who comes to swing a rusty scythe
From limbo, or beyond?

Clark Ashton Smith (1893–1961)

American poet and fiction writer Clark Ashton Smith published several volumes of poetry under the tutelage of George Sterling: *The Star-Treader and Other Poems* (1912), *Odes and Sonnets* (1918), *Ebony and Crystal* (1922), and *Sandalwood* (1925). These volumes created a sensation in his native California, but Smith did not establish a national reputation. In the late 1920s he took to writing fantastic fiction, producing more than 130 stories in six or seven years; much of this work was later collected in such volumes as *Out of Space and Time* (1942), *Lost Worlds* (1944), and *Genius Loci* (1948). His *Complete Poetry and Translations* appeared in 3 volumes in 2007–08. "Ode to the Abyss" and "The Eldritch Dark" first appeared in *The Star-Treader and Other Poems*. "The Medusa of Despair" was first published in *Town Talk* (San Francisco; 20 December 1913). "The Tears of Lilith" and "A Vision of Lucifer" were first published in *Ebony and Crystal*.

Ode to the Abyss

O many-gulfed, unalterable one,
Whose deep sustains
Far-drifting world and sun,
Thou wast ere ever star put out on thee;
And thou shalt be
When never world remains;
When all the suns' triumphant strength and pride
Is sunk in voidness absolute,
And their majestic music wide
In vaster silence rendered mute.
And though God's will were night to dusk the blue,
And law to cancel and disperse
The tangled tissues of the universe,

His might were impotent to conquer thee,
O indivisible infinity!
Thy darks subdue
All light that treads thee down a space,
Exulting over thine archetypal deeps.
The cycles die, and lo! thy darkness reaps
The flame of mightiest stars;
In aeon-implicating wars
Thou tearest planets from their place;
Worlds granite-spined
To thine erodents yield
Their treasures centrally confined
In crypts by continental pillars sealed.
What suns and worlds have been thy prey
Through unhorizoned reaches of the past!
What spheres that now essay
Time's undimensioned vast,
Shall plunge forgotten to thy gloom at length
With life that cried its query of the Night
To ears with silence filled!
What worlds unborn shall dare thy strength,
Girt by a sun's unwearied might,
And dip to darkness when the sun is stilled!

O incontestable Abyss,
What light in thine embrace of darkness sleeps—
What blaze of a sidereal multitude
No peopled world is left to miss!
What motion is at rest within thy deeps—
What gyres of planets long become thy food—
Worlds unconstrainable
That plunged therein to peace
Like tempest-worn and crew-forsaken ships;
And suns that fell
To huge and ultimate eclipse,
And from the eternal stances found release!
What sound thy gulfs of silence hold!
Stupendous thunder of the meeting stars
And crash of orbits that diverged,
With Lfe's thin song are merged;

Thy quietudes enfold
Paean and threnody as one,
And battle-blare of unremembered wars
With festal songs
Sung in the Romes of ruined spheres;
And music that belongs
To undiscoverable younger years
With words of yesterday.
Ah! who may stay
Thy soundless world-devouring tide?
O thou whose hands pluck out the light of stars,
Are worlds but as a destined fruit for thee?
May no sufficient bars
Nor marks inveterate abide
As shores to baffle thine unbillowing sea?
Still and unstriving now,
What plottest thou,
Within thy universe-ulterior deeps,
Dark as the final lull of suns?
What new advancement of the night
On citadels of stars around whose might
Thy slow encroachment runs
And crouching silence thunder-potent sleeps?

The Eldritch Dark

Now as the twilight's doubtful interval
Closes with night's accomplished certainty,
A wizard wind goes crying eerily,
And on the wold misshapen shadows crawl,
Miming the trees, whose voices climb and fall,
Imploring, in Sabbatic ecstasy,
The sky where vapor-mounted phantoms flee
From the scythed moon impendent over all.

Twin veils of covering cloud and silence, thrown
Across the movement and the sound of things,
Make blank the night, till in the broken west
The moon's ensanguined blade awhile is shown. . . .
The night grows whole again. . . . The shadows rest,
Gathered beneath a greater shadow's wings.

The Medusa of Despair

I may not mask for ever with the grace
Of woven flowers thine eyes of staring stone:
Ere the lithe adders and the garlands blown,
Parting their tangle, have disclosed thy face
Lethal as are the pale young suns in space—
Ere my life take the likeness of thine own—
Get hence! the dark gods languish on their throne,
And flameless grow the Furies they embrace.

Regressive, through what realms of elder doom
Where even the swart vans of Time are stunned,
Seek thou some tall Cimmerian citadel,
And proud demonian capitals unsunned
Whose ramparts, ominous with horrent gloom,
Heave worldward on the unwaning light of hell.

The Tears of Lilith

O lovely demon, half-divine!
Hemlock and hydromel and gall,
Honey and aconite and wine
Mingle to make that mouth of thine—

Thy mouth I love: but most of all
It is thy tears that I desire—
Thy tears, like fountain-drops that fall
In gardens red, Satanical;

Or like the tears of mist and fire,
Wept by the moon, that wizards use
To secret runs when they require
Some silver philtre, sweet and dire.

A Vision of Lucifer

I saw a shape with human form and face,
If such should in apotheosis stand:
Deep in the shadows of a desolate land

His burning feet obtained colossal base,
And spheral on the lonely arc of space,
His head, a menace unto heavens unspanned,
Arose with towered eyes that might command
The sunless, blank horizon of that place.

And straight I knew him for the mystic one
That is the brother, born of human dream,
Of man rebellious at an unknown rod;
The mind's ideal, and the spirit's sun;
A column of clear flame, in lands extreme,
Set opposite the darkness that is God.

Robert Graves (1895–1985)

British poet, essayist, and novelist Robert Graves served in the British Army in World War I and issued his first volume of poetry, *Over the Brazier,* in 1916. Several more volumes of poetry followed during and after the war. Graves gained celebrity with the brash autobiography *Good-bye to All That* (1929) as well as such historical novels of the classical world as *I, Claudius* (1934), *Claudius the God* (1934), and *Count Belisarius* (1938). He later wrote *The Greek Myths* (1955) as well as a controversial study of myth, *The White Goddess* (1948). He continued to write poetry prolifically and published dozens of volumes of his verse. "The Haunted House" was first collected (as "Ghost Raddled") in *Country Sentiment* (1920).

The Haunted House

"Come, surly fellow, come: a song!"
      What, fools? Sing to you?
Choose from the clouded tales of wrong
      And terror I bring to you:

Of a night so torn with cries,
      Honest men sleeping
Start awake with rabid eyes,
      Bone-chilled, flesh creeping,

Of spirits in the web-hung room
        Up above the stable,
Groans, knockings in the gloom,
        The dancing table,

Of demons in the dry well
        That cheep and mutter,
Clanging of an unseen bell,
        Blood choking the gutter,

Of lust frightful past belief
        Lurking unforgotten,
Unrestrainable endless grief
        In breasts long rotten.

A song? What laughter or what song
        Can this house remember?
Do flowers and butterflies belong
        To a blind December?

Frank Belknap Long (1901–1994)

American poet and fiction writer Frank Belknap Long published a slim volume of poetry early in his career, *A Man from Genoa and Other Poems* (1926); a later volume, *The Goblin Tower* (1935), was assembled and published by H. P. Lovecraft and R. H. Barlow. Long wrote numerous tales of horror and the supernatural for *Weird Tales* and other pulp magazines from the 1920s onward; some were collected in *The Hounds of Tindalos* (1946), *The Rim of the Unknown* (1972), and other volumes. He also wrote several horror and science fiction novels. His verse was collected in *In Mayan Splendor* (1977); uncollected verse appeared in *The Darkling Tide* (1995). "The Goblin Tower" and "The Abominable Snow-Men" (*Weird Tales*, June/July 1931) were both collected in *The Goblin Tower*.

The Goblin Tower

The Goblin Tower stood and stood
        And stood for years and years:

And it was haunted splendidly
    By twenty thousand Fears.

The Fears were tall and very old,
    With scars upon their faces;
And there were Greek and Hindoo Fears,
    And Fears of Saxon races.

The Tower's windows looked upon
    A moat of thunderous green;
And red lights shone behind the panes
    Where gallant ghosts had been.

The ghosts were shyer than the rats
    That lived in Roland's hall;
And they reposed upon the chairs
    Or walked upon the wall.

Until the Fears took up the lance
    And chased them screaming hence;
And now they wander in the moat
    Or climb the castle fence.

I dreamed the Goblin Castle fell
    And vanished in the night:
And yet for years and years and years
    It was a gorgeous sight.

The Abominable Snow Men

Blue shadows lay upon the crater's rim,
    And far above the town a traveler moved
In circles through the snow; his eyes were dim
    From glint of sun on ice in worlds unproved.

A thousand feet below him at an inn
    His host smiled wanly, said: "The fool will find
Small prints upon the snow—so small, so thin—
    He will not know that they are prints which bind."

"He will not know that they are prints which bind!"
    His very words gained substance on a height,

As to his knees the traveler fell, half-blind,
    And groveled in the dimness of his sight.

"They dwell in barrows on a skyward wold
    And make no sound; shrill hunger is their goad:
'Tis said they feed on men when men are bold;
    When men are scarce, on flesh of fowl or toad."

The silence on the heights gave way to shrieks
    As to a shattered cairn the traveler clung
And fought a shape with bright and slimy streaks
    Of blood upon its fat, protruding tongue.

They came in swarms from out the crater's rim;
    The thin snow men, abominable and cold;
They came in swarms, and tore him limb from limb,
    And strewed his flesh in ribbons on the wold.

Robert E. Howard (1906–1936)

American fantasy and horror writer Robert Ervin Howard began writing stories as a teenager and published many tales in *Weird Tales* and other pulp magazines. Most of his stories revolve around heroic figures such as Conan the Cimmerian, Solomon Kane, King Kull, and Bran Mak Morn. He wrote poetry sporadically throughout his life but never attempted to collect it in a volume; it was gathered posthumously in *Always Comes Evening* (1957) and other volumes. His collected poetry was published in a limited edition in 2008. "Dead Man's Hate" was first published in *Weird Tales* (January 1930). "Recompense" first appeared in *Weird Tales* (November 1938).

Dead Man's Hate

They hanged John Farrel in the dawn amid the market-place;
At dusk came Adam Brand to him and spat upon his face.
"Ho neighbors all," spake Adam Brand, "see ye John Farrel's fate!
'Tis proven here a hempen noose is stronger than man's hate!

"For heard ye not John Farrel's vow to be avenged on me
Come life or death? See how he hangs high on the gallows tree!"
Yet never a word the people spake, in fear and wild surprise—
For the grisly corpse raised up its head and stared with sightless eyes,

And with strange motions, slow and stiff, pointed at Adam Brand
And clambered down the gibbet tree, the noose within its hand.
With gaping mouth stood Adam Brand like a statue carved of stone,
Till the dead man laid a clammy hand hard on his shoulder-bone.

Then Adam shrieked like a soul in hell; the red blood left his face
And he reeled away in a drunken run through the screaming market-
    place;
And close behind, the dead man came with face like a mummy's mask,
And the dead joints cracked and the stiff legs creaked with their un-
    wonted task.

Men fled before the flying twain or shrank with bated breath,
And they saw on the face of Adam Brand the seal set there by death.
He reeled on buckling legs that failed, yet on and on he fled;
So through the shuddering market-place, the dying fled the dead.

At the riverside fell Adam Brand with a scream that rent the skies;
Across him fell John Farrel's corpse, nor ever the twain did rise.
There was no wound on Adam Brand but his brow was cold and
    damp,
For the fear of death had blown out his life as a witch blows out a lamp.

His lips were writhed in a horrid grin like a fiend's on Satan's coals,
And the men that looked on his face that day, his stare still haunts
    their souls.
Such was the doom of Adam Brand, a strange, unearthly fate;
For stronger than death or hempen noose are the fires of a dead
    man's hate.

Recompense

I have not heard lutes beckon me, nor the brazen bugles call,
But once in the din of a haunted lea I heard the silence fall.
I have not heard the regal drum, nor seen the flags unfurled,
But I have watched the dragons come, fire-eyed, across the world.

I have not seen the horsemen fall before the hurtling host,
But I have paced a silent hall where each step waked a ghost.
I have not kissed the tiger-feet of a strange-eyed golden god,
But I have walked a city's street where no man else had trod.

I have not raised the canopies that shelter revelling kings,
But I have fled from crimson eyes and black unearthly wings.
I have not knelt outside the door to kiss a pallid queen,
But I have seen a ghostly shore that no man else has seen.

I have not seen the standards sweep from keep and castle wall,
But I have seen a woman leap from a dragon's crimson stall
And I have heard strange surges boom that no man heard before,
And seen a strange black city loom on a mystic night-black shore.

And I have felt the sudden blow of a nameless wind's cold breath,
And watched the grisly pilgrims go that walk the roads of Death,
And I have seen black valleys gape, abysses in the gloom,
And I have fought the deathless Ape that guards the Doors of
    Doom.

I have not seen the face of Pan, nor mocked the dryad's haste,
But I have trailed a dark-eyed Man across a windy waste.
I have not died as men may die, nor sinned as men have sinned,
But I have reached a misty sky upon a granite wind.

Donald Wandrei (1908–1987)

American poet and short story writer Donald Wandrei began writing for *Weird Tales* and other pulp magazines in the later 1920s. His tales were gathered in *The Eye and the Finger* (1944), *Strange Harvest* (1965), and other volumes. He published two early volumes of poetry, *Ecstasy and Other Poems* (1928) and *Dark Odyssey* (1931); many years later he issued *Poems for Midnight* (1964). His *Collected Poems* appeared in 1988; an augmented edition was published in 2008 as *Sanctity and Sin.* "Nightmare" was first published in *Ecstasy and Other Poems.* *Sonnets of the Midnight Hours* first appeared as a unit in *Poems for Midnight;* many of the individual poems had appeared in the 1920s and 1930s in *Weird Tales.*

Nightmare

And after this, there came to me one green
    With all the dreadful cerements of the grave,
    Who shambled down the midnight's empty pave
With flapping tatters and long talons lean.
And of his face, there was no vestige seen,
    And all his flesh to rottenness was slave;
    He leered so vilely, Horror could not save
Itself from horror at those eyes' blind sheen.
And of that thing there came to me a fear
    So great, I clawed my face to bleeding strips,
        And turned to flee that corpse's hideous head.
But everywhere I looked, I saw it near,
    And saw it smile, with fleshless, gaping lips,
        For I was his, that horror of the dead.

From Sonnets of the Midnight Hours

The Old Companions

Amidst great cobwebs hanging everywhere
My old companions waited all around:
Stray hands and heads that crawled; in nests I found
Part human creatures creeping from their lair.
Out of a dusky corner came the stare
Of some gray form that made a rattling sound.
Along the walls dwelt living mummies, bound
In swathes of softly searching sentient hair.

What goal, what new companion did I seek?
Was it an hour? Eternity? A week?—
Until I felt that tongue or talon stroke
My neck, and heard that husky, gurgling choke
As of some ancient corpse about to speak. . . .
I could not move though mind and spirit broke.

The Prey

Vast wings were flapping in the night. I heard
Them fill the air with measureless strong beat—
What nameless hunter searching for its meat?
So huge the wings, I wondered what the bird
That clove through midnight where no other stirred,
What sight in later hours would haply greet
The dawn, when those great wings had made retreat;
For in the talons I was fast immured.

Though endlessly we traversed far abysses,
At length all motion ceased, upon a crag.
And when the talons loosened, I could see
The burning harpy eyes, head of a hag,
Before I dropped away, for I was free—
To fall amid colossal precipices.

The Hungry Flowers

The fleshly flowers whispered avidly:
This being's face is soft, he shall not pass;
And all the little jeweled blades of grass
Made mutterings that sounded like low glee.
I looked across the great plain warily.
Those glittering swords that shone like splintered glass,
Though singly impotent, might be in mass
A savage, indestructible enemy.

So hesitantly, I put forth my foot
To seek, beneath the flower-heads, a path.
I found my leg become a hellish root,
I saw the hungry flowers toward me crawl
With bright-eyed ecstasy, exultant wrath,
And on my flesh their mouths, devouring, fall.

Escape

Now was I destined after all to die,
I who had fought so hard to reach my goal?
Would maggots in my starved, gaunt body loll
When I collapsed beneath that burning sky?

The sun stared on me like a blood-red eye,
In all this hideous land the only soul.
Yet, when toward farther desolate wastes I stole,
I thought ironic laughter passed me by.

Though they who tortured me were far behind,
My bloodprints in the dead sand marked my trail.
Each step eternal, on I struggled, trying
To reach the haven I would never find.
I stumbled onward, knowing I must fail,
For they were deathless hunters, I the dying.

The Ultimate Vision

I dreamed the waters of the world had died,
The ocean beds were open now, and free,
And all strange things once covered by the sea
Showed everywhere, while flopping creatures died.
There lay a bed of shells and bones; I spied
A city of a vast antiquity;
Ten thousand ships and more; shapes great and wee
And weird encrusted forms on every side.

I saw the vales and mountains of the deep,
I saw the dwellers of the ocean night,
The weedy pastures and the drowned, the dead;
And in the fading vision of my sleep
I saw rise up a substance soft and white
That feebly moved its pulpy, eyeless head.

Joseph Payne Brennan (1918–1990)

American fiction writer and poet Joseph Payne Brennan began pub-
lishing horror tales in *Weird Tales* and other pulp magazines in the
1950s, among them such classic stories as "Slime," "Canavan's Back
Yard," and "Levitaton." His tales were collected in such volumes as
Nine Horrors and a Dream (1958), *Scream at Midnight* (1963), *Sto-
ries of Darkness and Dread* (1973), and *The Borders Just Beyond*
(1986). Brennan also wrote several volumes of stories involving the

psychic detective Lucius Leffing. He was a prolific weird poet, and his verse was typified by relatively traditional horrific motifs and an artlessly simple diction. It was gathered in *Nightmare Need* (1964), *Sixty Selected Poems* (1985), *Look Back on Laurel Hill* (1989), and other volumes. Brennan was also a publisher, running the small press Macabre House and the occasional journal *Macabre* (1957f.). "The Scythe of Dreams" was first published in August Derleth's anthology *Fire and Sleet and Candlelight* (1961) and reprinted in *Nightmare Need* as well as in Brennan's later collection, *Sixty Selected Poems* (1985).

The Scythe of Dreams

Sleepers are mangled by the scythe of dreams;
every spastic turning takes a knife.
Out of childhood's thicket creeps the ghost
we thought was banished with the hopscotch squares.
Out of the drunken tunnel of our loves
the old sad terrors slowly reel.
Fears have flaming faces; gains are lost.
Naked in our nightmare need, we know at last
the fissures never filled, the crevices we kept.
We glimpse again with eyes that lose their lids
the grey ineffable ghoul of all our days.

Stanley McNail (1918–1995)

American poet Stanley McNail was born in Illinois but moved to San Francisco in 1950, where he published such well-regarded journals as *Nightshade* (devoted to macabre poetry) and the *Galley Sail Review*. He also established the small poetry presses Galley Sail Press and Nine Hostages Press. He published several poetry collections in his lifetime, including *Footsteps in the Attic* (1958) and *Black Hawk Country* (1960). His weird verse was gathered in *Something Breathing* (1965) and *At Tea in the Mortuary* (1991). "The House on Maple Hill" was first published in August Derleth's *Fire and Sleet and Candlelight* (1961) and reprinted in *Something Breathing*.

The House on Maple Hill

The old house waits for no one.
It only seems to wait
Behind the weedy hedges
And flaking iron gate.

The window frame is sightless:
It only seems to stare.
Those are not really voices,
But tricks of summer air.

Yet something always makes us start
As though from sudden chill,
And hold our breath when we pass by
The house on Maple Hill.

Donald Sidney-Fryer (b. 1930)

American poet and critic Donald Sidney-Fryer published *Songs and Sonnets Atlantean,* a scintillating volume of poetry in verse and prose, in 1971. Since the late 1950s he had been acquainted with Clark Ashton Smith, and he became Smith's leading critic and bibliographer. In recent years Sidney-Fryer has published a second (2003) and third (2005) series of *Songs and Sonnets Atlantean;* all three series were gathered in *The Atlantis Fragments* (2008). "Midnight Visitant" first appeared in *Songs and Sonnets Atlantean: The Second Series.*

Midnight Visitant

The old grandfather clock out in the hall
Strikes twelve, then stops, its monstrous tick-tock stilled,
As if in answer to some daemon's call:

Silence profound . . . might it be daemon-willed?
He sits unmoving, but much more than chilled;
He feels such fright, he scarcely dares to breathe.

Will his own pulse be likewise daemon-stilled?
Why do such fears at midnight need to seethe,
Or as . . . in *whose* firm flesh some baleful daemon's teeth may
    teethe?

A prodigy comes forth, a presence out of time antique—
Whose tall and all-aspiring horns vertumnal flowers enwreathe—
A snub-nosed, goat-legged lad, moustached, with beard and bristled
    cheek:

The man leaps up, renewed; his heart from fear shall not convulse;
The shape moves out of view, beyond; the clock resumes its pulse.

Richard L. Tierney (b. 1936)

American author Richard Louis Tierney is a well-known name in weird fiction. A native of Iowa, Tierney spent his early years in Oregon, Alaska, and elsewhere in the U.S. Forest Service. He also traveled to Mexico and Central and South America exploring archaeological sites, a milieu he later used in his fiction. His first book publication, the novel *The Winds of Zarr* (1975), was followed by *For the Witch of Mists* (1978), beginning a series of collaborations with David C. Smith. A devotee of science fiction and sword-and-sorcery, Tierney counts H. P. Lovecraft and Robert E. Howard among his literary influences. His poetry volumes include *Collected Poems: Nightmares and Visions* (1981; an earlier version of this collection appeared as *Dreams and Damnations,* 1975); *The Blob That Gobbled Abdul and Other Poems and Songs* (2000), and *Savage Menace and Other Poems* (2009). Tierney is also the creator of a long-running series of stories featuring Gnostic heresiarch Simon of Gitta. "The Evil House" first appeared in *Nyctalops* (February 1972). "To the Hydrogen Bomb" first appeared in the *Diversifier* (March 1977).

The Evil House

The old house totters near the edge of town,
Enshrouded in a still and subtle gloom;
Gaunt, gaping windows seem to scowl and frown

Like sightless sockets from the face of Doom
On passersby who flitter up and down
Heedless of Those who watch from every room.
But townsfolk hasten quickly on their way
When dusk-winds usher in the close of day.

An unseen essence casts a dismal pall
Over this house of grim and mottled gray
Where furtive footsteps through each room and hall
Echo at dusk, though none can truly say
Whose steps those are that hover at the fall
Of night, or why no children ever play
In the old garden where rank weeds abound
And fungi bloat upon a curious mound.

Cold night-winds blow—the old house stands aloof,
Scowlingly scornful of each howling gust.
Old bones lie white beneath its creaking roof;
Between two ribs a pitted blade stands thrust.
The lightnings flash—marks of a cloven hoof
Are limned an instant in the thick-piled dust—
Then white bones clatter fearsomely and rise
To madly dance beneath the thundering skies.

Behind dark-looming clouds a dim moon hides,
And wooden shutters blow with dismal creaks;
A hate-mad poet in the loft abides
And taunts the whistling wind with gleeful shrieks;
But when at last the howling storm subsides,
A flute pipes eerily, a viol squeaks,
And from the attic drifts an evil tune
To mock the calm and greet the leering moon.

Beneath high gables of this bleak abode
Weird laughter from a lighted garret rings
And echoes down the drear and dripping road
To draw from darkness ancient, evil things.
The moonlight glimmers on a great black toad
That arches to the roof on monstrous wings,
Drawn from deep caves by necromantic spells
To that high room where the mad poet dwells.

Above the stairwell ancient timbers groan
And shadows hide a lurking form from sight.
The staircase creaks beneath a wheezing crone
Who drags her aged frame up the long flight
Where the black lurker waits, to her unknown,
With eyes that glitter strangely in the night.
Then morbid laughter sounds—a long knife gleams—
And silence shatters to mad, gurgling screams.

A fear-fraught stillness shrouds the huddled hulk
Which sprawls beside the stair to rise no more,
Till from deep shadows gnomish creatures skulk
And creep in stealth across the creaking floor
To lift and bear the hapless grandam's bulk
Silently through the gaping cellar door,
Down rotting steps to those black regions where
The foul-eyed Feaster slavers in its lair.

Now as the black-cowled steeples toll their bells
To stir the stillness of the midnight air,
And moon-mad witches cast their noxious spells
O'er dreamers wrapped in visions quaint and fair
To drag their fancies down to nightmare's hells,
There comes a footstep on the attic stair—
And one may glimpse against the window-blind
A shadow-shape whose source would blast the mind.

A slumbering beauty stirs in dreams of dread
Before she wakes to see the shape that stands
In shadowed darkness hunched beside her bed,
And shrieks with terror as its clutching hands
Grope icily across her huddled head
To grip her throat with claws like iron bands.
But screams are quickly stilled for want of breath—
And nightmare's terrors dissipate in death.

To the Hydrogen Bomb

O Mushroom-cloud unfolding o'er the world,
    No terrors in *my* soul do you inspire;

Within this breast a dreadful hate lies furled,
    Hotter by far than your atomic fire.

Beneath your shadow some crouch down in fear
    (Though most still go their mundane, maudlin ways),
But I await the day when all shall hear
    Your crashing peal and char beneath your rays.

I wait—for when your thunder shakes the skies
    And blafts the towering cities to the sands,
Then you, like to a new-born Sun, shall rise
    And blaze your radiance forth to all the lands!

Within the whiteness of your fiery core
    The dawning of a brighter age I see—
When, in the crescendo of all-ending War,
    Mankind shall all be gathered unto thee.

––––––––––––––––––––

Bruce Boston (b. 1943)

American poet Bruce Boston is a leading author of weird and speculative poetry. He received a B.A. and M.A. in economics from the University of California at Berkeley and lived in the Bay Area for many years. Among his many poetry collections are *Alchemical Texts* (1985), *The Nightmare Collector* (1988), *Sensuous Debris: Selected Poems 1970–1995* (1995), *Pitchblende* (2003), and *The Nightmare Collection* (2008). He has also written several novels and story collections, including *Stained Glass Rain* (1993), *The Complete Accursed Wives* (2000), and *Masque of Dreams* (2001). He has received the Rhysling Award, the Pushcart Prize, the Bram Stoker Award, and the first Grandmaster Award from the Science Fiction Poetry Association. "The Nightmare Collector" appeared in the poetry volume of that title. "Ghost Blood" appeared in *Pitchblende*.

The Nightmare Collector

Each night he calls you
for the leading role
in his gallery

of ancestral tableaus
that trails back
through the Pleistocene
to the red primeval.

From the endless slashes
in his voluminous greatcoat
you can feel the heat
of captured bodies
invade your rumpled bed
with delirium and fever,
you can smell a brassy
sediment of tears.

From the hollow blackness
of his flapping sleeves
you can hear the pulse
and thump of unborn shadows,
a dense hysteric fugue
winding up and down
the bones of your sleep.

The nightmare collector
waits on the landing
in the unlit hall
where the instruments
of ablation are arranged
on cold leather pallets,
where the dreamer's
balustrade of terror
rushes across landscapes
of a darkening retina,
where snakes coil about
your arms and ankles
and draw you down
bodily into a forest
of bloodstained hair.

Ghost Blood

It seeps into your life
from the wounded past,
from the etheric bodies
of dead friends and lovers
who tramp the corridors
of your dreams and nightmares.

Invisible to the naked eye,
its stains are ineradicable:
gathering beneath your nails,
rorschached in a passing cloud,
overheard in random scraps
of strangers' conversations.

Three parts sorrow,
two of self-recrimination,
a measure of dark imagination,
it flows with hemophiliac abandon
unstaunched by bandages
and tourniquets alike.

And on some grave day
unbeknownst to your
incinerated or embalmed self,
your own ghost blood will
acquire such morbid traits
for those who survive.

Brett Rutherford (b. 1947)

American poet and publisher Brett Rutherford founded the Poet's Press in 1971 and held many poetry readings in New York City. He has published many chapbooks of his own poetry; larger collections include *Whippoorwill Road* (1985; rev. 1998) and *Poems from Providence* (1991). He has also published *Night Gaunts* (1993), a play about H. P. Lovecraft, and two horror novels, *Piper* (1987) and *The*

Lost Children (1988). "Fête" was first published in the revised edition of *Whippoorwill Road*.

Fête

A thousand stars will blaze and sing tonight.
The livid day has blown before itself
all clouds to leave this sepulchre of sky
a barren bowl of paranoiac suns.
Come I this eve into my mirthless wood,
this colonnade of grey-striped masts,
to celebrate some lisping, rhymèd love?
I am Love's Antichrist—my barbed-wire heart
has never beat in time with another's!

Though it is June, I crave the bite of ice.
I send the Leveler, wind fanged by North
to sink its hoarfrost tooth into the world,
crisping the maple red, browning the oak.
I cannot pass tonight where green things hope.
I banish Persephone's corn bounties.
No leaf that has the glint of chlorophyll
can last a moment in my chilling gusts.
Precede me, airborne, wasting Nothingness,
lay for my feet a carpet sere and gray,
a trail of ash from my Hadean robe,
dust of the murdered summers I've renounced.

My eye sees all in inverse images:
the near is far, the far away my toy.
Each chink of sky leaps like a broken pane
from where it hangs suspended on a branch,
or like a painted sliver where the trees
thrust down to meet horizon—it is these stars,
my witnesses, who hover near, while elms,
by web-line weaving architecture thrust,
fade to infinity, night's palette mad.

I close my cloak about my throat, hold tight
the leaden box I bear. The curve of earth
blinks out the last scant gleam of the village,

save one blanched clapboard church, desanctified,
which grinds against Pleiades as they rise.
Its steeple breath exhales the lidless bats,
purblind, carnivorous doves of my court.
Fly up and out, and with your leather wings
make me an arbor black with rabid pride!
Along my way, an abandoned boneyard
lifts limestone paws and graven platitudes
against me. I laugh at hallowed places,
defying their passive, limp corruption.
My eyes spit fire. The unkempt grass explodes.
The crosses singe, the solemn obelisks
crack and shatter, the marble angels fall.
No crucifix or holy sign can stay
what I would call and consummate tonight.

Do you suspect me? Would even *your* fortress
of intuition guard against *this*?
My tentacles of ink reach out for you.
You send a moon, and in its sickly glare
the smoking earth rears up two night monsters—
four horns unfolding red, gigantic,
blood wet and throbbing as they block my way.
Horns become ears, I recognize the heads
of guardian owls, elm-high and screeching
as they snap their beaks, their eyes all-seeing.
I pass in silence through their talon clutch
for they are but conjured—and *I am real*.

Would you cast dreams against my greater force?
Hurl Elmo's fire against my juggernaut?
Ah, soon, comes my reward for nights denied;
for all the days I circled your dwelling,
outcast while others consumed your beauty;
for those half-loved because some hint of you
haunted an eye or a cheekbone—revenge,
my calm last gift for your squandered passion.

I cough a cloud and let it blot the moon
so that no distant star may hear and mock
the oath that is sworn in the hidden copse.

Here! now even fireflies are dimming out,
now ravens avert their ebony orbs,
now sputter and die, ye will o' the wisp!
Not even a random thought can penetrate
this furry arbor of my wretchedness.

Open the box,
be sure the sacred objects are counted.
Be sure the unspeakable ointments gleam
in the krater-shaped Plutonian cup.
Lay out the black and scarlet vestments now,
set forth another cup with water drawn
blind from a mountain spring in midnight oaths,
scoop graveyard earth burned free of worms and roots
into the center of the Pentagram,
light the black candle *now*,
step from the arbor and bid *you* come:

Hear me, ye formless, boundless nameless ones,
Ye captive essences of fire and air,
by this dread Ring and Stone which all obey
I conjure Ye to take the form I dream.
Give me NOCTURNE, bat-winged and silver-reined
(the beast whom once I saw lust-seeking Pan
ride round the earth in an hour's passing!).

I shall not move, yet on his back my will
shall leap these mountains, beat over cities,
hell-ride the hard Atlantic sea-line,
then swoop, then scan the forest
then fall with unrelenting speed
onto your lawn.

Touch not the door which has been daubed in blood
against my coming and going. Sing out
your piercing call to the shuttered window,
where the cat, whom I have collared a slave
of my impulse, will beckon you to look
at the flat fanged face of my messenger.
In an instant, you are borne away,
your scream to no avail, your bedclothes ripped
as you graze the upper treetops, held firm

in ten claws beneath the throbbing wing beats.

I am waiting for you,
for the sound of descending wings,
waiting for the years denied me
to curl into a wrinkled ball
that some hot maelstrom draws
into its belly.
I am dancing the death of romance.
Dizzily, you rise from your abduction.
You do not know me yet in this darkness.

I take your hand. You speak my name
in anger and astonishment. Your touch
is just as I imagined it, frail and terrified.
Your eyes would plead your innocence, your lips
would say that none but I have tasted them.
I would believe you for the sake of those eyes,
had I not left humanity behind.
Your arms invite my dissolution, death
in one touch of your supple shoulders,
but I dare to finish what I started.

Come, love, come stand by me,
let me anoint thy fevered brow,
kneel amid knives and Pentagram,
bowing your head for the severing blow
        or blood's obscene baptism,
and thus, and *thus,*
with what still trembles in the cup,
with earth, with fire,
with midnight waters I place to your lips,
with ivory rings I now produce
from soulless lead and velvet lairs,

as all the bats take mawkish flight,
as leaves drift down upon your hair,
as stars seal our troth
with burning glaze
I do
thee wed.

G. Sutton Breiding (b. 1950)

American author George Sutton Breiding is known primarily for his dark fantasy poems and prose, along with reviews and essays, in the amateur press. Born in West Virginia, he later settled in San Francisco. He has published several fanzines and appeared in many others. His books include *Autumn Roses* (1984), *Necklace of Blood* (1988), *Journal of an Astronaut* (1992), and *Hallucinating Jenny* (2000). "The Worm of Midnight" and "Black Leather Vampyre" were first collected in *Autumn Roses*.

The Worm of Midnight

Into this heady wine of solitude
A slow and gnawing Worm does oft intrude:
The Worm of Time that chews away the hours,
And leaves black stains upon spring's flowers;
The Worm of memory that poisons night's desire,
And turns to bone the fingers on the lyre;
The Worm of love whose breath makes roses sere,
And all love's honeyed kisses less than dear;
The Worm of beauty that flies with pricks of pain,
And fleeing, leaves its formless image in the rain;
The Worm of silence that wriggles in the heartwood
                 of the cadenced line,
And breaks all singing's splendour like a hollow spine.
Slowly, with the victor's patience, the Worm crawls by:
Its hunger, vast and bournless, sucks the cosmos dry;
A million suns have gorged its swollen throat:
Upon a thousand unborn systems it yet will gloat.
Blind and white, it spins its webs of awful slime,
And passing in the night, takes our cherished dreams,
                 and leaves the rotten husk of Time.

Black Leather Vampyre

Bloodred her lips in the lamplit fog
Black her hair as a charnel sun
Buried in the sepulcher of night

White her flesh as a dead lily
Her eyes are headlights of mystery and desire
Her leather pants hug her legs and hips
Close as sweat
Clutch at her vulva
Like an incubus
Her black leather jacket
Burns and bursts
With succulent and dangerous fruits
Through the windy husk of streets
She wanders in her search
Touched with the fumes of drugs
And the lunes of legend obsessed
At the first sight of a face
Shrouded white with melancholy
And shadowed by a sea of torsoes
Adrift in horrible decay
Her scarlet lips uncurl
Her hair falls round
The oval of her polished skull
Her breasts heave to a breathless mouth
Black leather grinds and screams
The accursed poet's blood flows
Down her deathless throat
In an ancient necrotic fellatio
Two spectres seethe
In the far end of an alleyway
And the myth of darkness
Is consummated
In the mausoleum
Of the streets.

W. H. Pugmire (b. 1951)

Wilum Hopfrog Pugmire is a widely published American writer of
horror fiction, most of it in the Lovecraftian tradition. Among his
publications are the short story collections *Dreams of Lovecraftian
Horror* (1999), *Sesqua Valley and Other Haunts* (2003), *The Fungal*

Stain and Other Dreams (2006), and *Uncommon Places* (2012). His work appears frequently in magazines and anthologies. In many of his tales Pugmire has created a region in the Pacific Northwest called Sesqua Valley, parallel to Lovecraft's imaginary New England topography. "The Outsider's Song" is one of a sequence of sonnets entitled "The Songs of Sesqua Valley," imative of Lovecraft's *Fungi from Yuggoth*. The sequence appears in *Sesqua Valley and Other Haunts*.

The Outsider's Song

Why have you brought me to this godless place,
This place of haunted shadow, haunted sound,
Where dream and dark reality compound
To breed a wild, a weird, a godless race?
Why do the shadows follow me around
And sink into the texture of my skin,
So that I feel a monstrous mannequin
Composed of poison bred of Sesqua's ground?

I sink to trembling knees upon the sod.
I claw the dirt that dares to call my name.
I feel the potency that aches to claim
My wretched soul for some chaotic god.
And you, you smile at me with silver eye
And whisper secrets to the hungry sky.

———————————

Gary William Crawford (b. 1953)

American poet and critic Gary William Crawford is the founder of Gothic Press, which has issued the scholarly journal *Gothic* (1979–80) and other works pertaining to horror literature. Crawford has compiled a bibliography of J. Sheridan Le Fanu (1995), co-edited *Reflections in a Glass Darkly* (2011), and written *Robert Aickman: An Introduction* (2003). Among his poetry volumes are *Poems of the Divided Self* (1992), *In Shadow Lands* (1998), and *The Phantom World* (2008). "The Formicary" was collected in *Poems of the Divided Self.*

The Formicary

Nightmare ants feed in my brain,
The sweet nectar of my life.
I smoke a cigarette,
Decide to hurt myself.

I will burn,
Scar myself.

I open the place in my brain
Where ants nest,
And burn it with the cigarette.

The ants fry,
And I scream.

The scars of my past lives
Are preserved.

Keith Allen Daniels (1956–2001)

American poet Keith Allen Daniels began writing poetry in the late
1960s. His first volume, *What Rough Book* (1992), contained poems
that had appeared in many little magazines as well as in such venues
as *Asimov's Science Fiction* and *Weird Tales*. Another volume, *Satan Is
a Mathematician*, appeared in 1998. Daniels also edited the poetry
of James Blish and the correspondence of Lord Dunsany and Arthur
C. Clarke. "Stonehenge" was collected in *What Rough Book*.

Stonehenge

The stones are mute—but I would have them speak
of sacerdotal madmen, foul and fey,
and tales of bloodshed from an elder day;
alas—they brood in silence, bare and bleak.
I dreamt of Stonehenge on the windswept plain,
and saw the very stones begin to bleed!

I dreamt of countless legions that were slain
by mad proponents of an eldritch creed.

The stones bore witness to a time when men
made gods of what they failed to understand.
Their pagan whims left bloodstains on the land,
and sleeping specters that will rise again.
I curse the story which the cromlechs tell—
that man himself will sow the seeds of hell!

––––––––––––––––––

Leigh Blackmore (b. 1959)

Australian poet and critic Leigh Blackmore has edited the journal *Terror Australis* (1987–92) and edited an anthology of that title (1993). He is now coeditor of *Studies in Australian Weird Fiction*. He has compiled bibliographies of Terry Dowling, Harlan Ellison, Jack Dann, and Brian Lumley. "Terror Australis" is included in his first published poetry volume, *Spores from Sharnoth and Other Madnesses* (2008).

Terror Australis

I
The Southern Land—where snow but rarely falls—
In Yuletide brings the threat of searing fire;
Where sun and heat with sweat and dust conspire—
No holly and no ivy deck the halls.
The ground is shrouded here with naught but dust
And—scorched beneath the sun's incessant glare—
The sheep that dully raise their heads and stare
May die of thirst; the barbed-wire fences rust.

The celebration of the birth of Christ
Is shadowed here by legends dark and old;
The nights can be both comforting and cold;
The days string out like rope, knotted and spliced.
It is an alien land, where Christmas cheer
Gives way to trepidation and to fear.

II
A land of painted cabalistic signs
That lead us into pitiless vast space,
Where near and far and dark and light change place,
While jagged serpents dance along our spines.
Ghosts dwell here of an unrelenting kind,
Survivors of the famine and the flood,
Which rob men of their last remains of food—
Thrice-vicious ghosts that prey upon the mind.

A land whose secrets yield and break apart
To only those who live and die alone
(Perhaps condemned by pointing of the bone)
And see the truth at last in its dead heart.
Horrors half-glimpsed through waves of scorching light
Give way to freezing, arid, taunting night.

III
A Christmas here is not a Northern Yule—
Hot foetid winds defeat the gasping breath;
The arid sands give warning of stark death;
The ocean's roar portends a fate most cruel.
Did Lovecraft dream in "The Shadow out of Time"
A tenth of all the burning, torpid fear—
The horrors that inimical lie here—
In wait for dwellers in this alien clime?

Antipodean nightmares strange and bleak
Fill dreamers' minds with eerie visions dire,
That fill their souls with recondite desire
And draw them on to leer and shout and shriek.
Oppressed and tortured, baneful and malign,
With their grim fate Australians must entwine.

———————————————

Ann K. Schwader (b. 1960)

American poet Ann K. Schwader has published her poetry in many
journals, including *Dark Regions*, *Studies in the Fantastic*, and *Weird
Tales*. Her numerous volumes of poetry include *The Worms Remember*

(2001), *Architectures of Night* (2003), *In the Yaddith Time* (2007), and *Twisted in Dream: The Collected Weird Poetry* (2011). Her short fiction is collected in *Strange Stars and Alien Shadows* (2003). "The Coming of Chaos" was first published in *The Worms Remember*.

The Coming of Chaos

None dare to speak of it, & few suspect
That shadow-claws clutch inward day by day
(Too subtle for man's science to detect)
Upon this world still wobbling on its way
Between dim pasts in which it played no part,
& grimmer futures gnawing at its heart.

Our hierophants of physics little know
Dread Chaos bears a nearly human face:
Lean as the East where nighted rivers flow,
Yet lightless as that nether void of space
Where muffled drums & tuneless pipers laud
The mad gyrations of an idiot god.

This deity alone does Chaos serve
As lying herald & as messenger
Whose lightest word speaks nightmare down the nerve
Of all who hear . . . and hearing, might prefer
Their ignorance new-polished & pristine
To hinted knowledge twisting toward obscene.

Fresh shrieks of horror haunt the urban night,
Dreamstalked by darkside visions of some end
Crouched formless, nameless till the stars spin right,
Then shatter from the pattern they portend
Of tortured oceans spattered to the sky
By that which should not live, but would not die.

Thus reason treats with madness to survive,
& knowing skirts the borders of unknown
As Terra's erstwhile masters now alive
Deny whatever dust they claimed to own,
But—being mortal—merely held in trust
For Others who esteem them less than dust.

Index of Poets

Acknowledgments

Charles Baudelaire, "The Phantom," translated by Clark Ashton Smith, first published in *Weird Tales* (May 1929), copyright © 1929 by Popular Fiction Publishing Company. Reprinted in Smith's *The Complete Poetry and Translations,* Volume 3 (Hippocampus Press, 2007), copyright © 2007 by Hippocampus Press. Reprinted by permission of CASiana Literary Enterprises, Inc.

Charles Baudelaire, "The Irremediable," translated by Clark Ashton Smith, first published in the *Auburn Journal* (23 July 1925). Reprinted in Smith's *The Complete Poetry and Translations,* Volume 3 (Hippocampus Press, 2007), copyright © 2007 by Hippocampus Press. Reprinted by permission of CASiana Literary Enterprises, Inc.

Joseph Payne Brennan, "The Scythe of Dreams," first published in August Derleth, ed., *Fire and Sleet and Candlelight* (Arkham House, 1961), copyright © 1961 by August Derleth; reprinted in Brennan's *Nightmare Need* (Arkham House, 1964), copyright © 1964 by Joseph Payne Brennan, and in Brennan's *Sixty Selected Poems* (New Establishment Press, 1985), copyright © 1985 by Joseph Payne Brennan. Reprinted by permission of Arkham House Publishers, Inc.

Stanley McNail, "The House on Maple Hill," first published in August Derleth, ed., *Fire and Sleet and Candlelight* (Arkham House, 1961), copyright © 1961 by August Derleth; reprinted in McNail's *Something Breathing* (Arkham House, 1965), copyright © 1965 by Stanley McNail. Reprinted by permission of Arkham House Publishers, Inc.

Richard L. Tierney, "The Evil House" and "To the Hydrogen Bomb," included in Tierney's *Collected Poems* (Arkham House, 1981), copyright © 1981 by Arkham House Publishers, Inc. Reprinted by permission of the author.

Bruce Boston, "The Nightmare Collector," included in *The Nightmare Collector* (2AM Publications, 1988), copyright © 1988 by Bruce Boston. Reprinted by permission of the author.

Bruce Boston, "Ghost Blood," included in *Pitchblende* (Dark Regions Press, 2003), copyright © 2003 by Bruce Boston. Reprinted by permission of the author.

CPSIA information can be obtained at www.ICGtesting.com
Printed in the USA
BVOW001125010413

316978BV00003B/16/P